Communications and Culture

Communications has been defined as the conveying or exchanging of information and ideas. This wide definition is taken as the starting-point for this series of books, which are not bound by conventional academic divisions. The series aims to document or analyse a broad range of cultural forms and ideas.

It encompasses works from areas as esoteric as linguistics and as exoteric as television. The language of communication may be the written word or the moving picture, the static icon or the living gesture. These means of communicating can at their best blossom into and form an essential part of the other mysterious concept, *culture*.

There is no sharp or intended split in the series between communication and culture. On one definition, culture refers to the organisation of experience shared by members of a community, a process which includes the standards and values for judging or perceiving, for predicting and acting. In this sense, creative communication can make for a better and livelier culture.

The series reaches towards the widest possible audience. Some of the works concern themselves with activities as general as play and games; others offer a narrower focus, such as the ways of understanding the visual image. It is hoped that some moves in the transformation of the artful and the scientific can be achieved, and that both can begin to be understood by a wider and more comprehending community. Some of these books are written by practitioners – broadcasters, journalists, and artists; others come from critics, scholars, scientists and historians.

The series has an ancient and laudable, though perhaps untenable, aim – an aim as old as the Greeks and as new as holography: it inspires to help heal the split between cultures, between the practitioners and the thinkers, between science and art, between the academy and life.

P.W.

The British Press:
a Manifesto

Edited by

JAMES CURRAN

© Acton Society Press Group 1978

First published 1978 by
THE MACMILLAN PRESS LTD
London and Basingstoke
Associated companies in Delhi Dublin
Hong Kong Johannesburg Lagos Melbourne
New York Singapore and Tokyo

Photoset and printed in Great Britain by
LOWE AND BRYDONE PRINTERS LTD
Thetford, Norfolk

British Library Cataloguing in Publication Data

The British press, a manifesto.–
  (Communications and culture).
  1. Press – Great Britain
  I. Title II. Curran, James III. Acton
  Society Press Group IV. Series
  079'.41   PN5118

  ISBN 0–333–23459–6
  ISBN 0–333–23888–5 Pbk.

Contents

    DAVE MURPHY
9   The Making of Foreign News   192
    HAROLD JACKSON

    Part 4   EXTERNAL CONSTRAINTS ON
    THE PRESS

10 Law for the Press   203
    GEOFFREY ROBERTSON
11 Advertising and the Press   229
    JAMES CURRAN

    Part 5   THE FUTURE OF THE PRESS

12 New Print Technology and Newspaper Culture   271
    BRUCE PAGE
13 Politics and the Technology Push   282
    LUKE ALEXANDER
14 Government Policy and the Mass Media   296
    JEAN SEATON

    Notes on Contributors   311
    Notes and References   315
    Index   336

The Acton Society Press Group, whose members and associates have prepared these essays, was initiated by the Trustees of the Acton Society, who also financed some of the research, but the opinions and arguments advanced are the responsibility of the writers alone.

Acknowledgements

I would like to thank Pauline Wingate for her help in putting this book together and Jackie Lebe for typing many of these essays.

JAMES CURRAN

Introduction

James Curran

The McGregor Principle

Almost without anyone noticing, the McGregor Commission on the Press has advanced a radical principle which, if extended to other media, would transform public policy. The McGregor principle is that all forms of public spending that are either *selective* or could result in *economic dependence on the state* are politically unacceptable because they might introduce state censorship.

The McGregor Commission did not rule out all forms of government action: to do so would have meant agreeing, from the outset, with the widely held view in Fleet Street that its investigation was a waste of time – a view that its report did little to change.[1] But it did impose strict limits on government intervention on the basis of a fixed and immutable principle. 'We are strongly against', the Commission declared, 'any scheme which would make the press, or any section of it, dependent on government through reliance on continuing subsidies from public funds. We are also opposed absolutely to the establishment of any public body which could, or might have to, discriminate among publications in such a way as to amount to censorship in the sense of preferring to support some publications and not others.'[2] All proposals, both practical and impractical, were rejected if they transgressed this sacred dogma.

Yet the extraordinary thing about the McGregor Commission, given the not immodest sum of £242,027 it spent on investigation and research, was that it never attempted to discover whether press subsidies or redistributive schemes introduced in other European countries to encourage press diversity had resulted in covert political censorship of the press.[3] It was left to Anthony Smith – supported by a public trust – to mount an independent investigation, the results of which were seized upon by Basnett and Goodman in their minority report to the McGregor Commission.[4]

The McGregor principle – or perhaps it would be more accurate to say the principle successfully pressed upon the McGregor Commission by press proprietors – was not exposed to empirical scrutiny. It was merely accepted as an article of faith. No attempt was made even to probe whether state intervention in other politically sensitive areas has resulted in political censorship. Indeed some members of the Press Commission appear not to have been aware of the profoundly radical stance they were taking. For if an embargo is to be placed on public funding that is either selective or induces state dependence in areas that are vulnerable to political manipulation, something close to a counter revolution in public policy would result. Nationalisation of book distribution in the form of the public library service would go: the McGregor principle does not allow public funding, selection and free loan of political material. The B.B.C. would go too, of course: its funding is regulated by the Government which fixes the licence fee. The Eady Levy and the British Film Institute would also be axed since they provide selective support for films and projects some of which have a clear political significance. Why stop here? The Arts Council and the Regional Arts Associations (relying heavily on public money) dish out grants to a wide variety of projects and institutions some of which are politically relevant. And what about state education? Why, in the name of McGregor, do we allow political indoctrination in state schools when education could be organised on neutral, free market lines?

This is not to make light of the possibility of state censorship inherent in certain forms of public intervention. The wider implications of economic intervention in the press need to be very carefully considered. But this is not the same as accepting the

McGregor principle as a theological tenet that defines the limits of government action before discussion even begins. For the McGregor principle has a long history. In the nineteenth century people opposed state funding of education on the grounds that it would lead to centralised political indoctrination.[5] In the 1920s opposition was voiced to the setting up of the B.B.C. on the grounds that it would be manipulated by government,[6] an argument that was revived in the right-wing assault on the B.B.C. in the post-war period.[7] If only the McGregors of this world had been heeded, some major achievements of reforming administrations over the last century would never have happened.[8]

Public Prejudice and Private Neutrality

Underlying the objection of the McGregor Commission to selective or ongoing public funding of the press is the belief that the market mechanism is essentially neutral, while public intervention is potentially manipulative. This belief is reflected in the double standards that are consistently applied in the McGregor Report. Public agencies are forced to make 'invidious' choices,[9] whereas private agencies merely take decisions.[10] Selection by a public body is defined as an act of censorship,[11] yet market allocation is assumed to be neutral.[12] Redistributive schemes imposed by a public agency can never be 'objective';[13] the same problem of 'objectivity' does not arise in the free market.[14] The trouble with redistributive schemes is that they have 'identifiable consequences' and therefore fall within the political arena;[15] the existing pattern of market distribution does not need to be identified, however, because it is impersonal and outside the political arena.[16]

This Alice-in-Wonderland logic can be illustrated briefly by the McGregor Commission's response to subsidies – both subsidies in the form of advertising allocated by the market and proposals for subsidies that would be allocated by a public agency. The first objection to the latter was that they involved an element of judgement:[17] as far as advertising allocation was concerned this was not seen as a problem.[18] The second objection to selective public subsidies was that they had identifiable consequences for the viability of particular titles:[19] this presented no difficulty in the case of the market distribution of advertising between titles, which was barely discussed.[20] The third objection was that the rules governing the allocation of public subsidies could be fixed to help papers of a particular political persuasion:[21] the fact that advertising expenditure per reader is (and always has been for as far back as detailed statistics were available to the Commission) much greater for Conservative papers than for Labour papers goes unmentioned.[22] In short, objection is raised to selective public subsidies on the grounds that they could be discretionary, could make the difference between life and death of individual papers, and could be fixed in a way that gives more help to papers supporting one political party than to another. The fact that advertising subsidies are discretionary, do make the difference between life and death for some papers, and do give more help to papers supporting one political party than another is accepted as the natural – and politically neutral – order of things

Similarly the fact that it requires millions of pounds to buy or start a newspaper in the competitive market is tacitly portrayed as natural and inevitable. It has no political implications, whereas proposals to widen market access to those without large capital resources through selective funding is considered politically invidious. A club that admits only the Murdochs, the Trafalgar Houses and the Altantic Richfields of this world is, after all, theoretically open to all: any change in the rules that makes this theory less of a fantasy apparently smacks of censorship.[23]

Of course, anyone with even a nodding knowledge of press history will recognise the absurdity of the assumption that the market mechanism is neutral. Ironically the last time the question of economic controls of the press was a major issue of public debate, advocates of the free market in parliament were at pains to emphasise that it was neither neutral nor free. The free market, it was widely proclaimed, would place control of the popular press in the hands not of penniless agitators but of 'men of respectability and capital';[24] it would boost papers 'enjoying the preference of the advertising public';[25] and these papers would be written by journalists who because they come from 'the comfortable part of society . . . will err on the side of making too much of their interests than on that of neglecting them'.[26] The result, they promised, would not be a distressing diversity of opinion. The free market precisely because it was not free would produce a press wedded to the free market system, biased in favour of moderation, and strenuously opposed to trade unionism.[27]

While these campaigners for a free market press perhaps overstated their case, few would deny the underlying accuracy of their predictions. The operation of the free market, with its accompanying rise in publishing costs, led to a progressive transfer of ownership and control of the popular press to capitalist entrepreneurs, while the new dependence on advertising encouraged the absorption or elimination of the early radical press and inhibited its re-emergence. Although the family controlled press chains are now being taken over or are expanding into large diversified corporations, the newspaper press continues to reflect a narrow range of perspectives and a political imbalance between left and right.[28]

Indeed, this would seem to be, at one point, the view of the McGregor Commission itself. In a key passage, the Commission declares: 'In the last fifteen years, the development of political news and discussion by broadcasting organisations . . . has certainly helped to counter the political imbalance of the press'.[29] This is a remarkable comment from a body which throughout its report assumes the impartiality of the market mechanism and the danger of political partiality inherent in extensive public regulation. With this one statement, the McGregor Commission blows wide open the basis of its argument.

'The Free Market World of Newspapers'

Underlying this assumption of market neutrality is an image of the free market in which the press supposedly operates. The Commission clearly wanted to believe that it is open to anyone to establish their own paper providing that they can get enough people to buy it; that everyone with a distinctive opinion can find somewhere to express it; and that the press is accountable to the public through the market mechanism, which allows us to pick and choose from a wide and diverse range of papers. Indeed it is partly in these terms that the McGregor Commission differentiates between broadcasting and the press. In 'the free market world of newspapers', according to the Commission, everyone has 'the right to buy or launch a paper'. In the closed world of broadcasting, on the other hand, the opportunity to broadcast is restricted because broadcast frequencies are few and valuable. Consequently, whereas the press is accountable primarily through the operation of the mar-

ket, broadcasting has had to be extensively regulated and controlled.[30]

But while the McGregor Commission fervently wanted to
believe in the free market, its own analysis led in the opposite
direction. Its long enquiry was, in a sense, a protracted struggle
against its own conclusions. Thus the Commission wanted to
believe that there was a free market solution to the political
imbalance of the national newspaper press. It expressed at regular
intervals in its report the pious hope that the gap left by the *Daily
Herald* and the *News Chronicle* will be filled by a new daily
launched by the trade union movement. The Commission's report
coyly admits, however, that 'no new national daily has been
launched recently', sensibly omitting to mention that the last time
this happened successfully was forty-seven years ago and before
that sixty-five years ago.[31] A telling caveat is also added that 'no
one knows whether the readership of such a paper would enable it
to survive commercially'. [32] No mention is made of the fact that the
Daily Herald died with 4.7 million readers on its hands – a mass
readership that was too small and too poor to sustain a popular
paper at a time when the cost and revenue structure of the popular
press was more favourable than it is now. These omissions were
omissions of tact rather than of knowledge. The Commission was
fully aware of the effective conomic barriers to launching a new
popular national daily.

The Commission wanted to believe that, at least in the regional
daily press, the free market would allow competition to extend the
diversity of the press. It reluctantly concluded, however, that even
to establish a new evening paper, with its own plant, in a town
without direct competition would cost £3 million; that there was
direct competition between evening papers in only two urban
centres; that most evening paper monopolies were impregnable,
and that starting up a rival evening paper in direct competition to
an established paper would, in most places, merely have the effect
of making both run at a loss.[33] In short, the great majority of
evening papers are in the same monopolistic position as most local
radio stations – the only difference being that the latter are
publicly regulated monopolies.

If 'the right' to start a new daily paper is rapidly being denied
even to millionaires, at least the Commission wanted to believe
that the existing range of choice, narrow and imbalanced though it

is, would be maintained in the newspaper press. Reluctantly, it came to the conclusion, however, that increased productivity arising from new technology and reduced manning levels would not, in the long term, guarantee the diversity of the press. While also anxious to establish that the advantages of size were not as great as theory might suggest in eliminating competition, the Commission still concluded that underlying competitive pressures resulted, all things being equal, in a dwindling range of titles, shrinking consumer choice and declining diversity. Noting the contraction of choice and diversity in the daily and Sunday newspaper press since 1947, when the first Press Commission was appointed, it offered little hope of things getting better in the future. At least it had the tact not to mention that the number and diversity (in its own terms) of daily and Sunday papers has been declining steadily since 1918.

This is not the place to discuss in detail the other economic problems confronting the Commission – the growth of chain ownership, the centralised control of some chains, the growth of multi-media monopolies, and their amalgamation with other economic interests. It is sufficient to note that the Commission was unable to recommend any effective action to repair the free market it so wanted to believe in.[34] Its proposal for a one-off state aid scheme to facilitate the introduction of new technology and reduce manning levels was, it confessed, only an alleviating measure.[35] Other proposals to strengthen the vetting and regulation of mergers, and limitations on joint ownership of press and broadcasting, were not intended to facilitate the launch of new papers or neutralise the underlying economic pressures that make for contraction. These were problems for which the Commission had no answer : indeed, by a curious irony, its very *laissez-faire* commitment prevented it from coming to grips with the admittedly formidable and complex difficulties with which it was faced. For a philosophy built on inherited faith in the free market and suspicion of government precluded forms of economic intervention that could have encouraged a greater measure of press diversity.

Coming to Terms with Failure

The Commission was placed in a further quandary. The tradition of an outspoken, combative and partisan press has always been justified on the grounds that the free market enables a free and equal interchange of views and information. Yet even its own analysis led, as we have seen, to the conclusion that market access was severely restricted and unequal between those with and without large capital resources; and that press diversity was shrinking and reflected a political imbalance.

The Commission could not repudiate partisanship in the press because this would mean jettisoning the traditional ideology of the free market to which it still clung and which justified, in its opinion, why broadcasting should be publicly controlled and the press should stay in largely private hands. It continued outwardly to espouse the free market values of partisanship and outspoken comment. But at the same time, it made a crucial mental adjustment that enabled it to come to terms with the absence of a free market. While paying lip-service to the free market ideal of partisan diversity, it advanced at the same time an ideology of social responsibility and public service, borrowed from broadcasting. The press, it solemnly proclaimed, should behave 'with proper restraint' and provide 'its readers with the fair and accurate information and comment essential for responsible judgements'.[36] To this end, newspapers should recruit, like broadcasting, more graduates; young journalists should 'learn about society' in new courses in which 'industrial problems and relations' should be 'a central part'; and the Press Council should be reconstituted yet again and asked to insist on stricter standards.

To advance a public control ideology without public control does not get us very far. To call for 'fair and accurate information' begs the question of who should regulate this information; to advocate 'comment essential for responsible judgement' leaves unanswered who has the right to define what is 'responsible'; to call upon teachers to correct bias in industrial relations coverage in the press is both inherently absurd and a parody of this well meaning approach. But a vague, woolly and, at times, contradictory espousal of public responsibility was of crucial importance to the McGregor Commission. It provided a rationale for doing nothing, a gesture in favour of reform, and a way of putting something in place of the threadbare and tattered ideology of the free market.[37]

Shape of the Book

The conservatism and lack of imagination of the McGregor Report provoked a minority report – the first of its kind amongst the now numerous official enquiries into the press – in which David Basnett, leader of the General and Municipal Workers Union, and Geoffrey Goodman, the distinguished Fleet Street correspondent, called for practical intervention to expand the diversity of the press. Their proposal for a national print corporation and launch fund to seed new publications has gained widespread support, and is the basis of the proposal outlined by Peter Golding and Graham Murdock in this volume.

This book is, in a sense, an extension of this minority report. The aim has been, however, to provide more than merely a reply to the McGregor Report. The book offers an alternative analysis of the British press and its role in contemporary society. In doing this, it challenges the political values, liberal economic theory and cultural assumptions that framed the McGregor Commission's response to the press. And in the belief that criticism needs to be related to positive action, it outlines various proposals for reform as a contribution to the ongoing debate about the press. Each of the articles express the views of the author alone. Although a certain degree of consensus has emerged, this is more accident than design.

The first section provides a number of introductory perspectives The opening article by Raymond Williams argues against interventionalist proposals designed merely to maintain and service the existing press and calls for a new approach that will explore ways of liberating the press from its class division between printer and writer, its metropolitan domination and cultural polarisation between elite and tabloid journalism. Stuart Hall is also critical, by implication at least, of attempts to service the capitalist press. He examines the growing crisis of press capital and the conventional framework of analysis in which the crisis and its wider implications are perceived, concluding with an examination of the role of the press in maintaining class hegemony in British society. Writing from a different ideological perspective, Anthony Smith sets the current debate about press intervention in Britain in its European context. He points out that, whereas proposals for intervention usually come from the left in this country, many forms of intervention enjoy consensual support across the political spectrum in other liberal democratic countries. While we are locked inside a Victorian debate that does not take into account the changing economic structure of the press and of communications generally, he argues that other European countries have been busily attempting to defend and promote newspaper diversity.

The second section focuses upon different aspects of control of the press. Peter Golding and Graham Murdock provide a critique of the liberal, free market theory of the press and propose a Public Press Authority which would print at subsidised rates and provide capital support for new publications in the monopolistic press. The market power of press corporations is critically examined also in a key article by Stuart Holland who proposes the break-up of the major monopolies, the establishment of an Independent Press Authority (with a role comparable to the Independent Broadcasting Authority), a Press Distribution Service, National Printing Corporation and Press Development Agency in order to make the ideal of consumer sovereignty a reality. Neal Ascherson's article examines various ways of democratising the press, arguing that internal democracy has become a vital safeguard against the threat to diversity represented by both the major media monopolies and an interventionalist government. Philip Elliott, Dave Murphy and Harold Jackson all provide critiques of the way in which news is manufactured. Philip Elliott criticses the uniform, repetitive and derivative character of national news reporting and argues that the demands for social responsibility will do little to improve it. A similar theme is developed by Dave Murphy in his examination of the local press in which he takes issue with the simplistic notions of accuracy and objectivity that are sometimes said to characterise responsible journalism. Both argue for changes in the practice, orientation and organisation of journalism as a way of encouraging a more diverse, probing and evaluative style of news reporting. On the other hand, Harold Jackson, who provides a critical examination of foreign news reporting, implies that we should adjust our expectations and accept that 'newspapers are shoddy goods'.

In the section on external constraints on the press, Geoffrey Robertson criticises both the McGregor Commission and the press for their willingness to accept excessive legal restrictions on freedom of expression and outlines a programme of legal reform. James Curran also criticises the McGregor Commission for its complacent attitude to the influence of advertising on the press, and proposes a way of dealing with some problems raised by advertising in the press.

The last section is devoted to considering certain aspects of the future of the press. Bruce Page examines the creative potential of new print technology to improve the quality of journalism. Luke Alexander considers the implications of the technological convergence between print and broadcasting systems. And Jean Seaton, in the concluding article, examines the haphazard evolution of British media policy, arguing the need for an integrated approach to mass communications as a whole.

Part 1

Introductory Perspectives

Part 1

Introductory Perspectives

Chapter 1

The Press We Don't Deserve

Raymond Williams

There is now no difficulty in agreeing that there is a crisis in the British press. But this, paradoxically, is why it is so very difficult to think about it. The symptoms of the crisis are so many and so various that our responses are always in danger of drifting into mere opportunism. As in the related crises of the political system and of the economy, so many things are so evidently wrong that it is easy to establish a quite spurious unity of concern. When it comes to remedies, of course, this unity does not last, and we have the familiar situation of British society over the last twenty years, in which there seems to be an almost functional relation between general recognition of the need for change and a persistent inability to make any real changes. Thus our years are punctuated with deep crises, decisive turning points, in-depth enquiries, radical reorganisations and bold new starts which, as they settle, and as the general problems persist, fade into the angry banalities of cynicism and frustration. This mood, which is now so prevalent, does not exclude, however, the further opportunism of yet newer starts, yet broader turning points, yet in-deeper enquiries. The crisis, at most levels, comes to feed on itself.

It is then time to assert that there can be no unity of concern about the state of the British press, any more than there can be unity of concern about the 'British' political system or the 'British' economy. In each of these cases, and in the press quite evidently, different kinds of crisis have become entangled with each other, and the consequent multiplicity of symptoms have to be distinguished rather than assembled. There have been times, as in the early 1960s, when it seemed reasonable to try to generalise our concerns and our campaigns. Now, in the late 1970s, it is necessary to distinguish and particularise them, since the other, more consensual mode, while serving to focus initial attention, has only, through the years, led us back into the labyrinth of the crisis.

Three distinct kinds of crisis have then to be named. First, there is a longstanding but still important set of problems about the relationship between the press and the state. This includes several old elements but also, as the state itself changes, several new features. Second, there is a deep and persistent crisis of the press as a capitalist industry. In some of its central problems – profitability, monopoly tendencies, corporatism, difficult industrial relations, changing ratios between technology and forms of employment – this crisis is closely related to more general industrial problems, but has to be seen in some respects differently, if only because of its connections with the first crisis, in the relations between the press and the state. But then, third, there is quite another form of crisis, which can be summarised as a set of unsolved problems about the modern national newspaper as a social and cultural form: problems deeply affected by each of the other crises, but in no way limited to them. It is in this area, most clearly, that any unity of concern breaks down. Most actual and proposed solutions to the generalised crisis take their cues from the problems of the press and the state or from the extreme difficulties of the press as a capitalist industry. What the solutions then commonly envisage is the survival, maintenance or at most modification of the existing forms. It is then only in the third area of crisis and analysis that we can add a different dimension: one in which most of the things that are really wrong in the British press, and that are properly matters of general public concern, can be defined.

It is necessary to look briefly at each of the first two kinds of crisis, even though they have been so widely discussed. Any useful analysis of the third kind has, in any case, to be protected from misunderstanding in terms of the other two, and some real connections have also to be made.

The freedom of the press, even in its most traditional definitions, can by no means be taken for granted or as assured. The newspapers we now have can trace their history to a period in which certain critical freedoms had to be fought for, and this has affected a whole area of current thinking. The difficulty now is that this old struggle is still relevant and indeed urgent, while at the same time new and more complex questions of freedom are also being negotiated. No radical and especially no socialist can be equivocal about the older questions. There are still serious limitations on press freedom, of a kind which it has been the task of a bourgeois and capitalist press, as well as a radical press, to fight. By comparison with many other capitalist countries, the British press is barred access to or prevented from reporting issues of evident public importance. The Official Secrets Act, the D-notice system, the state of the law on libel are all formal barriers, with continuing serious effect. The deliberate indirectness and occlusion of many parts of the political system, in local as well as in national government, are less formal but no less effective barriers. These are seen, quite properly, as problems of the relationship between the press and, in broad terms, the state. We have to add some related problems which are not definable in the same simple terms. There are substantial limitations of freedom in news and opinion of the activities of capitalist corporations and companies and of some major professions; limitations which overlap with other limitations, centred mainly on the law of libel, on news and opinion of individual activities. At any time, in discussions of the press, it is possible to assemble an apparent consensus in which the keywords of criticism are intrusion, irresponsibility, inaccuracy, even impertinence. But while there are certainly cases of intrusion into matters which are not really of public concern, and while there is often inaccuracy, the balance of danger lies heavily in the other direction. Radical critics have then to be especially careful not to join what is always, finally, an establishment consensus. Politicians of all colours, civil servants and state functionaries, company directors and trade union officials, judges and the police, professional organisations: all, as their interest or convenience serves, can hate or despise both newspapers in general and the relatively feeble and enfeebled newspapers we have. And on any such issue radicals must stand with the press; socialists, including revolutionary socialists, must also stand on that side. For socialists in particular have, in this matter, an ironically heavy responsibility. Every necessary campaign against the capitalist press, every attempt to move beyond its specifically restricting forms, must begin from an unequivocal acknowledgement of what a capitalist and bourgeois press has historically achieved. There are freedoms which by its nature it can not attain, but this is no warrant for underplaying the freedoms it has and the attainable freedoms it still needs. Every proposal for public intervention in the press as an institution or as an industry stands to be tested at this first point. The radical confusion between popular interest and the state, or, more plausibly, between public interest and the state, has already gravely weakened the socialist challenge, over a range from Fabian to Marxist forms. Neither the growth of a public bureaucracy, as in the Fabian model, nor the achievement of a workers' state, as in most Marxist models as hitherto defined, diminishes in any degree the historical challenge of a free press. The problems of its attainment, in radically altered social conditions, can not be left to verbal solutions, in which public representatives masquerade as the public interest, or in which the party equals the truth. What is at issue, really, is something very general in the current crisis of capitalism: that forms of post-capitalist thinking and organisation, emergent and embattled as they must always be, can turn for false comfort or support to pre-capitalist forms, and in this case to all those who hate the press because it is intrusive, embarrassing, irresponsible and even disruptive, or because it is vulgar and brash. The undoubted fact that the capitalist press is often, indeed, all these things must be no base for a consensus with those who, for their own reasons, want a more visibly controlled and 'protected' society.

And this is the more necessary to say when, looking at things as they now really are, we have to register the irony that in its main pressures, indeed in virtually every sphere of activity but its own, what the capitalist press is reporting and arguing for is just such a protected consensus and such controls. I will come back to the source of this primary contradiction, which lies deep in the social and cultural forms. But it is still no warrant for equivocation on the issues of press freedom. We must avoid the false opposition between a free press and a responsible press, that equivocal term of the false consensus. The question we have to put, to break the consensus, is responsible to what and to whom?

It is the right question, in any case, to bring to the crisis of the press as a capitalist industry. Here the shape of the crisis is by now well known. There has been a radical decline in profitability, indeed a quite general movement into chronic loss-making. The range of newspapers has steadily declined, and there are still periods of acute crisis, accentuated by radical changes in technology, which tend to promote a new kind of consensus: that the national press must be saved. Orthodox diagnoses, by the owners of the press, by capitalist economists, by a majority of political leaders, highlight such problems as overmanning, restrictive practices, the difficulties of rationalisation. Locally fierce conflicts break out between owners and unions, and still the consensus seems to hold: the national press, in essentially its present forms, must be saved. It is at this point that I now find myself standing back and asking why. Do I really give a damn if the *Express* folds, or the *Mail,* or . . . ? If the press, or that part of it, is as bad as I know it to be, why should I worry if it crashes into failure or drags on through its decline?

The traditional liberal answer to this question is that maintenance of the range of the press is crucial; that we shall have a free press only if we have an extended and various press, whatever the quality of some of its parts. This is still a strong and convincing answer, but what has then to be said is that it is the specifically capitalist organisation of the press, and especially its proposals for resolving its crisis of profitability, that is making the answer hollow. The range of the national press has shrunk dramatically through this century. Combine ownership has reduced the range of control as well as the range of publications. Moreover, combine ownership has itself moved, recently, into a new stage, in which even the large newspaper or newspaper and magazine corporation is itself only a part of a much larger fixed corporation, in which there are comparisons of profitability between the press and other areas of investment. In this new situation the liberal answer loses most of its relevance, since to support, in any way, the existing and emergent organisation of the press is to underwrite a form which is certain, by its own powerful internal criteria, to rationalise in the direction of profitability rather than of range. The consequent internal struggles between owners and workers are then only at one level a problem of changing technology and the necessary changes in working conditions. At a deeper level they are strug-

gles within a captitalist organisation which is itself steadily re-
nouncing the conditions which have made it a special case: that the
'newspaper industry', though it produces commodities, produces
commodities of a special kind which are crucial to political
democracy. As the corporations which now include newspapers
among their investment areas come increasingly to make not only
profitability (the condition of ordinary survival) but *comparative*
profitability their stated public intention, the liberal answer begins
to fade to an illusion or even a complicity. Certainly the dangers of
letting this process develop towards its inevitable result, with no
attempt at intervention, are severe. But there can be no useful
intervention along orthodox Labour lines. It is not even the same
kind of case as that for supporting a capitalist automobile corporation, where there is a balancing factor of the competition of
imports. No intervention within the terms of late capitalist corporate organisation is defensible, since the rationale of such
organisation is at once the reduction of its products to an increasingly standardised range and, with this, the reduction of total
employment. Both standing by and watching this, or, in the name
of 'doing something', actually assisting or subsidising its com-
pletion, have to be firmly ruled out. And it is at this point that we
have to restate, radically, what is really wrong with the British
press: why it is, centrally, a press we don't deserve.

All the basic faults flow from the central factor of corporate
capitalist ownership. But it is not enough to state this abstractly, or
to suppose that so general a diagnosis can be followed by some
such general remedy as the public ownership of the existing kinds
of organisation and publication. We have to look more specifically
into the real failings.

First we have to notice the radical contraction of the political
range of the British press. If we look back over thirty years we can
see that although a number of national newspapers have failed the
really significant losses are political: the *Daily Herald,* the *News
Chronicle, Reynolds' News.* It is now the case that in the popular
press the Right is more powerfully represented than at any time
since the early 1920s. It used to be said that aggregate circulations
corresponded quite closely to the distribution of votes as between
Labour and Conservatives. The development of the *Herald* into
the I.P.C. *Sun* and then the Murdoch *Sun* has radically shifted that
distribution, and the loss of the *Chronicle* into the *Mail* had

already made it probable. It is difficult to establish precise statistical ratios between circulations and votes, since in any particular election (for example, October 1974) certain newspapers of the Right may advocate Conservative – Liberal or 'all-party' coalitions, which prevents any definite assignments to separate parties. The Royal Commission's Table 10.1 (see Table 1.1 below) gives figures for all post-war elections. On their basis, we can examine the post-war trend. But this is only the broad ratio, in terms of established political parties. The right-wing popular papers are, in general, on the right wing of Conservative opinion, while the *Mirror,* supposed to be the countervailing force, is, again in general, on the right wing of Labour opinion. Thus the popular press, as a whole, has moved in the last thirty years decisively to

TABLE 1.1

	Labour		Conservative	
	% *Press*	% *Vote*	% *Press*	% *Vote*
1945	35	48	52	40
1951	39	49	52	48
1955	40	46	52	50
1959	38	44	54	49
1964	42	44	57	43
1966	43	48	55	42
1970	44	43	55	46
1974 (Feb)	31	37	71	38

The figures for October 1974, affected by support for coalitions, are 31/39 and 47/36.

the Right. If one told a visiting analyst that this had happened during a period of intensive monopoly-capitalist reorganisation, adding perhaps that it was surprising and regrettable, it would be difficult to survive his polite shrug at one's naïveté, let alone his impolite look of contempt. What else, he would have to ask, would you expect to happen? Yet most discussion, since the fifties, has been centred on the market consequences of the latest corporate phase. These remain important, but the political consequences have now to be brought into the foreground. The political spectrum, day in day out, is very significantly different from declared electoral opinion, though its variation from some electoral trends may be less extreme. Moreover the electoral categories, while revealing one kind of built-in bias, conceal another. In the crucial area of industrial politics there is really no significantly distributed newspaper which represents the views and interests of the trade union movement, with its eleven million members. In virtually all disputes the majority of the press is hostile to the workers' interests from the outset. (A different but not entirely contradictory view of this situation is expressed in the Royal Commission Report (213); see especially Table C33.)

This is, as has been said, what might be expected from a capitalist press. But there are two significant special factors. First, there seems in the last ten years to have been a structural change in the calculation of the relativities of market and political factors. The achievement of a predominantly right-wing press seems to have been given a specific priority, in certain critical areas, even when market forces might have produced a different result. The entry of the mixed corporations, the willingness (even through the drive for profitability) to bear heavy losses to keep right-wing papers going, is surely most readily explained in straight political terms. But then the second special factor is the extraordinary indifference of the organised Left. Every attempt to redress or even maintain some sort of political balance has been ignored or rejected by the Labour Governments. It is a mark of the capitulation of the Labour leadership to the terms of a capitalist economy that the only significant effort it has ever been persuaded to make is in terms of the maintenance of capitalist employment, and even this has been negotiated, except by unions with special interests, in terms of an inevitable reorganisation for corporate profitability. It is then difficult to overestimate the extent, in this area, of the social and political victory which has been gained by the organised Right in this country. That it is a victory for which both the Labour Party and the trade union movement are likely to pay very heavily is no comfort, even when they have most clearly brought it upon themselves.

One common way of evading this uncomfortable but inevitable conclusion is the argument that people do not or do not necessarily take their political opinions from the newspapers they read. And indeed, on the compared evidence of circulations and votes, this has often been the case. Moreover, theoretically, it is of course true that political opinions and actions are generated from a whole body of social experience, and not simply from overt organs of opinion. Yet amid so much else that is changing the first fact, at least, can no longer be complacently repeated. In the extraordinary intricacy and mobility of the current deep crisis in British society, the 'traditional', 'family' vote which was largely responsible for the older kind of disparity is being steadily and in some areas rapidly eroded. The broad objectives of alternative social and economic policies can no longer be so readily distinguished in received terms. Resistance to a policy can be generated where there are direct but then characteristically localised conflcts of immediate interest. Indeed this kind of militant particularism has sharply increased. But there is then a broad gap between the details of any such action and the necessarily general political and social policies within which the great majority of local actions will be determined. It is in this difficult and often seemingly intractable area that the deep political bias of the press – its effective consensus over and above party differences and specific issues – is likely to be crucial. The survival of a country is so solidly presented as the survival of a rationalised capitalism, with its imperatives steadily extended to those areas that had been considered reserved from it, that even the inevitable consequence of sustained structural unemployment has not produced the anger and determination which, before this phase, virtually everyone would have predicted. A distributed Left press would not necessarily shift this situation in the short term, but it remains a fact that the great majority even of those who might, on past record, be inclined to consider and support it, never hear, day in day out, any alternative perspective and policy. This victory of the capitalist press is so complete that even to mention it seems either banal, to insiders, or in public terms utopian and impractical.

This already dangerous situation is made worse by another consequence of the latest phase of press capitalism. Under the pressure of the economics of newspaper advertising, which has assumed an increasingly significant role in the finances of newspapers, there has been a marked cultural polarisation, within national daily newspapers, which seems to go against every other observable cultural trend. There are now virtually no national newspapers of the old 'middle' type, such as the *News Chronicle*.

The more expensive newspapers have increased their circulations significantly, broadly in line with the development of higher education, which in one way sets their readership, content and style. But the cheaper press, led notably by the Murdoch *Sun,* has if anything moved back towards older cultural styles. It is true that at both poles there has been some internal expansion of range, but it is significant that most of this expansion has been in direct relation to new trends in consumption and its directly related advertising : notably travel, wine and new foods. In the level of its treatment of political, economic and social news the popular press has moved hardly at all since the 1920s, while the society around it has been becoming significantly better educated and informed. All the devices of sensational simplification and spurious personalisation are still regularly practised. Moreover, through a prolonged social crisis, the proportion of such news in the total selection of content has remained remarkably low : even in the most serious papers rarely exceeding 25 per cent. The specific adaptation of the newspaper as a form, through a period of many social changes and through the significant development of television as an alternative source, has been, in fact, towards the magazine and away from the *news* paper which is still taken as its central definition. This is as observable in the more expensive as in the cheaper press. Material directly linked to advertising, again notably 'travel news', has markedly increased. So, very significantly, has 'financial news', in which the concerns of the stock exchange, the banks and the insurance companies have come to be much more centrally represented. It is no surprise that some readers, including some socialists, now find the *Financial Times* the most serious national daily newspaper. One factor, there, is that it presents these central concerns of a capitalist economy more directly, without the spurious identifications common in 'magazine' treatment. (For a further discussion of this, see James Curran's chapter 'Advertising and the Press'.)

Two points have then to be made. The very marked cultural polarisation within the surviving national newspapers has taken place within a significant overall decline in total readership. Every new phase of the decline seems to be met by a further degree of polarisation. In the 1950s there was a broad classification of tabloids, middle populars and 'heavies'. Most of the middle has now gone, and the popular press is overwhelmingly tabloid, and not simply in format. Yet this is only a tendency within the *national* press. Regional and local newspapers now largely occupy the middle ground which the national press has moved away from. The evidence of this more significant representation of an actual public is also directly comparable with the evidence of broadcasting audiences. *News at Ten* is regularly among the television programmes with the very highest audiences, yet in selection and even more strikingly in method and style it is in the middle ground that has been largely lost from newspapers. If we add to news bulletins the whole range of broadcast current affairs coverage, for all its faults, we find a level of sustained presentation and discussion which is in fact more comparable with the expensive minority press than with the popular press, yet which still finds audiences fully comparable with the latter. What has then happened to the popular national newspaper is more likely to be a result of its internal adaptations, within a fiercely competitive and shrinking market and with advertising revenue a major and even decisive factor, than a result of some projected 'popular taste'. While its general decline continues, we can expect these features to become even more pronounced.

The significant disparity between the development and the fortunes of the national and the regional/local press has to be related to a longstanding special factor in British newspapers. In no other capitalist country was there so rapid and apparently so complete a movement towards a centralised metropolitan press. The historical reasons for this are complex but include the relatively early centralisation of industrial capital, the coincident expansion of a national distributive system through the railways, and certain specific characteristics, through the imperialist phase, of the British nation–state. If in style and method the national popular press still reminds us directly of that phase, it is probably no accident. These newspapers are the products of a centralised imperialist urban culture, and their whole cultural and political emphasis is still on that bearing, even while, though slowly, this deep social form is breaking up. What had to be found, and what is now more and more frantically sustained, was a package of interests at that level: an intense nation–state patriotism, a displayed monarchy and plutocracy, a centralised but then personalised politics, the spectacles of large-scale sport and of scandal. Many other agencies are still tied to these interests, but the specific form of the national popular newspaper is more directly tied to them and, even in decline, can only re-emphasise them.

In objective terms, many of the political and social factors which were the conditions for that kind of package have been visibly weakening. Yet, as in other fields, great energy and substantial investment are still given in attempts to sustain this residual version of a metropolitan British consensus. The irony is that a substantial part of its economic support, most directly in advertising, comes from the paranational corporations, many of them foreign-based, which are among the most important objective forces now breaking up the earlier phase. The all-British voice, disseminated in its millions of copies from London as imperial capital and metropolis, is being cut across by other voices – on the one hand American, at the centres of the culture; on the other hand Scots, Irish and Welsh, the English North, in the areas previously drowned by it. Under these pressures the London-based popular press cannot really adapt, since its structure is bound up with the survival of its selective version of 'Britain'. This is a crucial factor in both the cultural polarisation – the promotion of ever simpler and more stereotyped versions of the 'common interest' – and in its observable movement to the Right, which corresponds, in a period of great confusion and difficulty of adjustment, to ever more shrill reassertions of a lost 'Great British' greatness. The observable tendencies of a weakening of the centralised press and some strengthening of the regional and local press are certainly welcome. But we can never overlook the continuing dominance of economic structures of press ownership and control based on a centralised form. This still limits what would otherwise be a very rapid shift of emphasis. Moreover, under these conditions, it seems to be easier to find a contemporary national voice, still of great political importance in this period of transition and struggle, on a limited class basis, as in the *Telegraph* most obviously, or on a very limited educational base, corresponding to a deliberately limited higher education, as in *The Times* and the *Guardian*. Thus, as in other areas, the dominant and residual structures may buckle or even disintegrate, but there is as yet no assured basis for any advantageous alternative structures. It is in this area, above all, that public intervention must be concentrated.

The crisis will probably be fast moving, since we are already in the first stages of a crucial period of technological change. This is already affecting newspaper production itself and is the source of the drive for 'rationalisation'. But what is about to be outdated is the crucial class division inside press production, and at the same time the false class consensus inside the product itself.

In production there can be quite rapid movement towards a significant lessening of the division of labour inside writing and printing. Editors and politicians are now indignant that 'manual workers' on a paper can 'interfere' with its production or content. The indignation is based on a simple class assumption that these workers are unthinking machines which transmit the writing of others. In the short term, of course, there are many established job interests to protect within existing structures. But new developments in electronic composing and typesetting can supersede the structure which demands the division of labour into those who 'write' (and are therefore entitled to ideas and opinions and a certain autonomy) and those who merely 'print'. Within the present structures these can lead only to prolonged industrial struggles and unemployment. Within alternative and then necessarily decentralised and more various structures, the technical opportunities could be remarkably liberating.

At the same time that this battle between alternative futures is being fought, the package which is now the modern newspaper, 'popular' or 'quality', will be likely to be further untied. Already the newspaper has been outdistanced by radio and television for speed of news and for actuality. It was against this background that it moved towards a 'magazine' type of package. With the remarkable growth of specialist magazines, all that remains as an advantage to the modern large-scale newspaper is the fact of the package itself : a multi-interest convenience which is then subject to crucial calculations of cost. The introduction, in the next few years, both of Ceefax, for more detailed immediate news, and of Viewdata, for a very wide range of information and enquiry, will affect newspapers radically. Both are television systems, the latter a combination of television and telephone. The combined effects on newspapers will be radical, both generally and in the field of 'mail order' and classified advertising. The political and commercial decisions made during their early years will be decisive for an already weakened press.

The survival of good newspapers must then be distinguished from the survival of newspapers in the forms in which we now have them. What is fundamentally wrong with most of the British press as it now exists is that it is cast in profoundly residual forms : politically, geographically and technically. But there are extremely important political and economic interests whose future is now tied up with the maintenance or minor adaptation of these residual forms, and this is why they are being sustained in a market situation in which they would otherwise have collapsed. In a truly contemporary perspective, the faults of the residual forms are readily seen: the in-built and increasing political bias, in conventional terms; the propagation of a falsely centralised and falsely personalised version of the nature of political and industrial life; the cultural polarisation within an actual cultural diversification; the dominance of the mixed corporations; the dominance of 'London' (meaning a small class sector in London, near the centres of political and economic power); the division of labour between writers and printers, which corresponds to a wider division between originating writers and a public seen only as consumers; the technological lag, now masked only by the altering relation between the convenient package and the acceptable cost.

Yet many of the 'faults' lead us directly to possible alternative future forms. We are looking for an end to the insanely magnified voices and the absurdly simplified content of the commercial popular ('mass') phase. We are looking for a new political, geographical and cultural diversity. We are looking for organs of news and opinion in which genuine interaction and collaborative contribution are possible, as distinct from magnified one-way transmission and 'penetration of the market'. Only one thing is certain: that if we do not get these things in newspapers, we shall get them in other ways.

Chapter 2

Newspapers, Parties and Classes

Stuart Hall

There is a major debate now in progress concerning the present
condition and future prospects of the British press. This debate
touches issues more profound than a general expression of concern
by those who work in the industry about its viability in a period of
economic recession. The problems now being confronted are
deep-rooted, structural rather than contingent in manner and
scope. Indeed, nothing short of a major restructuring of the
newspaper industry is presently on the agenda: and this is a
process calculated to affect every feature of the press as we know it
today – its size and shape, its management and conditions of
work, the organisation of its labour process, its technical and
financial structure, its role in society. The Royal Commission on
the Press has not resolved these issues. It is, indeed, as much a
symptom of the crisis, as a contribution to its resolution.

This crisis of the British press relates to the internal structures of
the newspaper industry, but an analysis of it cannot be confined to
this level. For the crisis is crystallising in a very specific political
and historical conjuncture, and must in the end be understood
only in this wider context. Even when the question of the press is
fiercely debated within its own terms, everyone concerned is aware
that it has a relation to the wider crisis of hegemony in British

society; and its resolution will have consequences for how the wider crisis will be resolved. I hope to show in the course of this article how and why the crisis of the press must be seen as part of wider tendencies and contradictions which are fusing with it at the present moment. I shall try to demonstrate that the present debates about the 'future of the press' are part of a more general ideological struggle, which has already been joined, whose terms are already 'in play' in the ideological field.

Several different aspects of the substantive crisis of the press are discussed in the chapters which follow. In this essay, I want instead to direct attention, first, to the *general* nature of the crisis which is developing; and then to the *terms* in which the 'debate about the press' is presently conducted. Why has this crisis arisen at this moment? More fundamentally, how is the crisis being represented in the current ideological debate? Are these terms adequate to grasp the real relations and conditions which they purport to 'express'? If not, why are these the terms which currently structure the debate, and what are the consequences of this mode of ideological representation?

The first aspect concerns the financial structure of the press – a problem which is more effectively defined as a crisis in the structure of British press capital. Post-war conditions – including the rising costs of raw materials, production and distribution, and the competition from the new, emergent forces in the communications industries – have *already* precipitated a massive reconstruction of British press capital. The principal effect here has been the break-up of the old press empires, the formation of new conglomerates, with the leading sectors in the electronic-based communications systems and their leisure ancillaries, with the press as a relatively backward and unprofitable sector. This had led, in turn, to a strong tendency towards monopolisation – a tendency which, while combining the press with other sectors of the communications–leisure complex, has sharpened the competition for advertising, reduced the number of national newspapers and polarised the press towards one or other of its two extreme poles – the 'elite' and the 'popular–tabloid' newspaper. This re-structuring has not been sufficient to lift the industry free of its economic problems. The press is no longer the 'leading fraction' of that sector of capital tied up in the communications industry. Even those national dailies with relatively high circulation figures and quite strong advertising positions are, nevertheless, daily threatened with extinction.

This declining relative position of press capital has been undermined further from two distinct but related directions. The first is the rising costs of production and distribution. These include both the cost of necessary raw materials, like paper and pulp, of which there is now a world shortage; and high labour costs – the latter sustained through the long-standing but still effective unionisation of the labour force employed in the industry. The second factor is the so-called 'technical' solution to this problem. Faced with a comparable barrier to further expansion and development – factors which limit the press as a profitable site of investment – there has emerged a 'classical' solution. This is the attempt to by-pass the limit by the introduction of new machinery and new processes, with the consequent restructuring of the labour process and a secular reduction in the ratio of men to machinery. This means, in effect, raising the ratio of (new) machinery to 'living' labour – that is, intensifying the productivity of labour or intensifying the rate of exploitation, by the combined strategies of pushing through new technologies and decreasing the labour force (i.e. adding to the size of the reserve army of labour) through a process of 'technological unemployment'. The various recipes for the solution to the crisis of the press all involve, in one form or another, some variant of this process of substitution and dilution – a classical solution to a classical form of the capitalist crisis.

This 'solution' is, however, blocked from two different directions. First, by the extremely high cost of installing the new machinery and working it cost-effectively. This can only be met by, in effect, opening the press to the penetration of fresh capital (mainly, in the present conditions – though, as the recent case of the *Express* shows, not exclusively – overseas or multi-national capital – American, in the case of the *Observer,* Australian, in the case of Rupert Murdoch). This triggers an internal crisis between competing capitals – the present holders resisting the admission of new kinds of capital not 'schooled' in the traditions of the British press families and empires. Another alternative is that of some form of state intervention or support. But this would represent a shift from private ownership to some unholy combination of private capital and state capitalism – a form of ownership which is currently, in general, the site of a major political struggle (again,

between different fractions of capital), and which, in the special
case of the press, has the added disadvantage of appearing to
undermine its very *raison d'être,* the economic source of its traditional independence.

But the 'solution' is also blocked from another source: in effect,
by the corporate power of unionised labour, which quite correctly
does not see why the costs of 'modernisation' should be borne
exclusively on the backs of – and at the expense of the hard-won
position and long-established skills and differentials of – the print
workers. Print workers are not only highly unionised. They have a
tight hold over entry to the industry, and the internal division of
labour – as represented in manning levels per job and a well-
defended scale of skills and differentials – has been effectively
defended by the chapels against technological dilution.

This is where the class struggle is effectively joined in the
newspaper industry, and where it sets limits to the forms in which
capital is free to resolve its own accumulation and realisation crisis
at the expense of its labour force. That struggle has been, for
several years, the subject of protracted and unresolved negotiations. As should be clear from the sketchy outline given, resis-
tances to the adoption of any of these solutions arise from different
forces locked in the struggle. Some arise from within the press
itself – from the different fractions of capital involved. Some arise
from different levels within the press – managers here having a
different set of interests from owners. Some arise from the
organised workforce itself. The state, through its frequent con-
sultations with the newspaper proprietors, and with the different
managements at times of crisis, is now itself an active political
force in the struggle, though not yet either a direct, or a decisive,
force. If any combination of the available solutions is to be
adopted and successfully pushed through, this will require the
bringing to a conclusion of a major ideological struggle, with its
own pertinent effects in terms of the mobilisation of public consent
for 'tough but necessary measures'. The need to lay the basis for
such a resolution at the ideological level is all the more acute,
because of the contradictory double nature of the press. Commercially, like any other business, the press must compete and
succeed. But its products – newspapers – are not ideologically
neutral commodities. They hold a special, position because they
are the medium through which 'public opinion' is held to crysta-

lise, and thus they perform critical work on behalf of 'our democratic way of life'. Classical monetarists, who would generally argue that those sectors which cannot effectively compete and survive ought to be forced out of business, have to recognise that the press is, in this respect, a 'special case'. In short, the future of the British press will be decided, *in part,* in the field of ideological struggle. This is the aspect which most directly concerns me here.

The attempt to restructure press capital is a process which largely proceeds out of sight of public debate. It is only at key moments, when bids are being cobbled together, or when the big battalions of international capital are making their final tactical moves, that these structural movements come to light at all. Such turning points are elaborated, linguistically and ideologically, within three modes of discourse. They are fleetingly revealed in the spectacular discourse of the *Insight* and 'insider'-type features, which allow us briefly to revel in the dramas of high finance, in the blow-by-blow, minute-by-minute reconstruction of 'how the fate of the *Mail* was finally decided'. These moments are also the subject of financial commentary and speculation in the financial columns and business supplements. These employ the language of economic necessity – of relative costs, liquidity and investment – a realist language, fundamentally derived from ownership and markets, where the laws governing its movements belong unquestionably to the domain of private capital and its imperatives. Print workers – whether journalists of the lesser rank or compositors of any rank – are external to this discourse: 'notified', 'kept in the picture', but not principal actors on the stage where bids and counter-bids from Sydney, New York and places further west are being composed. Third, there is the editorial language of 'standards and quality'. In this mode, one end of the press may curl its lip in disdain at the thought of the depth of vulgarity of the new press entrepreneurs: but when the chips are down – and they usually are – the Murdoch machine proves unstoppable by any effective combination of British capital, however impeccable its lineage.

Other aspects of the press crisis are, however, subject to a major ideological reworking. It is useful to look at these here, since the terms involved are by no means confined to the debate about the press. The principal dimensions of this ideological representation concerns the *technical* solutions proposed and the *political* barriers to their adoption. The orchestration of the dispute between these two poles is the key to the ideological logic at work. The introduction of new machinery, the restructuring of the labour process, the dilution of existing historically created skills and the 'neccessary redundancies' are all represented as a technical question. Industry must advance technically to keep up and survive in 'modern' conditions; the logic of technological innovation is unstoppable and irreversible; neither social nor political criteria are relevant – only the rational calculation of the most cost-effective means to the most competitive ends. Modernisation is thus a cause for which all good men and true must stand up and be counted, for the future of industry, and thus the fate of the nation, stands or falls with it. It is in the 'national interest'. The enemy in the path of this inevitable march of progress is the entrenched, backward-looking and restrictionalist power of organised labour. Thus, there is a *technical* problem, with a *technical* solution, blocked by a *political* barrier. In short, the vested power of the unions is, once again, holding the press and therefore the nation up to ransom.

This is, of course, a representation of the forms of appearance of the crisis, cast within the discourse of 'technological rationality'. It is an ideological discourse. It offers terms, counters, categories within which ordinary folk can 'think' the problems of the press. These representations not only fill out the ideological field of discourse: they divide and regroup the field into significant oppositions – positioning the press on the side of the nation–people, the unions on the side of narrow, vested class interest. In effect, this draws one side in the crisis together, under the banner of a coherent representation, on which is inscribed 'The National Interest' at the expense of dividing and disorganising the opposition forces. By identifying the interests of the press with 'the general interest' and with the interests of technical modernisation, and casting the role of labour with sectional interest and a restrictionist, defensive posture, this mode of representation at one and the same time raises the issue 'above politics', and so organises the field of discourse as to favour the general tendency of a solution in capital's interest, which can now appear as 'technically neutral'. Of course, this is also a *credible* way of representing the struggle – and as such, does grasp *some* aspects of the crisis, though it does so *one-sidedly*. From the viewpoint of a solution favourable to capital, labour costs *are* 'too high', machinery *would* be 'more efficient' at current rates of profitability, there *are* 'too many men employed per job', etc. It is also 'true' that the unions, from their suboɪdinate position in the struggle, find themselves defending a division of labour in the industry which is archaic from the point of view of the potential capacity of the new forces of print production. But this is only one of the many – and necessary – contradictions in the current position. The language of 'technical necessity', however, has no space within it for the necessarily contradictory interests of capital and labour in the newspaper industry. Indeed, the function of its 'technicist' character is precisely to purge that language of all antagonisms. It cannot show that a 'solution', imposed on capital's terms, necessarily entails 'defeat'. It must re-present this necessary contradiction in the relation of capital to labour in the print industry as a technical solution, which could be good for *everyone* (including, presumably, the scores of print workers thrown on the scrap heap of the reserve army of labour in a period of rising unemployment) – a universal solution, in the general interest, to which particular, sectional vested interests are opposed. This discourse thus colonises the elements of the argument, and rearticulates them in a discourse which favours capital's solution.

To this we must now add another contributory factor. For the long-term structural crisis of the press has been accentuated by a second thrust: the limited push for greater 'journalistic power' against both owners and management. This second thrust has arisen in the wake of the cultural revolution of 1968, with its claims for greater 'worker participation'. At the same time, it reflects a longer secular movement within the journalistic profession. Journalism is one of those key sectors which has been moving steadily in recent years, alongside other white-collar professions, towards a more thoroughgoing professional unionisation. This in turn reflects the growing 'proletarianisation', or at least the tendency towards a degree of de-skilling, within the ranks of the journalists which has brought in its wake a greater degree of co-operation than would have been possible a decade ago between editorial and industrial staffs. The growing power and militancy of the NUJ, and its decisive movement – in the context of economic recession – towards the 'closed shop' is one aspect of this trend which fills the hearts of both newspaper managements and traditional senior journalists with fear and dismay. Another aspect is the growing claims, by journalists as well as in certain chapels, for greater control, not only over wages and conditions, but also over the 'product of their labour' (in this case, newspapers and what they print). When the resistance by the unions to technical innovation is combined with a movement, amongst journalists, towards a stronger 'closed shop' position, it becomes clear why the situation in the newspaper industry has become one of the paradigm cases of the 'misuse' of professional and industrial power for political ends: a sign of the overweening power and dictatorial practice of the trade unions, and a token of the encroachment of 'organised labour' into the domain of the traditional independence of the fourth state and an unwarrantable restraint on editorial freedom. It is not difficult to imagine, therefore, how and why these separate strands fuse together into the greater general thematic of the *threats to the freedom of the press*. Nor is it difficult to see how this theme can be made to articulate with the wider terms of the current ideological struggle, with its powerful populist appeal against the defensive organisation of the working class, its fear of the 'drift into collectivism', its nightmare vision of 'our democratic liberties' being so undermined that they are in danger of slipping and sliding into some imaginary Gulag archipelago.

The principal ideological articulation of the crisis in the press is currently to be found in terms of this great mobilising theme of the defence of the freedom of the press. It is worth deconstructing this theme a little, exposing some of its ideological connotations. This has everything to do with a certain received history. Summarily, this history may be represented as follows. In the 'bad old days', the press was a 'kept mistress', the organ and agent of political factions and parties. It was also limited and restricted by legal and legislative constraints. Against these limitations and restrictions, 'the press' fought a noble and heroic battle; and, in winning the 'right to publish' and the 'freedom to comment' it won an essential liberty on behalf, not only of its owners, but of the whole society. The creation of this 'fourth estate' is therefore part and parcel of the story of the great reforming, democratic liberalisation of, especially, the last century. Like the imposition of a universal 'rule of law', and other fundamental rights such as the 'freedom of assembly', it both marked the triumph of the reforming impulse, and the willingness of vested interest and power, when pushed, to yield to a more universal form of the democratic state. It is now one of the great fundamental liberties of 'our democratic way of life' – the bastion of public opinion against the powers of the executive. In this reading of the history, the freedom of the press is one of the central unifying themes of the Whig view of the evolution of the British state.

This 'history' is itself underpinned by what we might call the economic theory of liberty. For it was – and is – the private ownership of the press which is said to provide the final guarantee of the press's independence from political pressure and from executive interference: and hence the basis of that 'freedom of the press' which all free-born Englishmen have inherited. The privately-owned character of the press has therefore been firmly linked with the preservation of this democratic right – a coincidence of private property and a certain definition of liberty which enhances (and not only because in part it derives from) the political theory of John Locke. It is the location of the 'free press' in what Locke would have recognised as 'civil society' (an institution of private commercial association, separate from the state) which is said to guarantee and institutionalise the expression of the widest spectrum of opinions on major topics of the day. The press is thus the organ of 'public opinion', and, as such, sustains the society of free and plural opinions, giving the ordinary citizen access to power through the influence which the press can bring to bear within the arena of executive decision. Hence the private ownership of the press is indissolubly linked with the liberties of ordinary citizens against the state. The massive, real disparities of property and power – which alone permit a very small 'association of individuals' to bring together the men, means and materials necessary under modern conditions to produce the national newspaper – are magically dissolved into the image of this great, equivalent conversation of 'free and equal men' out of which public opinion spontaneously arises. It is this contradiction, at the root of the theory of 'possessive individualism', which the tide of democratic discourse has long since rolled over, rendering it invisible. It was, after all, the 'printer's devil' in Locke's theory of possessive individualism too.

We have called this selective re-reading of the history an aspect of the Whig view of English liberties and the English state. This school may have long been discredited in serious historiography, but it lives on as a powerful myth in popular consciousness, and has been deeply enshrined in the various institutional histories of the evolution of the British state. We can find its parallel in the history of the 'giving of the suffrage', in the establishment of an impartial judiciary and a professional police force with the consequent 'conquest of violence', in the re-reading of the history of British trade unionism and the 'right of combination'; and in the great story of the 'origins' of the modern welfare state. What is so powerful about this ideological structure is that it is fully able to take into account an earlier period when these liberties did not exist – before the great reform of English society. This is counterposed to the modern position, where these liberties have not only been widely established, but constitutionally and legally sanctified. This means that English society has *become,* through this long process of improvement, a society of full democratic rights, in which the ordinary citizen has been fully enfranchised. Many of these liberties, however, depend on modifications in the nature and structure of the state itself. In this galaxy, therefore, the press stands out as a pure and special case. For it only required that the constraints and restraints on the freedom to publish be lifted, for this particular liberty to flourish. Of course, the laws of libel and some other official constraints still remain – and there is a powerful press lobby at present pushing for a further reform of these remaining limitations. But, aside from these legal limits, the freedom of the press requires no intervention or guidance by the state – indeed, its freedom is defined precisely by the degree to which the state does not encroach. The institution of private property and the competitive laws of the market themselves mysteriously maximise the general conditions of freedom for all free individuals. These freedoms are preserved through 'the collision of unfettered individuals who are determined only by their interests – as the mutual repulsion and attraction of free individuals, and hence as the absolute mode of existence of free individuality in the sphere of consumption and exchange'.[1] No wonder Mrs Thatcher and Sir Keith Joseph regard the issues of the closed shop and union power in the print industry as undermining the very fabric of democratic society, and see the press as the paradigm instance of 'social market forces' serving as the guarantor of our liberties.

Now of course there are real and substantive differences between those societies in which the formal right to 'publish and be damned' is widely guaranteed, where citizens enjoy the freedom to express opinions which are not to the liking of the powers that be, and where the press is not subject to direct, daily censorship, surveillance and executive interference; and those where such freedoms do not exist or are severely curtailed. These are *significant* differences, with real and *pertinent* effects – effects even upon the forms which the class struggle (which of course continues) assumes under such conditions. The Whig historians are right at least in this: that the growth of a privately-owned free press has certainly gone hand in hand with, and is an intrinsic part of, the emergence of the democratic class state in its fully 'representative' modern form. However, far from taking this at face value, it is precisely this coincidence which we must explain. Certainly the maintenance of such freedoms cannot be simply attributed to the machinations of a clever ruling class which dupes and deceives the subordinate classes. Nevertheless, it is necessary to subject this great, abstract and universal theme in the ideologies of democratic class society to a rigorous and searching critique, for a great deal of mystification surrounds it.

Such a critique must begin by setting the abstract and formal 'right' of free expression within the context of the real relations (both historically and at the present) through which this formal relation is concretely realised, under definite and determinate conditions of existence. The form in which this relation is ideologically represented is through the image of the 'free market' – in this instance, the 'free market in opinions', with the press as a sort of third chamber (or fourth estate) where each individual free citizen is represented and can bring his influence to bear on society and the state – one voice, one opinion per citizen, so to speak – in the great democratic conversation between free individuals. This represents the situation with respect to the formation of public opinion as one in which each citizen is constituted as the formal equivalent of every other citizen. But it does not require a great deal of research to show that, in the real conditions of democratic class society, to conceive the real relations between the classes as a set of equivalent relations between equal individuals is to represent (to re-present, in the active sense) the real relations in which the classes stand to one another in the form of an 'imaginary relation'.

To put the point more generally: the 'freedom of the press' happily coexists with the maintenance of capitalist relations of production and exploitation, in the economic organisation of society, and with the maintenance of a complex system of class relations in its social and political life. What the ideology of the doctrine of 'rights' implies is that this coexistence of formal freedoms with the real relations of class domination and exploitation has the merit, over alternative social arrangements, of moderating and limiting the latter's most excessive and arbitrary features. The mechanism of this moderating influence is, of course, the formation and influence of 'public opinion' which the freedom of the press guarantees to each citizen. The press also guarantees that, in such societies, the powers of property and privilege will be exercised under the restraint – and thus with the consent – of the great mass of the population which is without either property or privilege.

There can, indeed, be no question that, in democratic class societies, the various forms of power *do* require to pass the test of popular consent before they can be legitimately exercised. The problem remains – how are we to understand this form of the state, and the role of the press within it? The press, that is to say, in its real relation to power, to classes and masses, rather than in an 'imaginary relation' with them. In such forms of the state, must we understand the press as it understands itself – as the *limiting* fourth estate, with an essentially democratising thrust, a major representational function, curbing the excesses of the arbitrary exercise of power by government, property and the state? Or are we to understand the press as the principal mechanism by which is mobilised and organised that consent to power and property – i.e. as articulating the relation of the popular masses to the dominant classes, without which democratic class societies would lose all legitimacy?

To the notion that competition and the free market had created the historic conditions under which 'unfettered individuals' could compete on equal terms with one another, 'determined only by their own interests', Marx counterposed the scandalous proposition that 'it is not individuals who are set free by free competition; it is rather capital which is set free. As long as production resting on capital is necessary, hence the fittest form of the development of the forces, of social production, the movement of individuals within the pure conditions of capital appears as their freedom'[2]. If modern daily newspapers disappear or are rescued, it is certainly not because any individuals require them in order to form opinions which can actively moderate and influence the disposition of power. What dictates these fundamental movements – and what, under modern conditions of concentration and monopoly, essentially *limits* these movements – are the laws of motion, the necessities and contradictions, of capital itself, and the conditions of its profitable reproduction. Before competition is the imaginary relation of free and equal citizens competing to maintain their opinions in the market place of ideas, it is 'the way in which the many capitals force the inherent determinants of capital upon one another and upon themselves.' It is the movements and dispositions of capital which essentially determine the *specific distribution* of newspapers which confronts the individual citizen as the means of social and political influence. That is, capital determines the structured field in which individuals compete to be heard. Competition under present conditions has indeed had the principal effect of *narrowing* the already narrow available spectrum of press channels. It has also had the effect – noted earlier – of dismantling an already simplified spectrum of *types* of newspaper, driving the press further into its two extremes. The density of capital now required to launch or successfully to sustain a national daily newspaper ensures that very few, if any, *new* forces can appear to be represented at the level of the daily press. Alternative channels have little real chance of breaking into this structured field, for they simply cannot command the capital resources required to stay effectively in the game. Far from maximising the range of outlets, in keeping with the increasingly complex and 'plural' society of opinions it is supposed to represent, the present structure of the capitalist press limits and restricts the organs through which the great conversation between free and equal citizens is supposed to be sustained.

Nor is the structure which results from the way 'many capitals force the inherent determinations of capital upon one another and upon themselves' a random one. The restrictions and limitations have been systematically of a certain kind, operated in a certain direction: namely, towards the marginalisation of alternative channels and virtual disappearance of anything remotely like a working-class national newspaper. The fate of the *Herald,* the failure to sustain the *Scottish Daily News* and the token position of the *Morning Star* are telling instances of the principal direction in which the 'logic of capital' has operated since the war. There is, of course, a massive national daily press directed *at* the working-class reader: but it is in essence a bourgeois press *for* a working-class market. Certainly, for a newspaper like the *Mirror* or the *Sun* so effectively to colonise certain sectors of the working-class market, it must address itself to the concerns, adopt the language, representative registers and tones of voice of that class strata, and to some degree articulate selected working-class themes, experiences and values. The difference between the *Mirror* and the *Sun* in the ways they articulate with their working-class readership is a complex matter, touching the precise nature of the representational relationship of the press to the complex fractions of a class. This point will be taken up again later. But it is sufficient to say, at this point in the argument, that if the spread of newspapers is supposed magically to reproduce and replicate, however roughly, the broad strata of classes and opinions in society – thus fulfilling its democratic-representational function – then the most striking feature of the present disposition of the press is the *structured absence* of the working class from any direct representational presence through the national press. Class interests, themes and experiences are 'present' here only in a highly mediated and transposed form. The formal play of 'equality of representation' through the mysterious hidden hand of the market must therefore be set against the real relations of representation: in which, side by side with the structured *absence* of a working-class press as such at the national level, there is the massive over-representation of the various strata and fractions of capital – including (with the virulent emergence of the revamped *Mail*), at least two daily papers which are, to all intents and purposes, 'working-class newspapers', so-called, *for capital.*

This structured position of the British press in relation to the disposition of classes and class forces is no recent phenomenon. The fact is that, throughout its historical development, the press has *always* stood in some specific, representational position in the equation of the relations of class forces. The so-called 'history' of the press could be (but never has been so far) written in terms of an account of the succession of positions, and the shifts between them, in which its leading sectors have stood to the equations of class power. There is no need to stress how different a set of 'histories' this would be from the Whig account of the great march of English liberties which has informed the history of the British press to date. We cannot reconstruct those histories here: but it is worth simply indicating them, even in the most sketchy and crude fashion, in order to mark the difference.

The emergence of something like a modern newspaper in the eighteenth century, governed principally, though not exclusively, by an approximation to commercial and market conditions, is very closely linked with the emergence of an urban and a landed bourgeoisie, and the related formation of the party system. For a major part of that period the close links between the press and the party factions were indeed one of its principal articulations. It is, of course, also in this period, that one finds the first great enunciation of the *universal* value of 'press freedom'. That is, with the freedom of the press as with the other great bourgeois freedoms, the struggle of an emergent bourgeois class against the old order was represented as a universal freedom on behalf of mankind as such, within the language of 'natural rights'. The force which was most dissolving those older social and political relations was, of course, the slow and uneven penetration of capitalist free market relations, and the growth of that corresponding form of 'civil society' in which private egoistic interests created a sphere of 'freedom' free of the limitations of both custom and the absolutist state. The press itself, and the struggle for the 'free press', in this period is a powerful articulator of these emergent elements. The coincidence between the 'free' individual, the 'free market', the 'free' press and the 'freedom' to accumulate private property is forged in this moment, and provides the basis of the real relations in which the press stood *vis-à-vis* the struggle of the classes. As Marx observed about this phase 'every new class which puts itself in the place of one ruling before it, is compelled, merely in order to carry through its aim, to represent its interests as the common interest of all the members of society, that is, expressed in ideal form: it has to give its ideas the form of universality, and represent them as the only rational, universally valid ones'.[3] It would be hard to establish, historically, that the eighteenth century press stood in an equal and universal relation to *all* the classes organised within the parasitism of 'Old Corruption'.

The press at the turn of the eighteenth century into the nineteenth stands in a very different position – indeed, it is not the same press at all. Here, alongside the emergence of the urban and industrial proletariat as a social force on the historical stage, and indeed in the most active, formative, *educative and organisational* relation to it, stood the radical and working-class press. This is the press of the new forces, the press of the radical sects, of the early unions and corresponding societies, of Jacobinism, of reform and political agitation and later the press of the Chartist movement. It is a press which specifically articulated the great economic and political movements of the working class in the period of its 'making' – an agitational, and frequently an *illegal* press – the great and lesser unstamped, the 'poor men's guardians' – which a whole generation of publishers and printers and sellers faced legal trial and incarceration to defend. Though the main enemy of this press was the unreformed state, in a phase of severe repression, it also stood opposed, in form, relationship and tendency, to the whole of the bourgeois press which was frequently found ranged *against* it – in the name of another set of 'freedoms': the freedoms of *laissez-faire* individualism and the inevitable laws of political economy.

The decline of the working-class press of this period does not belong within the limited 'history of the press' as such. It is part of the much wider history of the containment, and transformation of the emergent classes to and for whom it spoke. The victories it won – breaking both legal–administrative and tax constraints – were maximised by the great middle-class reforming press which comes into its own from the mid-century onwards. The hegemony of the mid-century liberal press is clearly part and parcel of that deep transformation of English social, political and economic life which made England an industrial capitalist society; it was established on the back of the defeat and decline of the working-class press. It is this decisive shift in the articulation of the press to the classes which has, subsequently, been redefined and absorbed into the heroic story of the triumph of Whig liberties.

The dismantling of this Liberal press of 'politics and opinion' into the more commercially oriented press of the modern era belongs properly to the closing period of the nineteenth century and the opening decades of the twentieth. This is a period of major transition and transformation, marked above all by the 'high noon' of imperialism, and by the beginning of that complex shift into the phase of monopoly capitalism about which so much has recently been written. The press of that period – in both its reformed economic structure and basis, and in its content, themes and preoccupations – articulates in the most integral manner with both those aspects of 'the transition'; and thus with the classes which stood in a directing relation to them. The new 'popular' press of that period owes *more* to the themes of popular imperialism, and to the debate within the ruling classes and its subaltern class fractions, concerning competition and restriction, than it does to the much-heralded theme of the great reform in popular education – which is held, in the received wisdom of our times, not only to have 'created a readership' for the popular press in its new forms, but even to be in some way directly responsible for its quality.

Later, as soon as we find the great development of the new mass markets, the rise of the surburban lower middle classes and the massive concentration and integration of capital required to support the new technologies of mass production and distribution, we also find the press in something not remotely dissimilar from the press of our own time. Papers addressed to the different sectors of the population, mirroring in their internal structures and languages the class strata to whom they were directed; a fierce competitive struggle for supremacy in these stratified markets; with the commercial exploitation of newspaper readers as 'consumers' now in a more dominant position as compared with the direct articulation between newspapers, parties and classes. But this is also the period of the great enfranchisement of the masses, and the resulting emergence of a democratic state in something approaching its present form – forced, by the very established presence of an enfranchised working class, to appear to stand as a neutral, objective and *universal* force, above and outside the struggle between the contending classes – 'apparently reconciling them'. Classes and the struggles between and within classes continue into and through this phase. And the press continues to be articulated in its complex way with them. But the forms *assumed* by those class relations are qualitatively different in the period after formal enfranchisement as compared with earlier periods, for now those relations are obliged to 'pass through' the formal democratic process, winning and organising consent to the equations of power struck in the relations of force. This fact about 'mature' class democracies is the result of the struggles fought, through the previous century and a half, to make real and concrete certain 'rights and liberties' by and for classes of men and women for whom they were not originally designed, who previously stood outside of the formal equation of power in the successive stages of the development of the capitalist state. It is the result of certain concrete victories which made such freedoms real – rather than the result of the magnamimity and far-sightedness of the ruling classes of successive historical blocs. Of course, these real and pertinent conquests – pertinent in the sense of having a *real* regulatory and transformatory effect on the manner in which power operates and is legitimised in 'fully mature' class democracies – are stopped short of a profound social transformation. They have, in short, been worked back into, or worked through into new recuperative forms of hegemony which now operate, not through the exclusion, but through the *incorporation* (a tendency, never of course a totally completed process) of these classes which have forced their way on to the stage of history.

The terms and forms, then, in and through which the modern press articulates with this complex structure of class power and hegemony are profoundly different from those at previous stages of this turbulent and uneven 'history'. But this is quite a different thing from suggesting – as the contemporary ideological representations do – that *therefore* the equations and equilibria of power and hegemony have been wholly dismantled, leaving only in their place the free conversation of free and equal men, speaking through a free press. The rewritten, truncated and displaced history is precisely one of the ways in which this ideology effects a closure upon itself – how it wins its own kind of legitimacy as a way of 'making sense' of the current situation.

The modern press, then, remains an integral part of the equation of class power in our society. It is articulated – in new and complex ways – with the relations of class forces in society. As in its mirror image – the representative institutions of parliament – every one does indeed have the 'right' to express himself or herself, through the ballot, on the one hand, or the purchase of a newspaper, freely available, on the other. And indeed – again, as in the parliamentary system – all the classes and class interests and positions are 'represented' somewhere within the spectrum of available expressions. This is the qualitatively new phase or stage – the form, alike, of press and of parliament – in the fully mature democratic class state. But since classes, class struggles and class hegemony continue in and through this phase, the decisive question is not how the press can be preserved as an 'independent sphere' *free* of these determinations, but rather how precisely does the articulation between a 'free press' and the disposition of class forces actually now operate?

It is in the understanding of this question – a problem of the real relation of the press to the maintenance of class hegemony in the democratic class state – which has puzzled left- and right-wing critics alike; often leading both sides to false simplifications; and thereby making space for the themes of freedom and consent to operate. This question cannot be settled here, but a provisional solution must be sketched if the character of the ideological struggle outlined at the beginning of this article is to be properly understood. It requires us to abandon two attractive but over-simple ideas. The first is the notion that classes exist as whole blocks or groups, defined essentially by their economic status or even by their position in the system of economic production, with ascribed, class fixed 'world views', internally coherent and unchanging. The second, following on from the first, is the idea that the press, to be understood in relation to classes and class struggle, must then be conceived as passively reflecting these 'whole' classes and their 'interests' in a narrow, direct and given sense. For if so, we would have no need of anything but a single newspaper of the bourgeoisie, a paper of the working class, each with its predictable, ascribed ideological position on all issues – positions which could be identified simply as 'expressions' of ascribed class interests. Clearly, the existing structure of the British press is only comprehensible in these terms at the expense of a massive and tendentious simplification.

The fundamental classes of modern capitalist society do not exist in this pre-given form. They are not whole and coherent blocks, whose status is determined by their economic position. They are complex formations. Though their position in the structure of a particular mode of production provides the necessary condition, it does not provide the sufficient condition of their position and practice in society. Their political and ideological positions cannot be taken as fixed and given by their economic designation. What classes are in fact is what they *become*, through the effects upon them as homogeneous categories of the practices which produce them: and these depend in turn on the political and ideological as well as the economic practices of the class struggle. Their effect, as classes, depends on the manner in which they are articulated and represented, in political and ideological practice, that is through the practices and institutions which have this specific function of *representation* in relation to them. Far from passively reflecting and expressing class policies and ideologies, in forms given by their economic position, *everything* depends on the means and apparatuses through which they are articulated and represented as class forces in the political and ideological theatres of struggle. Further, there are no whole classes as such – homogeneous and uncontradictory entities – to be found in the field of political and ideological struggle. Classes are complexly fractured and/or unified (it is an active *process*) through their practices. The ruling bloc in any particular period is not the direct representatives, the managing committee, of some unified 'bourgeoisie'. It is precisely a *bloc,* composed of particular fractions of the dominant classes and class fractions: which have managed, first, to unify themselves in practice; then, to exert their hegemony over other fractions within the ruling class and in subaltern classes; and which, then, on this basis – and through the organs of the state and civil society – are able at certain moments to exert their hegemony over the social formation as a whole, welding it into a unity, of the kind which enables, not narrow class interests but the mode of production as a whole to expand and develop and be realised.

It is only when the nature of class hegemony within the framework of the democratic class state is understood in something like these terms, that we are able to understand the articulation of the press to this 'equilibrium of power'. The press, then, serves both an *organising* function, and a 'relatively autonomous' or independent function, with respect to this hegemony. That is to say, it has real and pertinent *work* to do; work which is not given by the existing classes, which cannot be reduced to a passive reflection of already organised class expressions, on behalf of this hegemonic function. It has the 'work' of articulating, resolving and exploring the *real* contra-dictions of interest, direction and tendency – between the many and complex alternatives available – within the various fractions of capital, and within the political bloc. It has the organising function of bringing certain views to a coherent expression – of working through their ramifications and welding the alliance of class forces together into a cohesive strategy. It has the role of organising and articulating these coherences in such a way as to mobilise behind them the support and consent of other classes and class fractions, which stand outside the equations of power, but whose consent is necessary to their functioning. It has, that is to say, the role of the organiser and mobiliser of 'public opinion', organising and orchestrating it in such forms as to allow the social formation to be cemented in support of those strategies which are emerging as the coherent and necessary ones, from the point of view of the successful reproduction and expansion of the mode of production. Finally, it has the role of so representing the oppositional forces, as to *disorganise* them, face to face with an emerging hegemonic consensus. It is above all in its role of articulating various positions on the major issues of conflict and struggle in society *into a coherent class discourse,* orchestrating this discourse as a discourse not of a narrow class interest but of the nation–people – the 'general interest' – and, in that way, demobilising alternative viewpoints, that the press can be understood as playing a critical role in the reproduction of class hegemony in the democratic class state.

It is important to add that this function is not, and cannot be reduced to, the willed or conscious *intentions* of those professionals who actually produce the press. Indeed, the very proof, on occasions, of an explicit class orientation or bias, is as likely to be regarded among such professionals as a breach of their professional ethic and ideology. That is because, in taking their stand on the various issues and themes of the hour, they orient themselves, but in a profound unconsciousness, to the way the field of struggle has been defined by the forces involved. And, taking this as the natural, 'given' ground of controversy and debate, they can – in full consciousness – really (that is, 'really') explore 'all the issues', from 'all points of view'. If the professional journalists thus perform a role in the reproduction of class hegemony, it is only because the professional ideology' of objectivity effectively *brackets them off,* in a sphere of professional freedom and uncommitment, from the direct play of class interests. Their relation to classes, class interests and class struggle is necessarily *displaced,* as all such relations are displaced in and through the institutions of the democratic class state 'standing above the struggle and reconciling it'. Professionalism, neutrality, the 'clear distinction' between facts and values, reports and judgements, is the unconsciousness – 'that specific form of consciousness called unconsciousness'[4] – through which professional men 'live' their real relation to the struggles on which, with due impartiality, they report and comment.

Within this equation of power and consent, the press has a very specific role to play. For, despite the many protocols governing the direct expression of particular class interests, the private nature of the press, and its position in civil society, give it a freedom not possessed, for example, by television, actively to campaign, organise, orchestrate and mobilise its disorganised publics behind certain positions, tendencies and calls for action. It is not governed by the stricter protocols of due impartiality' which monitor and regulate the more state-oriented sphere of television. And, especially in a period of sharpening class struggle, this 'freedom' (not the one normally cited in the litany of 'natural rights') is a vital one, which the press and only the press can perform, on behalf of the present organisation of society.

Gramsci once spoke of the active, *educative* role of the press in these terms. He said the press had, in relation to the fundamental classes, something very much like the representational role of the democratic party.

> This function can be studied with greater precision if one starts from the point of view that a newspaper too (or a group of newspapers), a review (or group of reviews), is a 'party' or 'fraction of a party', or a 'function of a particular party'. Think of the role of the *Times* in England; or that which the *Corriere della Sera* used to have in Italy; or again of the role of the so-called informational press', with its claim to be 'apolitical'; or even that of the sporting and technical press.[5]

Gramsci means here that the press always has this active educative role in relation to the classes and class fractions it 'represents'. He means that the representational role is never a passive, reflexive one. It is actively educative in relation to its class tendency – actively forming, articulating, working up a set of ideological representations which serve to clarify and unify, giving coherence to specific class forces in a particular conjuncture. And indeed, as the example of the *Times* indicates, the very relative freedom from narrow class or party commitment is precisely that room for manoeuvre which makes the press so effective an organiser of the supporting consensus.

It is in this sense that we can now return to the problem of the 'working-class press' of the bourgeoisie. Within the structured field of representation marked out by the distribution of newspapers on the national scene, there is – one may say at the ideological level – no single 'working-class viewpoint'. The working class is not only 'represented' in and through the capitalist press whose sectors are in part directed to the working-class reader: it is also 'represented' in more than one form. One could say that it appears, ideologically, structured through its *corporate* class representation (the *Mirror*), its apolitical, fun-loving class representation (the *Sun*) and indeed, in a peculiar petty-bourgeois representation (in the *Mail* and some parts of the failing *Express*). These are all 'working-class positions' in the sense that it is possible to articulate these contradictory facets of 'the working class' – to work them up, representationally – in these displaced or condensed discourses. Each facet has real credibility, and thus awakens real recognitions, in the identifications of working-class readers with the forms in which their class positions have been *interpellated* in these discourses. Each, of course, also works up these positions in a systematically distorted way. That is, they actively produce representations of the class in which class members can 'recognise' themselves as the bloody-minded 'Us' of the *Mirror,* the bingo-and-bare-breasted subject of the *Sun,* the respectable, law-and-order militant of the *Mail.* They also actively do *not* produce representations which allow class members to recognise themselves as working people, as the producers of wealth, as an exploited class, as the producers of surplus value, as a subordinate culture, as active and militant trade unionists, as men and women 'who have nothing to lose but their chains'. These are interpellations which are structurally *excluded* from the field of class representations at the ideological level. It may be said that, so long as this field of structured absences and presences is taken for granted, as the ground and presupposition on which the press operates, it is 'free' to do and say what else it likes. And that 'freedom', at once real and imaginary, will work to reproduce society in its already given class structured form. That will be the 'freedom' of the present structure of class hegemony to reproduce itself to infinity. It is just worth remembering, when the great voices in defence of English liberties are raised, which particular 'freedom' it is that is being defended. For, in and through the great upheavals and restructurings of the press which are before us, if it is this 'freedom' alone which prevails, everything will have changed but the pivotal relation – the hegenomic role of the great, liberal free press, that jewel in the crown of British liberties.

Chapter 3

State Intervention and the Management of the Press

Anthony Smith

A subtle reversal of phrase in the terms of reference of the McGregor Commission (1977) from its predecessor (1962) provides an important clue to a major and international change in thinking about the press. The Shawcross Commission was invited to 'examine the economic and financial factors affecting the production and sale of newspapers, etc.' in order to find out whether these tended to diminish diversity of ownership and control 'or the number or variety of such publications'. Its successor, a decade and a half later, set out to 'enquire into the factors affecting the maintenance of the independence, diversity and editorial standards of newspapers and periodicals', *with particular reference* to questions of economics, management, labour practices, etc. With the passage of time, priorities had changed. In order to secure continued diversity, a much wider range of possible governmental interventions was now thinkable (although most of them continued to be rejected). It is no longer possible for any enquiry into the future of the press to dismiss such notions as subsidy or anti-concentration measures as a matter of principle. In fact, throughout the whole of the industrialised world, the relations between government and press are being re-thought, and in many societies profoundly wedded to traditional ideas of press freedom, a new set of social needs have been identified in the field of information which can only be provided for, it seems, as a result of decisions taken at the level of society as a whole.

History provides many examples of trends which have begun as a trickle of sporadic anomalies, and of major transformations which are composed of an accumulation of long-established trends. The history of the relationship between the newspaper press and the governments of western democracies affords us an illuminating example of this principle. Looking back over the last century there is now clearly visible a growing tendency for government to take the crucial decisions which underpin the prevailing structure of the newspaper and other information industries; such a trend runs counter to the notions generally accepted in democratic societies enjoying press freedom as to the appropriate relationship between authority and journalism and has therefore tended to be, as it were, overlooked as a matter of exceptional circumstance involving, for example, the control of newsprint in wartime, the establishment of national news agencies, the subsidising of party newspapers, the manipulation of government advertising. In fact, the anomalous intervention of government in the transactions which constitute the newspaper industry can now, in the age of the 'new technology' and the increasing use of telecommunications in the press, be seen to have turned into a major international trend, occurring with increasing force of example everywhere in Western Europe, and, indeed, elsewhere. What has still to be made clear is the way in which this trend is now turning into a major transformation, which in due course, may result in a situation in which it is considered normal for government to control the provisioning of society with printed and other media, without, of course, entailing day-to-day government control of the content, although the two roles may turn out to be hard to separate. It does not necessarily follow from this that the 'freedom of the press' which has long been thought to be inseparable from the essential private sector position of the newspaper will disappear; on the contrary, there are signs that those societies most aware of the changes taking place are also those most concerned to see that journalistic and informational freedoms are enhanced and updated to take account of the other changes. At least, that will be the argument of this essay.[1]

There are four major spheres in which public policy and media provision converge, in which circumstances provide the spur for government to intervene in the privately owned industries of the press. The four are telecommunications, monopoly supervision, the provision of information on the processes of government, and the organisation of political debate. Decisions taken at the level of society as a whole in all of these areas have gradually broadened the scope of the role played by authority in the governance of the press. In some cases there are ancient traditions legitimising intervention, in others there are modern economic emergencies which have invited official intervention. Throughout Western Europe, with a few important exceptions, government is, in the late 1970s, already being looked to as the primary guarantor of the press's existence. There are instances where a traditional monetary support to the press, so entrenched as to have become ignored, has been pushed into the limelight in recent years and newly established as a legitimising precedent. There are other cases where a traditional government support has been re-examined with a view to its being withdrawn and redistributed differently within the press industry.[2] There are also important cases where government is intervening very directly in the transactions between advertisers, readers and newspapers in order to redress by administrative means the free working of the very same market mechanisms which have traditionally been thought to be the mainstay of a free press, but which are now coming to be seen as the underminers of journalistic diversity. What is becoming clear is that each act of intervention necessitates further acts, especially where intervention is designed to compensate for damage inflicted upon existing private press institutions by historic market changes or by government activity in other spheres (for example the inauguration of commercial radio or television). Put in its broadest context, we are seeing a single complex of institutions private, public and mixed, evolving in modern societies as mediators of information and entertainment, mutually dependent, mutually abrasive, with functional overlaps and newly emerging demarcations. There is thus a kind of cultural–informational complex growing at the heart of modern societies, which does not in itself spell any kind of doom but which profoundly alters the way in which we should think about the role of government and the press.

In the case of Britain, there is one important distinction from most of the other countries of Europe in regard to the increasing power of government over the newspaper and periodical press: whereas all the countries of Western Europe are aware of what is happening and are taking steps to adjust to the new situation, British politicians, administrators and newspaper editors and publishers continue to think and speak as if nothing had changed, as if the press in Britain were utterly unsubsidised, as if media policy over the last quarter century had left the press in the same essentially private position as before the Second World War, as if the changes in the structures of ownership had not fundamentally altered the relationship of the press with society as a whole. In fact, the British press has become one of the more heavily subsidised newspaper systems of Europe, enjoying a wider diversity of state privileges and concomitant risks than most other societies.[3] The divisions of the market in Britain between different enterprises are such as to have warranted, in the context of other societies equally dedicated to press freedom, further measures of official intervention to safeguard political diversity. One further contrast between Britain and other societies is that in the former nearly all discussion of intervention as a means for reforming or rededicating the press has been the prerogative of the left. Ideas of redistributing advertising revenues, for aiding the entry of newcomers of the newspaper market, for changing by statute the relationship between journalists, owners and editors and for encouraging co-operative ownership and control of newspapers, have nearly all emerged from the left and died within the left to a chorus of public disapproval. In many European societies the construction of national media policies, encouraging co-operative ownership, redistribution of advertising, the subsidising of newspapers as a branch of party activity, all in the context of improving the laws protecting journalistic activity against interference or hindrance of government or administration and guaranteeing the presentation of information by government to the press, have generally been a matter of national consensus – schemes for improvement emerging from parties of the right as well as the left and centre. At the same time it requires to be emphasised that in such societies (such as Norway, Sweden, France, Italy, Finland and Switzerland) a much higher proportion of the press itself is owned or operated by parties of the left who thus are concerned with intervention as a matter of practical administration as much as of ideological commitment.

In many European societies, telecommunications was one of the earliest of modern public utilities to be subjected to national monopolies. It was also the first area in which international institutions took a major role in defining functions and in sharing a kind of sovereignty with national governments.[4] Britain was unable to participate in certain international conventions on the telegraph and telephone because, she, unlike her partners, had not nationalised the telegraph at the same time as France, Prussia, Belgium and other countries.[5] Thus Britain was absent from the great international gathering at Paris of 1865 which created international standards for telegraphy and established Morse as the international language of the air. In the 1880s, international telephony started up, necessitating further action at government level, and within twenty years the birth of wireless telephony (and an accompanying scramble for patents) encouraged the German Government to take the initiative in establishing international standardisation and therefore governmental supervision of all the apparatus, institutionalisation and allocation of the electro-magnetic spectrum. Throughout the second half of the nineteenth century, therefore, the newspaper press was coming to rely more and more for its informational input on a series of contrivances over which government held control.[6] Reuters' control of the telegraph installations of several foreign countries was short-lived. The newspapers of the provinces had come to see, in the 1880s, the distinction between operating a news agency which supplied content and operating the telegraphs themselves which were becoming national resources with multiple applications. Reuters was able to develop as a supplier of information for business as well as newspaper purposes and gradually passed into the direct ownership of the newspapers themselves, as did the Press Association. However, many European countries came to face a choice between reliance upon a foreign source of international news and the construction of their own (necessarily subsidised) national news agencies. The establishment of a news agency, like the acquisition of a parliament, a flag and a currency, became one of the *sine qua non* of modern European nationhood. Thus, in the aftermath of the Versailles Treaty a cluster of new news agencies emerged, which all depended upon one form of subsidy or another, and have done so ever since. By this means government in those countries has been able to develop a major role in providing the input, the basic content of the papers circulating within their boundaries.

Telecommunications services thus came to serve as one of the early channels (and excuses) for government subsidy to the press. In France for example subsidies are given direct to newspapers to reduce their telephone bills and telegraph costs. In Britain reduced telegram rates to provincial papers were once a mainstay of the non-metropolitan press, enabling it to survive the arrival of the big national dailies in the age of the railway;[7] this form of subsidy was soon whittled away, however, until it finally disappeared with the triumph of national over small-town papers. In countries with large and difficult terrain the story has been different: Norway,[8] for example, has decided that its essentially small-town press is to be preserved (it has never developed a national press) together with the political diversity upon which it is predicated. In order to deter the development of large regional or national papers and to preserve small newspapers with adequate information from outside the country, the government decided to defray the entire telecommunications costs of the national news agency, N.T.B. Each subscribing newspapers pays N.T.B. a fee based upon its circulation rather than upon its distance from Oslo, the capital. In this way a small newspaper within the Arctic Circle can receive the same news from N.T.B. at the same cost per head as a paper in Oslo.[9] For N.T.B. the subsidy is a subsidy to the communities which benefit rather than to itself. It provides an apt example of the way in which governments have found themselves alone available to guarantee the media policies required by a nation as a whole.

In the case of France, telecommunications and other subsidies began in the 1880s, not as a means for keeping newspapers alive (they were then at the beginning of a period of exponential growth as an industry) but as a means of guaranteeing the *reader,* the new citizen of industrial society, adequate information upon which to exercise the franchise.[10] It was a policy designed to create popular knowledge following the Press Law of 1881 rather than a tool for manipulating the market for newspapers; between 1880 and 1914 France increased the number of newspapers circulating per thousand of the population from 73 to 244 (a higher number than prevails in the late 1970s) and total circulation from two and three-quarter millions to nearly ten millions (close to today's total).[11] The early subsidies were thus part of a process of social decision-taking in France which enabled its press to achieve, by international historical comparison, a very early 'peaking-out' in newspaper development.

Today the A.F.P., France's national agency, operates without apparent subsidy, which it enjoyed in previous decades. Since 1957 France has helped the A.F.P. by obliging all *mairies, prefectures,* embassies and other official institutions to take out subscriptions to A.F.P., thus guaranteeing an income adequate to its needs as an international agency.[12]

The relevance of these examples of government involvement in telecommunications is considerably enhanced when one considers the implications of rapidly arriving systems of satellite printing. Already several Paris papers are partly printed in provincial districts by modern telecommunicated devices. Fourteen French newspapers are working on systems of facsimile printing. Five Scandinavian papers, several Italian and four British newspapers are all operating page transmission systems to remote printing plants.[13] These systems make it possible for the markets within which morning and evening papers circulate to be less dependent upon geography and public transport. With the arrival of printing via communication satellites distance is eliminated altogether as a factor within cost:[14] it becomes as cheap for a Hamburg newspaper to print copies remotely in Munich or Paris as in Limburg or Berlin. The arrival of these telecommunications devices could thus transform the historic markets of the press throughout Europe; language areas alone, rather than zone or city, will become the natural boundary for the printed word. However, this new facility depends upon three new earth resources: satellite capacity, which is a matter for inter-governmental and industrial arrangements within regions, geo-stationary orbits and microwave spectrum allocation which are subject to international treaty. The new newspaper market system of the 1980s and 1990s will thus depend permanently upon government. In time the satellite may come to *feel* as available as newsprint or telephone time, but in reality it will become quite rapidly a moderately scarce resource permanently dependent upon skilful diplomatic initiatives and dextrous international dealing, especially when the developing countries begin to demand more satellite and orbital privileges for themselves.[15] One question which has already arisen to reinforce this interconnection between governments and newspaper industries is whether the existing telecommunication subsidies will apply to remote printing by satellite and terrestrial link; in the case of France, the answer has already been given – yes.[16] Newspapers will be able to claim back part of the costs of remote printing as an entitlement within the national newspaper subsidy sytem. At a still later stage when home facsimile and teletext services become general, a large part of the information input of the press will be disseminated not merely to remote printing plants but direct to the reader's home by over-the-air links. Telecommunications services will thus have passed through three stages: first in providing information to the newspapers, second in helping the newspaper through its stages of production and finally in sending out the material to the audience.[17] Government agencies will come to operate as the essential enabling institutions, through whose hands all the transactions which comprise a newspaper must pass. A national agency will be the inevitable intervening mechanism between all information and its reception.

The newspaper has always been designed to meet the needs of two separate markets; advertisers and readers. In the period since the establishment of adult suffrage and the creation of mass marketing economies the newspaper has come to play a dominant role in the mediation of both forms of information. Without it the whole world of sport, for example, could not have been developed, still less the efficient distribution of new models of manufactured consumer goods. It was in the inter-war years in most European societies that newspaper diversity reached its peak: at that cultural moment it was possible for two extra strata of newspapers to exist side by side, the new post-Northcliffe 'demographic' papers and the much smaller political papers identified with specific political groups and often subsidised covertly by those parties or more openly by the owners of profitable mass distribution papers.[18] Contraction in the diversity of owners as well as in plurality of titles brought about demands even before the Second World War for government intervention.[19] During the war years the entire newspaper industry was socially controlled simply as a result of newsprint rationing and this form of control created an overall scarcity of titles and indeed of circulation too, to the extent that all papers were profitable and had difficulty in meeting all the needs of advertisers.[20] In Britain the consumption of newsprint did not regain the levels of 1939 until well into the 1950s,[21] and at this point the newspaper industry, freed from controls, was having to face the new rivalry of commercial television, as well as fundamental changes in the structure of advertising. With the abolition of retail price maintenance manufacturer consumer advertising began to decline, in relative terms, while the trend towards classified advertising began to accelerate; changes were occurring in the age structure of the readership of certain of the mass papers (*Daily Herald* and *News Chronicle*). The concatenation of new circumstances meant that certain categories of newspaper enjoyed a period of rapid growth (most notably the quality dailies and Sundays, provincial dailies and weeklies) at the expense of other categories. Overall circulation began to fall.[22] Middle-class spending power was able to command media in a way working-class spending power was not. The result was a spate of vertical and horizontal mergers within Britain's press, combined with one or two closures. The Monopolies Commission investigated several of the more important of the mergers, in particular that involving the combination of *The Times* and the *Sunday Times* in a group which already owned major provincials.[23]

Much of the ensuing public discussion revealed that large areas of opinion believed newspaper concentration to be inimical to the public interest. In a period dominated by the factors alluded to above, however, there was little that public policy could achieve other than to investigate and to obtain assurances from proprietors. Thus, Lord Thomson gave undertakings to the Monopolies Commission that it was not his policy to interfere with the editors of papers under his control.[24] The owners of the *Daily Mirror,* on acquiring its competitor, the *Daily Herald,* gave a public undertaking to keep the paper in existence for seven years.[25] Thomson was fortunate in holding large amounts of stock in Scottish Television, most of which he was permitted to keep after the refranchising of the commercial television companies in 1967; newspaper groups were allowed to acquire sometimes substantial holdings in other television companies (for example, Southern T.V.).[26] Public policy found it impossible to grapple with the problem of concentration; at the point of merger it was generally too late for intervention and the 'public interest' in the preservation of titles could only be met by the extraction of promises from proprietors.

In other societies monopoly control systems have experienced similar set backs. In the Federal Republic of Germany any merger between two newspaper interests which bring their combined annual turnover to the level of 25 million marks must be reported to the Kartellamt;[27] a combined circulation of 60,000 to 80,000 daily would be sufficient to reach this figure. However, in no case hitherto reported has this led to the ending of a proposed merger. The Kartellamt is generally faced with the choice of allowing the merger or letting one of the papers collapse. In December 1975 the *Westdeutsche Allgemeine Zeitung* (700,000 circulation) merged with two smaller papers and created a virtual social democrat newspaper monopoly from Hesse across the Ruhr and as far as the Dutch border.[28] The number of separate editorial entities in Germany has dropped from 225 in 1954 (when the post-war reconstruction of the press was complete) to 122 in 1976[29] In terms of visible titles the number of papers has dropped from 1500 to 1200 in that time, but increasing numbers of papers are only notionally distinct, their contents being shared by groups of papers. In the same period the average circulation of German papers has increased from 60,000 to 158,000.[30]

German press policy, like that of virtually all other developed societies confronting the diminution of newspaper titles or editorial entities, has observed the failure of admonition as a tool and has seen that the only apt alternative lies in direct subsidy to those papers which cannot survive the historic tendencies of the market. The German newspaper industry planned to set up a Press Foundation with the German Government to produce unpoliticised grants of cash to the press, but the plan was not put into effect.[31] Denmark, Austria and Switzerland, traditionally countries with a huge diversity of newspapers and firmly disposed against the introduction of subsidies, went through a veritable newspaper carnage during the late 1960s and early 1970s. At the end of the war Denmark had 150 papers but today has only 45.[32] Austria has watched four of its nineteen daily papers gradually acquire 50 per cent of the entire market between them and has been able to respond only with modest subsidies.[33] Switzerland, where the multiplicity of newspapers is an inextricable element of its unusual system of direct consultative democracy, its citizens voting on innumerable issues themselves, has watched hundreds of its tiny newspapers disappear since the end of the Second World War.[34] Where there were 300 papers with circulations below 5000 there are now only 160; where there were only six papers with more than 50,000 there are now twelve.[35] One element in public policy which has acted as a brake on the tendency towards the large conventional local or regional daily in Switzerland has been the Swiss Government's decision not to introduce commercial radio; thus, in its efforts to hold back the tide of mergers Switzerland has stumbled across the important contemporary fact that media policies exist negatively as well as positively. Government control over telecommunications is in certain circumstances a powerful anti-monopoly regulatory weapon.

A direct connection between television advertising and the viability of newspapers has been drawn in several small countries; in the Netherlands arrangements were made to pass a certain proportion of television commercial revenue over to the press, as 'compensation' for damage caused to the latter by the existence of the former.[36] Complex calculations were made as to the amount of advertising which newspapers would have collected in the first years following the introduction of commercial television. Gradually the system disappeared when the causal connections became difficult to draw and when the revenue position of a large part of the press was evidently restored. In Belgium, however, the whole of the newspaper subsidy allocation is described as 'compensation' not for revenues lost to the press but for the simple existence of rival editorial entities in television.[37] Thus, the Belgian Government has formally 'admitted' that by setting up broadcast services at all, it has damaged the interests of the newspapers; 200 million francs are distributed annually in lump sums, broken down equally among the separate registered editorial entities.[38] In countries which have eschewed commercial television, on principle, such as Sweden and Norway, the connections between media are not established in compensatory terms. There, local monopoly is simply recognised as an undesirable consequence of certain developments in the market for which society must take responsibility. This brings us to the third area of public policy, the intervention of the state in guaranteeing the freer flow of information within society.

The first country in which public discussion focused on the connection between concentration in press ownership and the ability of the press to fulfil its democratic functions was the United States. The early post-war Commission under Robert Maynard Hutchins[39] formulated a set of roles which newspapers undertook on behalf of society, and concluded that these could not be adequately fulfilled with an inadequacy of newspaper coverage. It asserted a clear role for the state in guaranteeing that the *roles* were performed. The Hutchins Commission's line of thought was rejected for quarter of a century although it helped to influence the thinking of Britain's first post-war Royal Commission on the Press[40] which led to the establishment of the Press Council, an instrument which has subsequently been re-imported, in a different form, back into the United States. The same themes, however, have cropped up all over Western Europe in the period of newspaper financial difficulties when country after country has instituted investigations into whether and how the state should help support the enterprises of the press. In countries in which the norm for the newspaper market consists of two or three newspapers of different political persuasions competing locally, the growth of concentration and therefore of local monopoly appears to be much more serious than in countries where plurality is supported by the presence of many national titles. Sweden, for example, in the early 1960s saw extreme dangers to the flow of information within society in the movement towards local press monopolies. The sense of emergency developed there and in Finland and Norway much more quickly than in Britain with her numerous national press.

Where state financial intervention in the press is established on the basis of the general difficulties of the newspaper industry, subsidies tend to develop of a 'general' kind. Sums of money can be distributed, as at times in Italy and in France,[41] on the basis of newsprint consumed; money can be provided to help defray the costs of distribution. But when the state is considering aid on the argument that diversity of outlet is an essentia' prerequisite to the free flow of information, then it logically follows that the financial aid must be organised in such a way as to guarantee the desired results; that is, the preservation of some newspapers which are losing the battle for life in a particular market. Swedish press policy after its first Parliamentary Commission (1963)[42] was to pass out moneys through the political parties represented in Parliament; it was soon seen, however, that this tended to over-emphasise the party loyalties of individual papers. The subsidy continued as a subsidy to party activity rather than to the press and a second Commission (1967)[43] brought about another form of subsidy, cheap loans for technical improvements and aid with the costs of newspaper distribution. The wave of financial difficulties which hit the Swedish press in the late 1960s, however, was such as to render these new forms of aid nugatory. A wave of closures took place and it became clear that money would have to be found to help the second and third papers *against* the first papers, community by community. The Centre and Social Democrats accepted this dramatic switch of policy, the Liberals and Conservatives opposing it; within five years, however, the Liberals came round to supporting the idea of selective subsidy and the Conservatives greatly modified their opposition.[44] The 1972 Press Commission argued that national policy must be based upon the needs of representative democracy; diversity of media did not fulfil these needs, which demanded a representative press as such. The press served to facilitate communication between groups and scrutinised the holders of power among its various functions. Sweden thus came to develop and strengthen her laws relating to freedom of information: journalists are *obliged,* under the latest press law, to preserve the confidentiality of their sources. Government departments, including the Prime Minister's office, are *obliged* to open all of their files to the press. The dangers to the press of the libel laws have been greatly softened. At the same time the 1972 Commission recognised that these roles could be fulfilled only if press subsidies were directed at minority papers. Newspapers needed to be free politically and this entailed a *slackening* of the dependence upon party-oriented subsidy. They fulfilled purely economic functions also and these required local diversity. Under the new Swedish subsidy system, a Press Support Board receives an equivalent in money terms of a 6 per cent tax imposed by the Swedish Government on all forms of advertising in the country; all newspapers are taxed on advertising revenues received over and above three million krone per year. The Press Support Board then pays out the money to newspapers occupying less than 40 per cent of the household coverage in their particular zone of distribution, the zones being mapped by the independent

Press Support Board. The Board is also empowered to help new titles come into existance and all changes in ownership tending towards the creation of newspaper chains must be reported and investigated. However, working collaboration between papers is encouraged; competing papers are provided with additional help if they agree to use the same system of co-operative distribution and if they agree to use new technical processes jointly. Thus Sweden has come to provide the state with a dual role in the press, that of guarding against interference by authority and that of guarding against a dimunution of titles. So far since the new policies were adopted scarcely any papers have closed.

Italy is another example of a society in which state intervention, now of ancient lineage, is seen to be inadequate to meet society's current expectations of the press's role; the state is being invited to take stronger measures of financial support, in the context of stronger measures to guarantee the functions of the newspaper. State involvement in Italy goes back to the days of Mussolini when journalists became a kind of registered profession with restricted entry and with enormous financial and functional privileges.[45] Journalists to this day have enormous salaries and enjoy travel concessions by air and rail; they also enjoy rights within their newspapers as members of Editorial Committees who have to be informed of any impending changes in ownership or management; they also enjoy a wide measure of intellectual rights over their written copy which may not be altered without their permission.[46] The newspaper industry also enjoys other privileges: the price of newsprint is regulated by a state commission on paper[47] and the number of news-vendors throughout the country is also controlled in order to avoid wastage of copies.[48] The Italian newspaper works within a complex mesh of controls, all designed to ensure its freer operation. Italians read fewer newspapers per head of population than any other country in the developed world and it is difficult to decide whether this is a result of or the cause of the system of controls. In the context of the present international financial difficulties of the press the Italian newspaper enjoys one serious disadvantage: the presence of the newspaper in the 'basket' of goods which comprise the cost of living index means that there is enormous pressure imposed by the Italian Government on the special Commission which controls the prices of those goods which have been removed from normal market forces to keep down the cover price of newspapers. Thus the Italian press is constantly having to demand permission to increase its price to meet its current losses, entailing an endless spiral of intrigue and counter-pressure. The newest and most comprehensive plans for press subsidies in Italy (the Arnaud proposals)[49] involve strengthening journalistic autonomy as well as providing larger sums of direct aid, paid out according to newsprint consumed: under the Arnaud plan no newspaper owner would be allowed to acquire more than 40 per cent of the national newspaper market (although regional monopoly would not be prevented, since it has already almost occurred) and all journalists would have a say in advance of any takeover. The journalist would be given the same immunity in court in protecting confidence as the priest and the doctor, and his rights of intellectual control of his copy would be extended. But perhaps the most significant of all the proposed changes is that which encourages the formation of journalist co-operatives to take over control of failing papers: wherever a paper is due to close an opportunity must be provided for the journalists employed to inherit the paper and any resulting co-operative will henceforth enjoy additional subsidies across the board (covering newsprint, telecommunications, distribution, etc.). At the time of writing it is not known whether the Arnaud proposals will become law.[50]

The interconnection between subsidy systems and ownership systems was an inevitable development in European national press policies. Public policy intending to prohibit monopoly and maintain diversity falls down, as we have seen in the case of Germany, when prevailing financial circumstances offer no practical alternative to newspaper closure. Businesses cannot be obliged to live if their owners desire to go out of business.

The discussion of co-operatively owned newspapers and of 'newsroom democracy' in various forms is now over ten years old in Europe,[50] and it was inevitable that at some stage the development of this movement and the development of subsidy systems would become interconnected, as they now have been in the Arnaud proposals. Scandinavian policy would also support such developments, although none has yet occurred. Italy, however, has one very successful newspaper co-operative in Mantua[51] where the local newspaper has been owned by its staff for several decades and where the newspaper itself is three centuries old. The co-operative is effective morally and financially and the resulting newspaper is indistinguishable in general format and function from its contemporaries.

Perhaps the most interesting feature of the Italian discussion and situation is, however, the proposed institution of a powerful Editorial Committee within each newspaper enterprise, designed to safeguard the editorial integrity of the paper against sudden takeovers and changes in management or line. It appears inevitable that the enhanced role of the state in providing the revenue for the newspaper form will entail the reopening of the whole gamut of issues affecting editorial rights. We have seen in Britain how the legalised closed shop for journalists has evoked an intense debate over the rights of the editor, even where he remains directly the 'property', as it were, of the owner. Where the power over life and death of a newspaper is held by the state, much more fundamental questions arise as to the powers of the editor *vis-à-vis* the owner as well as *vis-à-vis* the staff. It is inconceivable that subsidies can grow much further within the context of increasing chain ownership in Scandinavia, Germany, Britain, France and Italy without this particular Pandora's box being reopened. It is open to question, furthermore, whether the opposition by publishers to the idea of subsidies in Germany and Britain is partly motivated by a desire not to open up this vista of questions, which would pass over to government a much fuller set of responsibilities to guarantee internal structures of control within the press as well as the general spread of titles.

However, it is the fourth area of public involvement, that of guaranteeing party debate, which has taken root most deeply in Western Europe. Across the whole of central and northern Europe, including Scandinavia, one can discern geological strata of newspaper formation from period to period, in accordance with the establishment of political parties.[52] Ireland, Belgium, Norway, Sweden and Finland are perhaps the countries whose modern press continues to evince most clearly the outcrops of this political geology. Let us take Finland, where the first newspapers sprang up after the Language Ordinance of 1850, part of the aftermath of the great trans-European national movement of 1848. When Finnish consciousness developed further in the 1860s a group of liberal papers were founded; then came the Young Finland movement with another group in the 1890s, the labour movement with its agitational papers at the turn of the century, followed by the

Agrarian Party and its newspapers. Before the First World War Finland saw a new group of illegal papers spring up under severe political repression and with the peace of 1918, the Young and old Finnish movements and their presses were transformed respectively into the Progressive and Coalition Parties; then came the great divide in the labour movement, causing a split between socialist and communist papers. In the 1930s came the development of politics on the far right with an appropriate press. With the firm if belated establishment of Finnish nationhood came the media counterparts: a national news agency, a national radio corporation and a national advertising industry.[53] Even in the 1950s the small population of Finland (5 million) enjoyed 130 newspapers, and today still has nearly one hundred, divided among eight distinct political groups, plus the independents. Now the important point to observe is that the papers which survived the first carnage within the earliest political groups to emerge have in general the greatest survival power. In fact, the *Helsingin Sanomat,* the largest circulating paper, which reaches many towns far away from Helsinki every day, was until the 1930s one of the Liberal organs; today it tries to serve a variety of non-socialist political audiences as the leading independent journal. Since the end of the Second World War, the Agrarians have increased the total circulation of their papers (from 219,000 to 383,000 per day) and the Conservatives have increased theirs very slightly (from 346,000 to 377,000) but the Social Democrats and the Communists have retained very small circulations (128,000 and 110,000 respectively) even though the former has become a major political grouping in terms of voting strength. The independent group of papers (including the ex-Liberal, *Helsingin Sanomat*) has almost tripled its circulation, from 505,000 in 1945 to 1,319,000 in 1972).[54] The big independent paper has become the largest circulating paper in Helsinki and the most important *second* paper in every other town of the country. What this brief analysis is designed to show is the principle that when party formation is the basis of newspaper formation, the older newspaper groups have the chance to hold onto their market and build on it long after the parties they adhere to have given way to more modern political alignments.[55] Thus, throughout the Nordic countries the Social Democrat papers (and the Agrarians in some areas) are the hardest hit even though they enjoy enormous electoral support. It is not surprising therefore that political support can be generated for government to take over the role traditionally performed when necessary by political parties of subsidising party organs. In the conditions of the modern consumer market the demand for government support takes the form of a more generalised cultural policy – that the 'state' must support the continuation of party political activity through the press if private industry, through advertising, is no longer minded to do so.

Many countries have adopted measures of support for political activity as such.[56] Several (including Sweden at an earlier stage) have built their newspaper support systems upon their party support systems. Finland is the society in which this tendency has gone furthest and where large quantities of cash are distributed to the press via the parties. This method has the additional convenience of denying funds to the wealthy independent papers, and there is fierce debate as to whether the traditional postal subsidies (reduced rates on newspapers charged by the Post Office) should not be removed altogether and redistributed in cash terms through the parties to the party papers, causing very severe damage to the circulation of the *Helsingin Sanomat* and other independent papers (not all of which are wealthy).

A very special strain is put upon newspaper industries which have been traditionally dependent on partisan loyalties among their readers in the conditions of modern consumer economies. In a country like the Netherlands with fourteen political parties, a multi-party press is essential; the country's broadcasting system is also predicated upon a supposed necessity for political and confessional groups to enjoy autonomous editorial outlets.[57] However, the demands of advertisers in the last decade in the Netherlands, as elsewhere, have been for audiences of a 'demographic' rather than a confessional nature. Party papers circulating throughout the geographical terrain of a nation are handicapped by high distribution costs as well as by other new advertising disadvantages: their readership is not homogeneous in advertisers' terms; it is increasingly expensive to deliver papers to it. The Netherlands, therefore, has a tension between growing regional papers without strong commitments and shrinking national papers with large but scattered readerships.[48] Proposals have been put forward for a special *Bedrijfsfond,* or enterprise fund which would assist papers to adopt the new techniques.

Prevailing public philosophy is opposed to comprehensive Scandinavian-type subsidies, although socialist opinion is now veering towards certain forms of direct subsidy, distributed according to rational neutral criteria. In Germany proposals for similar grants have foundered upon an inability to discover what such criteria should be; Germany however, has a unique press system with many quite different types of newspaper within its borders which are difficult to fit into the same kind of subsidy system.[59] The German press has been rescued largely from the current wave of newspaper disasters through the sheer efficiency of its management and its ability to negotiate new technology into a large number of its papers with the willing support of unions and workers.[60]

There is a fifth area of public policy which provides governments with powers over the financial governance of the press on a scale not previously thought desirable. In all countries which have adopted Value Added Tax (which includes all within the E.E.C. and several outside it) newspapers have been given certain tax advantages. The Republic of Ireland is the only exception.[61] In Germany VAT is halved on newspaper sales.[62] In France it is reduced to 2.1 per cent, a figure which enables the paper with small amounts of advertising (on which VAT is charged at the full rate) to recoup the taxes it pays on its editorial content and on the purchase of equipment.[63] Everywhere else VAT is reduced to zero on newspaper sales. In Britain alone is VAT zero-rated on advertising revenue as well as on sales.[64] VAT provides a government with endless opportunities to manipulate the finances of the press as a whole; it provides it also with a permanent responsibility for monitoring the revenue position of the press and registering structural changes. In Britain the total amount of money saved by the press (or for the press by government generosity) amounts to a sum approaching £100 million per year, although the state itself loses roughly half that figure in revenue foregone. The press of Britain, by virtue of its much-prized zero-rating on sales and advertising, enjoys not only a colossal fiscal advantage, worth between 5 and 10 per cent of total revenue, but leaves government with a permanent and powerful manipulative weapon. In many societies government advertising (which is everywhere of enormous importance to the press) is being distributed to all newspapers irrespective of readership. In

Norway, for example, it is now national policy for government to buy advertisements in all papers within a given market, even if it would not do so on business grounds alone.[65] Government advertising in that and other societies has thus come to take on the character of a subsidy to the press and one carrying considerable potential for embarrassment and manipulation. In this area as in others the balance between aid and interference has to be most carefully weighed. Public policy has developed to the point at which the state has taken on the role of providing the possibility for a newspaper to exist; where the press formerly depended on two markets, the reader and the advertiser, a third has now been added, the state administration.

State intervention has reached a stage at which a new formulation is required for the traditional press ethic based upon a total separation of powers between authority and media. We can no longer pretend that information or media enterprises are utterly private businesses existing at the convergence point of supply and demand. Somewhere at the level of society as a whole the great decisions are being made, willy-nilly, not of what shall be said today in this paper or that, but of how many different kinds of paper shall exist and what level of interaction there is to be in the ownership and control of newspapers and broadcasting installations. It would appear to be important, therefore, that the whole range of interventionist decisions taken by governments should be moved further towards the light, so that implicit policy may be made explicit, so that society may in some ways participate in the making of the policies which ensure a particular spread of media in a given society. It is not merely a switch from the secret to the open; it is a switch from the muddled and haphazard to the planned and avowed. It is not in itself a threat to the traditional freedom of the press, but it presents a very powerful case for the re-examination of the traditional ethic of journalism. We are witnessing a turning point in history which removes the media from the private to the public sector of society. It is no longer as clear as it once was exactly what the public sector now is and what its responsibilities truly consist in. We are not at the end of a discussion about press freedom but at the beginning of a completely new recognition of the nature of the problem.

Part 2

Control of the Press

Chapter 4

Confronting the Market: Public Intervention and Press Diversity

Peter Golding and Graham Murdock

Introduction

> The national press should comprise a handful of titles with roughly similar political views. Most should be economically unviable and dependent on the subsidies provided by the diversified commercial enterprises which own them. A proportion should be foreign-owned and any which face economic collapse should be auctioned to interested oil or property tycoons with an urge to disseminate more widely their views on national economic and moral recovery. The provincial press should be dominated by a few major chains and organised on the principle of local monopoly.

No enquiry into Britain's press has actually produced such a recommendation. But the Panglossian conclusions of the most recent Royal Commission come close to it. As in the past the economic diseases of the British press have been examined in minute detail, diagnosed as grave if not terminal, and yet all medicines are rejected as unsafe, untested or too strong. The question of diversity has been defined by successive Commissions as one of the central issues facing them. As the McGregor Commission puts it at the beginning of their Final Report, 'Among the questions that we have to consider are whether the public can obtain the information and opinions that it needs in this democracy without a range of diverse newspapers as wide or wider than at present available, and whether the public interest in diversity may not be so great as to justify removing or reducing financial constraints by some form of subsidy'.[1] They go on to cite a great deal of evidence to show that the present market structure has steadily eroded diversity and choice. At the same time they fall back on the prevailing axiom that any interference with this structure would pose a greater threat to press diversity than exists at present. Like the Shawcross Commission before them they conclude that however bad the system we have now, 'there is no acceptable legislative or fiscal way of regulating the competitive and economic forces so as to ensure a sufficient diversity of newspapers'.[2] The press is in crisis but nothing is to be done.

We wish to challenge this view that intervention is impossible for political or practical reasons. On the contrary we argue that only intervention can achieve the objective of diversity endorsed by public enquiries into the press. We make this challenge at two levels. First, we argue that the principle of non-intervention has not been adequately supported even in its own terms, but has been based on a wilful misunderstanding of the possible form that intervention might take. Second we suggest that insufficient care has been taken in marshalling evidence about the possible effects of various interventionist schemes. The McGregor commission claims to 'have finally laid . . . to rest' all proposals for government intervention in the newspaper market. This claim accompanies an apology for having spent so long examining such schemes, an apology which appears (p. 126) at the end of a ten-page chapter reviewing at least a dozen schemes of one kind or another. This is political prejudgement not analysis. Not surprisingly Fleet Street was delighted, trumpeting with great gusto the survey finding that most readers seem to like what they get, and making the most of the equation of a market-dominated press with 'a free press'. 'Hands Off, Royal Commission Warns State' (*Sun,* 8 July 1977), 'Why the Press Must Stay Free' (*Daily Mail*), 'Why Britain's Press Must Keep Its Freedom' (*Express*) were typical headlines in papers whose economic structure and journalistic performance had not of late given cause for rejoicing.

In the rest of this chapter we briefly review the Commission's own evidence on the ways in which the present market structure of the press has failed to guarantee adequate diversity. We then go on to examine critically the arguments against intervention in the market, and, more positively, to argue for its extension. Finally, we resurrect for consideration one particular form of public assistance. Our main aim is to suggest that this argument has not been, and must not be, 'laid to rest'.

The Failure of the Market

> . . . the ultimate good desired is better reached by free trade in ideas – the best test of truth is the power of the thought to get itself accepted in the competition of the market.

This quotation from Justice Holmes prefaces the crucial chapter on diversity in the McGregor Commission's Final Report and provides the implicit framework for their general argument. This ideal of a free market in ideas presupposes three things: that there is competition between independent producers offering a range of distinctive products to consumers; that the demands and choices of consumers are the major determinants of supply; and that entry is open to anyone who spots a gap in existing provision. As the Commission's findings clearly show, however, none of these conditions is met by the present market structure of the British press.

The erosion of competition

Within the provincial newspaper market competition has virtually disappeared. As the Commission point out, 'With the exception of London, no town in the United Kingdom now has more than one evening newspaper' and 'with the exception of Belfast and Glasgow, in every town where there is a morning and an evening newspaper, both are owned by the same company'.[3] This consolidation of local monopoly is part of a general erosion of competition. Instead of the 'classic' model of separate sectors each characterised by vigorous competition between independent producers, we have a situation in which the major newspaper markets are increasingly dominated by the battle between the same handful of large concerns, spearheaded by the proprietors of the national dailies.

As Table 4.1 shows, since the last Royal Commission reported in 1962, the companies owning national dailies have significantly increased their share of the other major newspaper markets. They currently account for the great bulk of Sunday circulation, well over half the circulation of the provincial morning papers and almost half the market for provincial evenings. Their share of the weekly newspaper market is still relatively low and currently stands at just over a fifth. Even so, this is almost treble the figure for 1961 and there is every reason to suppose that it will continue to increase in the future.

TABLE 4.1 *Percentage of total newspaper circulation controlled by the companies owning national dailies 1961–76*

| | Provincial dailies | | National and provincial | |
	Morning	Evening	Sundays	Weeklies*
1961	37.6	30.7	61.5	7.5
1976	57.8	45.9	84.5	21.8
Percentage change in market share	+20.2	+15.2	+23.0	+14.3

* The figures for weeklies are for 1974.
Sources: Royal Commission on the Press (1961) p. 179; Royal Commission on the Press (1977) p. 42; Press Council (1976) pp. 148–50.

Not only have the major press concerns considerably extended their control over the total newspaper market, they have also changed substantially in character. One after another they have either been acquired by multi-industry conglomerates or have diversified their activities to become conglomerates in their own right. Of the nine companies currently involved in publishing national daily or Sunday newspapers, only two – the Daily Telegraph Limited and the Guardian and Manchester Evening News Limited – can be properly called newspaper companies in the sense that newspaper publishing provided the great bulk of their profits. The remaining seven are all subsidiaries of diversified concerns with interests in a range of commercial and industrial enterprises. As the Royal Commission point out: 'Rather than saying that the press has other business interests, it would be truer to argue that the press has become a subsidiary of other industries'.[4] The nature of these non-newspaper interests varies from company to company. They include substantial holdings in other sectors of the communications industry, particularly book publishing and commercial television and radio, together with stakes in a wide range of general industrial and commercial activities, including construction, transportation, consumer durables, insurance, banking, property and oil.[5]

According to the 1976 annual reports of the respective companies, their non-newspaper interests contributed the following proportions to total pre-tax profits: the Thomson Organisation 34 per cent; News International Limited 37 per cent; Daily Mail and General Trust Limited 45 per cent; Reed International Limited 71 per cent; and S. Pearson and Son Limited 82 per cent. The Thomson figures were compiled before the company's interests in North Sea Oil had begun to show their current high levels of profitability, and there is every likelihood that oil will become the group's major profit base.

The two remaining national newspaper concerns – Beaverbrook Newspapers Limited and the Observer Limited – have both recently been acquired by conglomerates. Beaverbrook is now a subsidiary of Trafalgar House Ltd, the engineering, shipping and investment group (and the single largest industrial contributor to Conservative Party funds). As yet it is impossible to forecast its likely contribution to the group's total profit. However, since Beaverbrook made losses of £1.7 millions in the financial year prior to the takeover as against Trafalgar House's pre-tax profits of £33.6 millions, its contribution is unlikely to be substantial, even given a significant improvement in performance. The chances of the Observer Group making a sizeable contribution to the profitability of its new parent corporation, Atlantic Richfield, are even more remote in view of the fact that this company's net income for 1976 totalled £334.4 millions. This emerging structure of conglomerate ownership coupled with the major concerns' increasing control over the main newspaper markets, has several important implications for the overall diversity of the press.

The potential consequences of growing monopoly and concentration were discussed by both previous Royal Commissions and are aired again in the McGregor Report. Basically the argument runs, the more newspapers a proprietor owns the more opportunities he has to impose his own interests and opinions, and the greater the market share of his titles the more widespread his potential influence. As a result, the Commission argue, increasing concentration of press ownership carries with it a strong potential for further restricting the 'diversity of opinion and expression'.[6] True, the old style 'press barons' in the Beaverbrook mould have largely disappeared in the years since the Second World War and modern proprietors have generally confined themselves to defining overall policy, leaving their editorial staffs to translate their aims into concrete production decisions. However, as the Commission recognise, there is nothing immutable or sacrosanct about this arrangement. True there is a strong tradition of editorial autonomy and resistance to proprietal pressure, but it is provisional. Owners retain the right to hire and fire all employees, including editors. Moreover, the recent growth of conglomerate ownership considerably increases the likelihood that a proprietor may wish to assume a more directive role in editorial matters.

Previously the main threat came from press tycoons wishing to use the newspapers they owned as mouthpieces for their own opinions and prejudices. This threat remains, but conglomeration has added the further possibility that newspapers will become incorporated into the public relations and image-building strategies of their parent companies. The potential pressures include: giving editorial puffs to the group's products; ignoring or denigrating the products of rival companies; and putting a brake on investigative reporting of sensitive areas of company activity, in an effort to promote a positive image of the group and its interests.[7] The more broadly based the conglomerate, the greater the likely reasons for intervention. Pressure is likely to be particularly strong where the group's interests are threatened by government policies or where the legitimacy of their activities and policies are called into question.

How far these pressures are actually operative is open to dispute. As the Commission point out in another context, it is exceptionally difficult to obtain adequate evidence since it is not usually in the interests of those involved to publicise the situation.[8] What we can say with certainty, however, is that the growth of conglomerate ownership has added a new and significant source of *potential* restriction on the diversity and range of press coverage.

The myth of consumer sovereignty

> In the end control is with the readers. For my money, what makes private capitalism the least imperfect of the available systems of newspaper ownership . . . is that it is more responsive than other systems, through ordinary market mechanisms, to the wishes of its readers (Sir Denis Hamilton, Chairman, Times Newspapers Ltd).[9]

The ideal of the 'free' market assumes that demand determines supply. In practice however, this is far from being the case. The provincial newspaper sector, where local monopolies have virtually eradicated effective choice provides the starkest example, but consumer sovereignty has also been extensively undermined within the national market. According to the Commission's interim report, only four dailies and one Sunday were making profits in 1975.[10] The rest operated at a loss and only continued because their parent corporations were prepared to subsidise them out of the profits from their successful divisions. Clearly the supply of national newspapers has rather more to do with the interests and financial muscle of the proprietors than with the demands of readers.

The relations between demand and supply are further distorted by the dailies' chase after advertising revenue in an effort to keep pace with their rapidly escalating costs. Although this is sometimes a self-defeating strategy, since the revenue derived from advertisements is increasingly cancelled out by the costs of printing them, it has been vigorously pursued in recent years. Basically advertisers are only interested in newspapers which have a mass readership or which cater for affluent minorities. Papers which satisfy neither of these criteria are therefore the most likely to go to the wall, the *Daily Herald* being the best-known example. When it finally folded, the *Herald's* readership was almost twice that of the *Times, Financial Times* and *Guardian* combined. Unfortunately this did not add up to a mass circulation and the fact that *Herald* readers tended to be relatively poor and ageing made them an unattractive minority for advertisers. Hence the dynamics of the market deprived a substantial number of people of a newspaper which surveys revealed they were committed to, enjoyed and wished to continue reading.

With the closure of the *Herald,* the country lost the only major national daily to give consistent support to the interests and ideas of the democratic socialist tradition which lies at the heart of the Labour Party and the trade union movement. As the Royal Commission's content analysis reveals, the *Herald's* disappearance 'marked a significant loss in diversity of style and content as well as in political outlook'.[11] This loss was made all the more significant since as the Commission notes: 'There is no doubt that over most of this century the Labour movement has had less newspaper support than its right-wing opponents and that its beliefs and activities have been unfavourably reported by the majority of the press'.[12] Nor is this imbalance in the national press counteracted by the diversity of political opinion among provincial newspapers. On the contrary, it is further reinforced since, as the Commission points out, the provincial morning papers 'are all either uncommitted or right of centre'.[13] But, the free market argument runs, if significant minorities and currents of opinion are not adequately represented by existing provision, it is open to anyone to enter the market and rectify the situation.

The problems of entry

Supporters of the existing market structure of the press are fond of pointing to the emergence of 'alternative' newspapers as evidence of its relative openness and responsiveness to new and untapped demands. The Commission cites the instance of *Gay News* which has built up a strong and viable base within the homosexual community with a circulation of 18,000-20,000 per issue.[14] Although making a welcome addition to the overall range of opinions and interests represented by the press, the success of *Gay News* offers only limited evidence of the market's openness. In the first place, it appears fortnightly which makes it more akin to a special interest magazine. Certainly it is not a functional equivalent for a daily newspaper. Secondly, it caters for a self-defining social group rather than a general readership. And finally it is an exception. For every successful 'alternative' newspaper there have been a dozen or more failures. The list of

defunct general papers of the broad left, which includes *7 Days,
Ink* and *It,* is particularly long. Indeed, the only socialist
newspapers which have managed to survive are the organs of the
left minority parties. These include two dailies, the *Morning Star*
(Communist Party) and *News Line* (Workers' Revolutionary
Party). At first sight their existence seems to confirm the openness
of the market. In fact, their continuation depends precisely on the
fact that ordinary market forces are offset by the commitment of
party members, who are willing to provide financial subsidies and
other support in addition to their own regular purchase of the
papers. At the same time, the fact that these papers are party
organs and identified as such, effectively prevents them from
attracting and holding more than a token general readership. As
soon as one begins to think in terms of reaching a broad
readership, it is evident that the possibility of effective competition
with established titles is foreclosed by the prohibitive costs of
launching and sustaining a comparable product under the present
market structure. A potential general reader would need to be
exceptionally interested or sympathetic to buy a six-page *Morning
Star* for 10p when for 7p he can get a twenty-eight-page *Daily
Mirror.* Hence although theoretically open the major newspaper
markets are in reality closed to everyone except the most affluent
of organisations and companies whose opinions and interests are
already well represented within the existing range of titles. The
Royal Commission is well aware of this closure. They explicitly
point out that although 'anyone is free to start a national daily
newspaper, few can afford even to contemplate the prospect'.[15]
Similarly, they underline the fact that their 'studies of the
provincial press suggest that it would be very difficult to start a
daily newspaper in competition with those already established'.[16]

All in all then, the evidence amassed by the Commission clearly
indicates that the present structure of the press is very far from
being a 'free' market in ideas and that it has signally failed to
guarantee adequate choice and diversity. They fully acknowledge
this and throughout the report they are at pains to point out the
various ways 'in which market forces threaten the proper
fulfilment of the social and political functions of the press'.[17]
Having arrived at this juncture, however, they fail to pursue the
logic of their evidence to its conclusion.

It is clear that the situation will worsen unless the prevailing

structure and dynamics of the market are changed. It is also clear
that the necessary changes are unlikely to take place spontaneously.
Hence the only possible way of increasing diversity and choice is
through some form of public intervention in the market. The
Commission, however, refuse to draw this conclusion and
forcefully reject 'all the proposals for government assistance' put
to them.[18] They argue that all the schemes on offer would
eventually involve the government or its appointees in making
discriminatory choices between competing applicants for public
funds, thereby paving the way for an extension of government
control over information and opinion. Lurking behind this
argument is the familiar chimera of totalitarianism, the state as
'Big Brother'. Other commentators have voiced this fear more
openly. According to Nora Beloff for example; 'The way things
are going, the British national press seems to have reached a
crossroads and will have to choose one of two ways: either the
American system of Jumbo monopolies . . . or else a communist
style state control.'[19] But are these really the only effective
alternatives? Is it possible to devise a form of public intervention
which would address the major deficiencies of the existing market
system without extending government control over the range of
press content and commentary? We would argue that it is.

The Unproven Case Against Intervention

Opponents of intervention readily accept that the press is a special
case, whose unusual importance in the political process requires a
greater level of public attention than might otherwise be
warranted. That is why we have Royal Commissions. As Anthony
Smith has shown in this volume and elsewhere, press subsidies are
no rarity, and even in this country we set a zero VAT rating which
subsidised the press by £60 million in 1975. Similarly, nobody
seemed horrified by the implications of the recent (and
unsuccessful) application by the industry for help from the E.E.C.
Social Fund.

Interference with the economics of the press already exists
through the machinery of monopoly legislation. There seems little
opposition to the view that the growth of monopolies within the
press is of concern to the public and requires government

supervision. McGregor reiterates this belief quite categorically: '. . . we believe it is right that the press should be under closer scrutiny and subject to more stringent rules than other industries'.[20] In fact this machinery is seldom prohibitive. Since 1965 when the legislation was tightened up, only fifty cases have been referred to the Secretary of State, and of these only seven have been referred to the Commission on Monopolies and Mergers. Most unreferred cases involved smaller local evening papers, but among such cases was the acquisition of the *Sun* by News International.

Monopoly legislation however is in principle inadequate to cope with the economic shifts we have described. It only deals with concentration of ownership within one sector and not at all with conglomeration. An active programme of 'trust-busting' would not therefore be crucial. It would not be irreversible and it would not address the central problem of diversity. If you chop logs you still get wood. In the present market structure multiplicity is not a sufficient guarantee of diversity. The existing monopoly legislation and the further extension proposed by McGregor lay down a case for intervention. But to achieve the objectives of increasing diversity requires rather more than the supervision of concentration

We have described elsewhere the growing economic interdependence of media sectors.[21] Others, notably Rex Winsbury, have drawn attention to the blurring of technological demarcation lines between the media. Hence decisions about the allocation and use of technically finite resources in telecommunications may, by default, lead to government intervention in the press as newspapers become part of a communications industry which is increasingly diversified, not only financially but technologically. Consequently, the choice is no longer whether to intervene, but what form of intervention would be best.

What then are the major arguments against intervention? Many schemes have been dismissed as impractical or expensive, but most commonly objections are directed at the potential for editorial intervention which might accompany the involvement of the state in press economics. Such arguments are most often advanced by those who claim that existing managements do not exercise any control over editorial practice; that there is indeed a total functional divorce between editorial and managerial decisions. If this is true in the nature of newspaper organisation or by virtue of the sturdy and well-established autonomy of journalists, why would public as opposed to private ownership be more likely to erode editorial autonomy? If ownership is irrelevant then it is illogical to rule out public ownership. In practice, though, private ownership is by no means immune from the temptations of editorial involvement. When Jimmy Goldsmith of Cavenham Foods was bidding for the *Observer* he consistently affirmed that he would not attempt to influence the editor should he get control – merely replace him if he followed an unacceptable line. Victor Matthews of Trafalgar House, when adding Beaverbrook Newspapers to his collection, made clear what he meant by non-intervention by replacing the editor of the *Daily Express* within weeks of the acquisition. Explaining his position, Mr Matthews provided the motto for Fleet Street's version of guided democracy when he said that 'By and large the editors will have complete freedom as long as they agree with the policy I have laid down'.

In fact, as the Royal Commission has pointed out, within the newspaper industry there is 'broad agreement that in reality editorial and managerial decisions [are] inseparable'.[22] Certainly decisions about production or marketing strategy have direct and substantial implications for content. We have already outlined the failure of the private market to support the development of a press independent of commercial imperatives. It may well be, as Graham Cleverly has argued, that the root cause of the economic crisis in Fleet Street is the inability of newspaper managements actually to impose commercially sound judgements. But it cannot be good for democracy to depend on managerial ineptitude for the continued editorial independence of the press. In the evolutionary struggle it is the powerful, diversified companies that have emerged in control of the press, and their financial timidity cannot be relied on so readily.

A related argument against intervention by the state suggests that any further interdependence of press and government would mute the 'watchdog' function of journalism either by direct mechanisms of control, such as censorship, or by the more subtle creation of tacit 'understandings' of the kind many detect in the relationship between the state and the B.B.C. We reject this argument for two reasons. First it misleadingly overstates the existing critical role of the press. Second it assumes a necessary identity of state involvement in press economics with government control. We discuss the mechanisms which might avoid this latter problem below.

The critical role of the press is not wholly a myth. Clearly campaigning journalism and the daily scrutiny of the political process serve an important function in democracy. But the very partial accounts which journalism provides often mask more than they reveal. A growing body of research, both in this country and elsewhere, has demonstrated the frequent failure of news adequately to explain the major processes and institutions it claims to survey. Whether in particular areas like race, industrial relations, government or welfare, or in its general portrayal of the world, journalism has been shown to be seldom critical and often cursory and misleading. There is no space here to expand on or examine these critiques, but they cannot all be dismissed as academic, naive or utopian. Moreover, it is not only outside commentators who have expressed concern about the lobby system, the invisibility of Whitehall, the sketchy coverage of industry, the excessive adulation of entrepreneurs, the obscurity surrounding financial institutions, and so on. Certainly it would be wise to be wary of excessive claims about the watchdog role of newspapers as at present constituted.

A slightly different argument is advanced by those who claim that intervention would undermine the principle of reader sovereignty. We have already shown how limited this sovereignty is in practice. Nevertheless it remains a potent talisman for defendants of the 'free' market. But if, as Denis Hamilton argues: 'In the end wherever ownership lies, control is with the readers',[23] why worry about state ownership? How many will think of famous last words when they recall the *Daily Express* leader of 10 May 1977, just seven weeks before the Trafalgar takeover, which asserted '. . . we will not go far wrong if we always hold ourselves accountable to our readers and to nobody else'?

In fact, as we noted earlier, the readership of a paper is not the major determinant of its character or its survival. The readers of the *News Chronicle,* the London evening *Star,* or the *Scottish Daily News* would all testify to this. It is no longer true that the ability to get the right revenue (by serving readers attractive to advertisers) is the crucial factor. Rather it is the ability to sustain the losses which newspaper production entails which separates the weak from the strong. As newspaper advertising rates have lagged behind both inflation and production costs, the marginal cost of advertising has gradually overtaken marginal revenue. By 1975 the proportion of advertising revenue absorbed by costs had risen to 100 per cent for national popular dailies and to 115 per cent for national popular Sunday papers. Even for the quality papers, with their much heavier dependence on advertising revenue, the equivalent figures were 55 per cent for dailies and 60 per cent for Sundays.[24] As the volume of advertising grew at a faster rate than advertising rates the massive increases in newsprint costs (which more than trebled between 1970 and 1977) took a heavier toll, incidentally raising the threshhold cost of entry to the market. Papers got bigger, costlier and less profitable. Ironically this produced a situation where circulation revenue was more significant, so that for some papers the reader was subsidising the advertiser, not the other way round.[25] In 1960 advertising provided 45 per cent of total revenue to national popular dailies and 73 per cent to the qualities. By 1975 these proportions had fallen to 27 per cent and 58 per cent respectively.[26] Cover prices for national dailies have more than trebled since 1970, rising more rapidly than retail prices as a whole in the same period. Circulations have dwindled as a growing number of families ceased to take any paper at all. Over one and a half million fewer national dailies were sold in 1976 than ten years previously. But in what sense does this situation reflect the sovereignty of the consumer? The right to do without is not the same as the right to exercise the control of buyer over supplier. It is a similar fallacy that identifies viewer participation with the right to switch off a television set. In the end, *pace* Mr Hamilton, control does not lie with the readers. Control lies in the hands of those with enough financial muscle to shape or disdain market forces. Consequently intervention in the market via a democratic and accountable structure is the only possible way of genuine reader sovereignty to be obtained.

In the end the case against intervention is neither logical nor arithmetical but political, and so of course is the case for it. In moving on to suggest one possible form of intervention we do so on the grounds that the case against intervention is incompatible with the objectives set by those who oppose it. If communications in general and the press in particular are indeed a special case, then this can only be preserved by grasping the nettle of intervention.

Intervention for Diversity: The Idea of a Public Press Authority

The aim of intervention is to ensure diversity among newspapers so as to prevent financial power being a major constraint on the free expression of views and the presentation of news from various standpoints. Such a diversity does not at present exist. Our major objective, therefore, in designing a scheme to alter the existing market dynamics, would be to ease the cost of entry. Subsidy schemes, such as those intended to reduce the cost of newsprint, or redistribution schemes which aim to even out the spread of advertising revenue, are not the best ways to achieve this end. They would certainly assist some of the currently ailing papers. But our aim is democratic evolution not the preservation of dinosaurs. It is therefore necessary to intervene by extending production facilities. The objective is to increase access to the medium, not by forcing an entry into existing papers, but by encouraging new titles. This requires access to the means of production, not to existing products. Such an objective is met in part by the Basnett–Goodman scheme presented as a minority report in the McGregor Commission Report.[27] However we depart from their proposal on several points.

We suggest the establishment of a Public Press Authority (P.P.A.), responsible for the administration of printing plant available for lease. The Authority would itself be national, though the plant would be situated regionally according to demonstrable demand as discovered by prior research. Unlike Goodman and Basnett we see no virtue in buying up existing spare plant, possibly at inordinate cost and often outdated. The P.P.A. plant should be custom built and designed to take advantage of the savings in production costs promised by the new technology. Basnett–Goodman suggest a similar body and would make it a subsidiary of the National Enterprise Board. At present Section 9 of the Industry Act 1975 prohibits the N.E.B. from becoming involved in mass media. This may be no bad thing. By making the major concession that the new body should be cost-effective, i.e. profitable, one is merely extending the range of existing market pressures. Our object is to withdraw communications from these pressures to the point where they are no longer the main determinant of cultural production. Thus it would be better to make the P.P.A. responsible to a relevant ministry, preferably one with overall concern with communications. It is not essential that communications policy be unified at ministerial level, but it should be integrated at some level, possibly by a permanent commission akin to the Supplementary Benefits Commission in the Department of Health and Social Security. The P.P.A. would be a printing but not a publishing body. It would have no editorial powers and would be prohibited from itself producing a newspaper and from doing so on behalf of any government or government agency. Its sole aim would be to provide cheap printing facilities for outside groups, thus achieving the separation of editorial and production quite common in the book and magazine industries.

The usual and major objection to such a scheme is that it would inevitably invite political interference. If access to the P.P.A. was by price, then it would merely reproduce existing market power. If, however, it discriminated in favour of the weak it would be drawn into making selections which, however fair and wise, would inevitably be politically contentious and open to abuse. All this is true. It is not insurmountable however, and it is unfortunate to say the least how little effort has been put into inventing machinery to avoid these problems.

In principle it is merely necessary to remove from the P.P.A. any discretionary powers by drawing up firm criteria of qualification which would automatically select or reject applicants for its facilities. The criteria may be contentious but they can be thrashed out in debate and would be subject to parliament approval, and only alterable by consent of parliament. The major criteria we would suggest for consideration are as follows. First no applicant would be refused by virtue of known political or moral views. It is for other laws of the land to exclude views which transgress standards of tolerance, defamation and so on. Second, applicants should have a demonstrable level of support, possibly by setting a level of subscriptions like 50,000 or 100,000 which would have to be authenticated to establish the real need for the applicant's paper. Third, the structure of the applicants' organisations should be such as to ensure the return of any ensuing revenue and profit to the paper. This could possibly be achieved by insisting on some variant of the trust form of ownership. Hamilton has argued that existing examples (he cites the *Guardian* and the *Observer*) suggest that trusts are not a viable commercial form. But he presents no evidence to support the view that any commercial failings of these papers derive from their ownership by trusts. This criterion would have another implication. At first sight there seems no reason why, say, an ailing *Daily Express* should not profitably sell off its plant and equipment, reconstitute itself as the *People's Voice* and move in as a lodger with the taxpayer. By insisting on the ploughing back of profits and on trust structure this eventuality is minimised. If some group like Trafalgar House decided it was still worthwhile, then this would be quite acceptable, indeed desirable, increasing the effective range of P.P.A.-produced papers without diluting its purpose.

A fourth possible criterion would be that the new titles should not accept advertising. At first sight this seems extreme. But it has several advantages. Advertising, as we have seen, produces little profit for a popular daily. It is expensive to produce and merely uses newsprint. Instead of having to juggle unpredictable margins to make advertising pay, the new papers could reduce costs by producing only editorial content. By not competing with the advertising-based press for revenue they would avoid being drawn into following the same readership gathering strategies and the consequent bunching of papers at the centre of the market.[28]

Such criteria are only suggestions. They are intended to illustrate the point that a P.P.A. need not be left with discretionary and potentially contentious powers of resource allocation. It has been argued that such an Authority would have many of the faults of the Independent Broadcasting Authority. But the analogy is false. The I.B.A allocates broadcasting franchises which bestow a regional monopoly upon the successful applicant. It chooses by judging the potential merit of an applicant's product. Not surprisingly it has an unhappy history of having made bad choices, exacerbated by continuing acrimonious debate about what steps it should have taken once such mistakes become apparent. Rigid criteria would mean not good or bad choices, but correct or incorrect ones. Any dispute about the fair or accurate application of criteria could be tested in the courts of law.

One major objection to the provision by the state of additional printing plant is that such resources already exist in abundance. The

McGregor Commission argues that lack of printing facilities is not a barrier to new entrants because of the existing range of contract printing. There are two objections to this view. First the evidence is incomplete. The Commission has merely enumerated the printing establishments listed in the Printing Trades Directory.[29] But there is no evidence that these establishments are under-utilised at present, or that they could meet the needs of new newpaper-publishing clients. As the Commission notes '. . . a listing in P.T.D. may be for reasons of prestige, or as a precaution in case spare capacity arises'. Most importantly the Commission goes on to admit that 'those companies which are themselves newspaper printers and publishers may be unwilling to print a rival newspaper or freesheet'.[30] To this can be added their conclusion that 'there seems little doubt that the further decline of the independent publisher is inevitable . . .'.[31] So the case for the availability of contract printing is far from proven. At the very least more intensive research is needed.

In addition to incomplete evidence there is a second objection to contract printing, namely that it is not responsive automatically to demand. Not only is there no guarantee of access, but access is by price only. It is thus in no sense equivalent to P.P.A. printing. True, the case against contract printing is incomplete, but we feel that there is insufficient evidence not to consider alternative provision.

There remains the problem of ensuring that new launches survive their early and probably loss-making stages. For this some form of launch fund is inevitable. The history of new launches in the provincial press is unhelpful. The only new provincial daily launched in the last fifteen years was the *Scottish Daily News*. Twelve new evening papers were established in this period, but five of these were from the Thomson stable. The new launches had average circulations of 40,000 by 1975, well below the average for their class of publication. They survive not because of demonstrable demand, but because of the financial resources of their ultimate owner. The Commission estimates that a new paper requires five years to break even, and at 1976 prices a paper with 50,000 circulation would need at least £1 million to set up. A weekly based on existing facilities, however, would need only £15,000 launch capital plus £20,000 working capital.

The problem is that a big publisher can make a small paper more profitable than a small publisher producing the same product. His crucial production and marketing advantages could only be met competitively by making the small publisher into a big publisher, as a client of the P.P.A. Monopolistic chain publishers can exercise their market power to control market opportunities. The biggest problem for a small publisher is the lack of financial reserves to buy new plant and equipment. Here again the custom-built P.P.A. plant would be the answer. The launch fund would apply so long as the paper met its subscription guarantee levels, but could be limited either by a maximum period, or by a finite sum being allocated on a first come first served basis, or some other criterion (for example largest subscription level) which would again be automatic and not discretionary.

Conclusion

These ideas are clearly tentative and incomplete. They are offered merely to illustrate our claim that the case against market intervention has not been concluded. A great deal more research is required to investigate the potentials and practical problems of various schemes. It is no longer possible to bemoan the failings of the market and yet obstinately stick to a principle of non-intervention; this is fiddling while Fleet Street burns. We have suggested that the market has drastically curtailed free and diverse expression in the press. Some scheme of intervention, whether akin to the one we have proposed or not, is essential if a fully democratic and representative press is to be even a faint possibility in this country.

Chapter 5

Countervailing Press Power

Stuart Holland

One wonders what may have passed through the mind of Elizabeth R. as she greeted a Right Trusty and Wellbeloved Baron, a Trusty and Wellbeloved Knight, (Untrusted and Unbeloved?) miscellaneous Esquires and a plain unsuffixed woman in her archaically worded warrant for the third Royal Commission on the press in thirty years. Perhaps she felt sympathy for a predecessor who, surrounded by gullible ministers, took them down to the beach to show that he could not, by taking thought or issuing decrees, hold back the waves. Maybe she had a shrewder appreciation that, this time as before, Labour ministers had no real expectation of stemming the tide of press power in any case, and were responding to Party pressure in opposition by a time-consuming alibi for inaction in government.

The remit of the latest Commission was to enquire into the factors affecting the 'independence, diversity and editorial standards of newspapers and periodicals, and the public's freedom of choice . . . nationally, regionally and locally'. It was specified that this should consider the economics of publishing and distribution; the interaction of press and other economic interests; management and labour practices; conditions and security of employment; the concentration of ownership; and the role of the Press Council. The integrity and effort of the Commissioners in attempting to tackle such issues should not be in question. What can be questioned from their findings is the likelihood of success in countervailing private power and securing the public interest. This arises partly beacuse it is not just the measure in itself which counts (for example a strengthening of the powers of the Press Council). It is the nature of the measure in relation to the wider framework in which its need is perceived and accepted or rejected – by government, pressure groups, parties or the press itself. In turn this relates to wider perceptions of the role of the press and press power in society as a whole. In practice this means a wider framework of the concepts, values, ideas, assumptions, presumptions and prejudice with which the press and its role is viewed. In other words, the framework of the dominant ideology and the perception of the role of competition and monopoly, consumer sovereignty, the role of the state and the role of the unions all in turn affect perception of problems and solutions to problems associated with concentrated press power.

As suggested above, the dominance of a particular ideology does not have to be explicit (though it tends to be so in the editorials of most of the press). It can represent an implicit assumption or 'gut feeling' about what is right or wrong, legitimate or illegitimate in society. However generalisations about the nature of ideology can usefully take the form of abstractions from common perceptions and assumptions, as in the role of consumer sovereignty, capital–labour relations, and their role in the press.

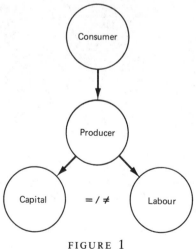

FIGURE 1

For instance, the implicit assumption concerning consumer sovereignty – and with it the case for the freedom of the producer to respond to the consumer in the manner of his or her choice – takes the form of Figure 1. The consumer expresses his choice through purchase to the producer – less demand if the product is poor quality or too highly priced, and higher demand in the reverse case. The producer in turn is assumed to draw upon capital and labour as factors of production in order to meet the demand from the sovereign consumer. Perception of the relative power of capital and labour depends on the viewpoint concerned. Some hold that big business is countervailed by big unions, with a relatively equal outcome; others that unions dominate business, and others the reverse. None the less, and certainly in conventional economic theory, the producer is perceived to enjoy a relative independence in his relations with both capital and labour.

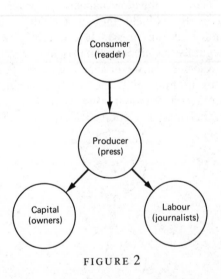

FIGURE 2

Translating this through to the specific context of the press, in Figure 2, a free newspaper producer would be dependent on a sovereign consumer/reader, while drawing on capital and labour as necessary for the efficient financing and operation of his enterprise. But advertising, which represents a cost for other enterprise, mainly amounts to a cash benefit for the press. In other words, the net gains from advertising receipts far outstrip direct advertising of the newspaper or journal. Yet by definition, this gain in terms of inward cash flow for the press also represents a dependency on advertising which is untypical of other enterprise. It also is commonplace that much of the press depends for its cash flow and survival on capital and income subsidy from owners. This is a second condition in which it contrasts with other enterprise.

There are two elements in the capital and income dependency from ownership which illustrate this contrast. First, it contradicts the alleged pattern of divorce of ownership from control under 'managerial capitalism', whereby the dispersion of share owner- ship in a pluralist structure is supposed to give management freedom to manage, rather than a dependent relationship with owners. Second, where private enterprise generally runs into a situation where it is dependent on ongoing subsidy, it is typically the pattern that the state either intervenes directly through ownership to salvage and attempt regeneration of the enterprise, or subsidises the profit level of the firm through tax relief and subsidy.

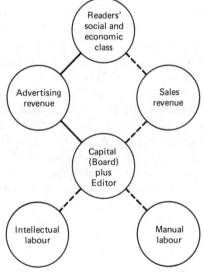

FIGURE 3

The two dependencies of the press mean a departure from the competitive, sovereign consumer model which is represented in Figure 3. The classic profitability of the *Financial Times,* with a readership but a fraction of struggling or failing papers with a far wider distribution also illustrates the important role of social and economic class in determining advertising revenue and viability. Crucially, it is not the affluence alone of its readership which is important in the *Financial Times* case, but the role which is played by its readership in the control and allocation of resources in the system as a whole: that is the control factor which, with ownership, is one of the key constituents of class power in the economy and society.

This is especially important in the contrast between the purchasing power of managers rather than workers – of capital rather than labour – to which advertising in such upstream 'quality' press is directed. Essentially, advertising in the *Economist* or *Financial Times* can meaningfully be directed towards capital goods or finance capital services, while advertising in the *Sun* or *Mirror* is towards consumer goods or personal financial services. Moreover, press advertising on capital goods and finance capital services is clearly perceived (with reason) to be more effective than television advertising, while this is not clearly so for the broad range of consumer goods and services. If the 'Abbey Habit' is encouraged both by television commercials and tabloid ads, few Eurodollar issues are notified in the tabloid press.

Put differently, the class structure of a capitalist society disproportionately benefits advertising and revenue in that section of the press whose readership is 'upstream' in terms of social status, income and power over the allocation of economic resources. In itself, this substantially qualifies the assumption of individualistic consumer sovereignty in the competitive model. Consumer power in the 'upstream' press is not so much a matter of direct purchasing power for the product itself – despite the fact that higher income groups can afford a wider range of papers and journals than the working class. It is the indirect power which derives from the concentration of class power in an oligarchic and hierarchical society of managers and managed.

Within the structure of the press itself, as further illustrated in Figure 3, labour is dependent on capital and its control of editorship, rather than a factor of production equal in status and power to that of capital (as in the common presumption indicated in Figures 1 and 2). There is no doubt that editors and journalists (as intellectual labour) and printers and typographers, etc. (as predominantly manual labour) exercise a degree of relative autonomy in relation to capital and ownership, just as there is no doubt that the degree of that autonomy (especially in the case of editorship and journalism) differs substantially between papers and journals. But there is a major relative inequality and disproportion in the power of capital and the power of labour – whether intellectual or manual. This inequality and disproportion is illustrated in Figure 4. This shows that the power of decision on content, criteria for production and service, frequency, location and type of market, the social and economic class of readership, control through ownership and the power of hiring and firing lie essentially with capital rather than labour. In other words, what is produced, why, when, where, to which class, in whose interest and with whom employed all lie with owners as controllers, rather than with intellectual or manual workers as producers of news, press content or the paper and journal itself.

Capital's power

1.	What	Type of paper or journal, news/editorial content
2.	Why	Private profit (primary); public service (secondary)
3.	When	Frequency of service (morning, evening, weekly, etc.)
4.	Where	International, national, regional, local distribution
5.	Which	Social and economic class of readership
6.	Whose	Owners' rather than workers' (journalists/printers)
7.	Whom	Editorial hiring and firing of journalists

Labour's power

1.	How	Technology and the production process
2.	How much	Wages as factor in production/distribution costs

FIGURE 4

As against these seven factors, labour undoubtedly exercises some power in two cases: the 'how' of production in terms of technology and the production process, and the 'how much' of wages and salaries. But even this 7:2 ratio overstates the effective power of intellectual and manual labour in the press. For one thing, the effectiveness of manual workers' opposition to new processes of production, and the feasibility of achieving improvement in wages and salaries depends on the seven aspects of the power of capital. The power of labour is mainly reactive rather than active. It relates not only to initiatives on technology taken by management, and to the real purchasing power of wages and salaries as determined by differences between general prices and incomes, but also to the kind of paper of journal considered viable by management within the framework of a predominantly capitalist press. In other words, they depend on decisions on viability or inviability taken by management boards within the framework of the dominance of profit rather than public interest. Where papers are subsidised by capital within a conglomerate framework, as in the case of Richfield and the *Observer,* or a multi-media market framework, such as Thomson Press and *The Times,* the decisions on viability or trade-off lie with management and capital rather than journalists, print unions and any representative institutions of the public interest.

In reply to such a case, it is maintained by those justifying loss-making papers such as *The Times* that they are serving the public interest in an independent and free manner crucial to the working of any effective democracy. But the conception of public interest and the manner in which it is served none the less is determined by private capital. Inevitably this brings into question the neutrality of the control exercised by ownership over editors and, through them, over journalists.[1] If those who subsidise the press see themselves as servants of the public interest rather than their own interest, refusing either public subsidy or the case for alternative modes of ownership and control in the media, it is important to question the extent to which their claim is independent of their private interest, either individually, or as a social and economic class.

It is in this context, again, that it is significant to analyse press control and press power in relation to the dominant ideology within a capitalist society. For instance Figure 5 represents diagramatically a common presumption on the role of politics, the state, capital and labour within a capitalist society. In theory, the political process heads the bill with 'sovereign' power. Like the allegedly sovereign consumer, the electorate via the ballot determines which party takes office and assumes state power. By analogy with Figure 2 (see page 96), the voter exercises consumer choice over who will 'produce' the goods in government. In turn, the government – via the state apparatus and its institutions – determines the relative weight to be given to the interests of capital and labour in a society in which these are seen to be relatively equal or unequal (depending on individual perception).

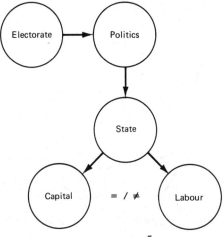

FIGURE 5

If the pretension of the controllers of the press were to match reality, it would amount to the exercise of both a genuinely autonomous and representative role within and between these power structures of society. In other words, the press would constitute not a sixth estate, but an intermediary role of both critic and advocate of the other five main estates within society: voters, parties, government, business and trades unions – i.e. electorate, politics, the state, capital and labour. However, the pretension and reality are in serious conflict. At present there are no institutional or other mechanisms whereby the press has an obligation to give a balanced representation of the views of any of the five estates as such. In cases of serious misrepresentation of an individual member of the public, a politician, a minister, a civil servant, a businessman or trade unionist, the individuals concerned can have recourse to a press conference of their own calling or to the Press Council. But the calling of a press conference, rather than writing a letter of protest, are beyond the real options of most individual members of the public, while civil servants are debarred from public representation of individual interests. Otherwise, the powers of the Press Council to date are notoriously weighted against individual complaint through both

delay and the wide range for discriminate judgement by the press
on the basis of alleged independent opinion.

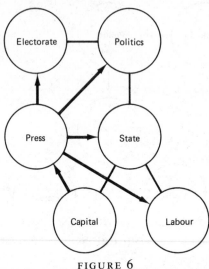

FIGURE 6

Apart from which, in practice, the press as at present
constituted fails to justify one of the primary conditions of genuine
independence in its intervention or judgement on the five other
estates within society. That is, it is not independent from capital,
either in the narrow sense of private finance or dependence on
advertising revenue. In fact, it is extensively inter-related with
capital in not only these senses, but also in the wider sense of
assuming the independence of capital to be a precondition for the
exercise of political freedoms. It thus has a pre-judged position in
terms of the role of capital in relation to both political parties and
the state. Also, either within the press itself, or within related
enterprise (where press power is conglomerate), it has a
pre-judged position in relation to a third of the four other main
estates within society – the trade unions as representing labour.

Even if one stays within the framework of pre-judgement rather
than prejudice, it is clear enough that the pretension of the press to
represent a neutral countervailing force within society is disquali-
fied by its own basic economic dependence on private capital. This
is especially clear if we represent the relatively dependent and
independent relations of the press with the other five estates in

Figure 6. Whatever the dependence of the tabloids on mass circulation, the very evidence given by the recent Royal Commission on the non-relation between voting and readership patterns indicates that the press controllers see themselves as relatively independent overall from the electoral preference of readers: that is, they can afford to weight their political preferences, or assume that they can do so, via editorials and comment, without fear of loss of readership. But they cannot afford predominantly to weight themselves against capital while dependent via advertising for finance and – in key cases – direct subsidy, *even* if this were the ideological or intellectual disposition of those who are appointed – by capital – to key positions of authority in the press. They can afford to offend fractions of capital – individual miscreant enterprises or entrepreneurs – but not capitalists as a class, nor capitalism as a mode of production.

At the level of casual empiricism, this is clear enough in relation to the relative weight given to overall support for political parties positively representing capital's interest and the free working of the market, rather than to parties and groups which claim to challenge capitalism. It also is clear enough in the extent to which the press is prepared to give qualified support to trade union leaders and Labour governments when these appear to be managing capitalism with effective restraint of organised labour, as in the period of the Social Contract between 1975 and 1977, while none the less making explicit their preference for a government which would be more authentically conservative.

But if one is to gain further perception into the power of the press in maintaining a prevailing capitalist mode of production and capitalist class relations, it is important to analyse the key role of the reproduction of the dominant ideology through the press: in other words, the way in which the press not only represents a particular and partial view of politics, the role of the state, capital and labour, but actually influences the public's views and perceptions by its own command of the press as medium. For instance, Figure 7 represents a distinction between the political and institutional superstructure of society, and its economic and social substructure. The functioning of the society itself depends on the legitimacy with which economic and social class view the role of politics and the state. These in turn depend on the implicit or explicit preconceptions, assumptions, ideas and values of those within society. Ideology in this sense is central to legitimation of a particular society. Within it, press power plays a crucial role.

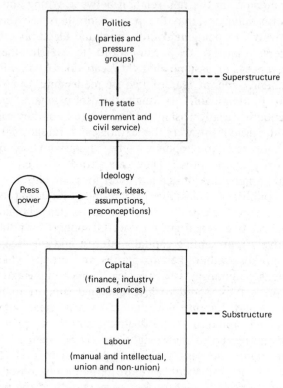

FIGURE 7

Unsurprisingly, a *capitalist* press tends to reproduce and reinforce a predominantly capitalist ideology and capitalist values. This is shown by the manner in which business entrepreneurship is valued through entire press pages on business news, without a countervailing section on trade union news (rather than news or feature items by industrial correspondents or non-union commentators on the unions); the space and role given to reporting on stocks and shares in a society in which 80 per cent of the personal shareholdings are controlled by only 2 per cent of the adult population.[2] In practice, this indicates the extent to which the press reproduces the interests of a minority class of owners and controllers of capital *as if* it represented the wider interests of the majority class dependent on capital for employment and income, yet excluded from its control. Such a literal bias in favour of the world of capital rather than labour, measurable in sheer page allocation, is reinforced by the extent to which there are grounds for claiming bias in selection, interpretation and comment on the role of organised labour or its representative institutions in society, whether trade unions or the Labour Party.[3]

But the critical role of press reproduction of a dominant capitalist ideology also can be illustrated by a further major misrepresentation of the structure of capital and its control of resources in society. For instance, as indicated in Figure 8, the predominant representation of the working of a 'free' market by an allegedly 'free' press takes the form of maintaining that the key mechanisms of the market represent the play of equal competition, consumer sovereignty, price competitiveness, an international struggle for survival by national capital, and a restraining role played by national unions.

Dominant ideology

Equal competition
Consumer sovereignty
Price competitiveness
National capital and labour

CONTRADICTING

Dominant capital

Unequal competition
Producer sovereignty
Monopoly
Multinational capital
National labour

FIGURE 8

In fact, this image of the competitive process – as widely reproduced in press reporting and comment – is contradicted not only within the dominant structure of capital as a whole, but also within the dominant structure of capital in the press itself. In both cases, the pattern is one of unequal rather than equal competition, producer rather than consumer sovereignty, monopolistic price leadership, and multinational capital versus national labour, rather than the more equal countervailance of capital by labour at a national level.

The dynamics of unequal competition in the press are analysed elsewhere in this book.[4] But in essence they amount to unequal access to finance, both in advertisement revenue and capital; unequal command of both intellectual and manual labour (journalists and print workers); unequal control of printing resources (plant and machinery); unequal command of retail outlets (where newsagents will carry bulk sale papers but not minority press), plus unequal power in price-making. The first and last factors are related to the realities of producer sovereignty and monopoly power, i.e. access to greater finance can enable a big group to ride out a temporary price war or period of price restraint more easily than a smaller group, before re-establishing prices at a higher level after elimination of the smaller concern, or deterring its entry from a particular segment of the market.[5] This is apart from the very real phenomenon of local and regional monopoly press power.

The concept of producer sovereignty is well illustrated by both the title and argument of the first chapter in Hirsch and Gordon's book on newspaper money, which is appropriately called 'The newspapers your money can't buy'. As they put it:

> It is too readily assumed that newspapers have a commercial incentive to reflect the views and interests of people at large . . .
> It depends on how profitable it is – and is not – to represent them. Minorities with high spending power find themselves excellently catered for. Minorities who have less pull on advertisers find themselves neglected. There is no newspaper their money can buy.[6]

The analogy with diminished consumer sovereignty in the broad range of household goods is very direct. For instance, in most kitchens, household electrical goods or processed and packaged foods, purchasers appear to have a wide range of choice. But from three-quarters to nine-tenths of what they buy under different brand labels will come from three, or at most four producers.[7] In Britain more than two-thirds of the circulation of daily newspapers is controlled by only four ownership groups. More than three-quarters of daily sales are controlled by eight groups. Most local press is either a duopoly or, more frequently, an outright monopoly of one group. Moreover, the apparent independence of many local monopoly papers disguises the fact that they are controlled centrally, in both editorial staff and content, by a central ownership structure and command, most notably the Westminster Press.[8] Thus readers may well be under the impression that they are reading 'their' local paper as it advocates and reproduces the dominant ideology of consumer choice and a free market, without being aware that the same message is being reproduced throughout the country by the same national–local monopolist.

Such monopoly domination contradicts the assumption of a plural, competitive press, representative in its commentary on politics, government or the role of interest groups within society in general. Even without direct misrepresentation, the simple under-representation of either minority groups or minority views – whether central or local – can in practice weight both the view of politics and state power in favour of the dominant power within the economic substructure, i.e. capital rather than labour. For instance, it is frequently argued that while clearly favouring the Conservatives rather than Labour, the national press is often unfair to the Conservatives. But it is so within the values and ideology of capitalism favoured by Conservatism. In other words, press criticism of Conservatives tends to be specific – of individuals or particular groups – rather than general. For Labour it tends to be the reverse. Criticisim is general, and individuals or groups gain press approval mainly where they support values, ideas or policies favouring capital and restraining labour. Also at local level, and especially where the Conservatives are relatively established in local government, a press monopoly sympathetic to capital rather than labour tends to reinforce a hegemonic control by conservative, pro-capitalist power.

The structure of press power in this sense is important irrespective of the specific form of both politics and government, whether national or local. Whether or not the main parties happen to be Labour and Conservative, or whether Labour in government makes a determined effort to placate capital and manage capitalism, the lack of effective consumer choice undermines the nominal pluralism of the democratic process. It reinforces the prevailing oligarchic structures in society through its reproduction of an ideology serving the interests of oligopolistic or monopoly power. In practice this tends to mean a reinforcement of liberal capitalist mythology, legitimating capitalism as a mode of production despite the dominance of economic ownership and control of a kind which contradicts the liberal myth.

One of the most remarkable aspects of the present degree of concentration of press ownership is that it needs but two more groups to withdraw from support of the daily press, to result in a literal duopoly domination of more than two-thirds of the market. In reality, if the quality and quantity press are differentiated, this would mean joint duopolies in both sectors of the daily press market, probably between the *Mirror* and the *Sun,* on the one hand, and the survivors from the *Financial Times, Guardian, The Times* and *Telegraph* on the other. Some who survive may do so through finding cracks in the market, either rising from depths to which others would not sink, like the *Sun,* or meeting the demand from relatively affluent non-business readers, like the *Guardian.* But key survivors are likely to to be bouyed increasingly on finance from non-press sources, either conglomerates or multi-nationals, or both, such as Thomson, Pearson and Richfield.

Some press barons show concern about the monopoly trend. Sensitive, perhaps, to classic charges of harlotry, Sir Denis Hamilton stated in a speech in California in 1969 that 'the trend towards high profit monopoly newspapers is open to appalling irresponsibility'. By contrast, Lord Beaverbrook, in evidence to the 1962 Royal Commission, seemed concerned that a literal press monopoly would behave less like a courtesan and more like the Queen, careful to offend no one for fear (perhaps) of democratic consequences such as disvestiture. As he put it, 'where you get a single newspaper you get slothful management and the desire to please everybody . . . newspapers do not care about competition any more; therefore they lose in efficiency. They do not care any more about opinion because they must not offend anybody'.[9]

Such fears probably are not so much about the probability of direct government intervention to break up monopoly power, as concern that the legitimacy of the press and its power of comment will be called into question, opening a Pandora's box of public pressures for reform. In other words, in general terms, there is concern that a more explicit monopoly structure in ownership and capital would question the assumed ideological neutrality or objectivity of the press. In turn, this could give rise to political pressure on the state, backed by the trade unions and organised labour, to intervene to give a New Deal or changed role for the press relative to more plural power groups in society. Put differently, the dynamics of unequal competition could provoke a legitimation crisis for the press, from which up to three of the four remaining estates of the realm (politics, labour and the state) might put to the fourth (the electorate) a credible case for countervailing press power.

So far, those commanding the heights of press power might well feel that the crisis will escape them. Certainly the most recent Royal Commission threatens them very little. Its well meaning majority and minority recommendations amount basically to an attempt to equalise competition by offering the Davids more slingpower versus the Goliaths of monopoly and multi-national capital. Unfortunately for the minority press, the majority groups have better defences against slingpower in an electronic and nuclear age. It is not the fringe press which will displace them, so much as themselves. The biggest problem for a monopoly press is not small press competition, however fleet-footed or bold. It is the big business dynamics of monopoly itself which bring into question whether Fleet Street rather than the state will play Big Brother in 1984.

Ironically, by the same token, big business in the press resists precisely those measures which could contribute to an equalisation of competition and a greater viability for minority or plural press interests. In opposing measures of state intervention or public countervailance which could support a wider number of papers, it is hoist on the petard of its own largely fictitious competitive rationale. For instance, in resisting public subsidy of private enterprise in the press it not only opposes one of the main measures which could give private ownership an indefinite transfusion, but also contradicts the reality of current public subsidy of private capital in general. This is apparent enough in agriculture, where no one familiar with support prices would maintain that Gulag has been unleashed by either deficiency payments or the less socially efficient system of E.E.C. intervention which has superceded it. More importantly, big business in the industrial sector of the economy survives today less on modern investment and high productivity than on public subsidy, without a notable increase in the state's capacity to determine what is produced, why, when, for which market, in whose interest and by whom.

Put differently, in terms of Figure 4 (see p. 99), the key prerogatives of capitalist power in resource allocation have not been challenged by the state through the broad range of industry despite the fact that total public subsidy of private industrial enterprise now is equivalent – in the big league – to virtually the whole of private corporate profits. The fact that such a phenomenon should not itself be common knowledge is a remarkable enough reflection on the claimed objectivity of the press in reporting on capital and its power (despite valiant efforts by Victor Keegan in several articles in the *Guardian*). But in practice, in the early 1970s, Mervyn King of Cambridge University estimated that the scale of investment grants, depreciation allowances, regional incentives and other state support had amounted to subsidy equivalent at least half nominal corporation tax in the private sector.[10] Since then, through one measure alone – tax relief on stock appreciation – a Labour government has rebated a total of more than £3.8 billions to the private industrial sector.

In practice, this amounts to a situation where British industry would not be showing any profit at all without government subsidy. Yet so far from resulting in a massive increase in central state power, governments in the 1970s have shown themselves quite incapable of significantly influencing even a key economic variable such as the level of investment, which remains lower in manufacturing at the time of writing (in 1977) than in 1970. Arguably this is a highly inefficient transfer of public resources away from public expenditure to private profit. Certainly it makes proposals for press subsidy in the millions look insignificant in comparision with the billions going without accountability to industry. But, above all, it suggests that industry has a shrewder intuitive appreciation of the merits of state capitalism, or public intervention to preserve capitalist profit and power relations, than the allegedly well informed barons of the press.

One explanation might lie in the extent to which the press lords believe what they read in their own newspapers. The hold of the prevailing ideology, of which they are the prime advocates, may literally blind them to the reality of current relations between big business and the state. Boardoom myths about the power of trade unions may actually persuade them that the disunited unions whom they schizophrenically rebuke for demarcation disputes within industry, have somehow managed none the less to combine on a global scale in the mid-1970s to bring capitalism to a halt. Seeking to justify the legitimacy of their monopoly hold, for so long, by resort to liberal competitive myths, they may finally have succumbed to a false identification of reality and illusion. If so, their failure should constitute one of the primary justifications for public intervention in the press. Those whose perception of reality is distorted by their own looking glass can hardly expect the continuing confidence of those for whom they should be the eyes and ears of the system. More importantly, it illustrates the manner in which the dominant ideology, perpetrated and repoduced by the press, contradicts not only the dominant mode of production (by monopoly rather than competitive capital) but also the dominant policies implemented at the level of state power.

The case for public intervention to assist some sections of the press is strong on both general and specific grounds. The general grounds have been argued already in terms of the dependency on private capital and its actual and potential conflict with the public interest. This has been illustrated by argument on the extent to which the nominal consumer sovereignty of the reader is contradicted in practice by substantial producer sovereignty. Sovereign editors, like sovereign consumers, are a thing of the past, if not indeed of fiction. Editors are dependent on management boards, and exercise the power to hire and fire journalists in relation to this overall constraint from private capital. Put simply, we not only lack some newspapers which money cannot buy (since private capital will not finance them), but we also lack the news and comment which many journalists would give us (since they lack editorial control over their own papers).

The specific case for intervention in the press relates to unequal competition, barriers to entry, barriers to distribution, inaccessibility of start-up and run-in finance, exclusion from certain categories of advertising revenue, high fixed costs of printing and equipment, and so forth. In other words, it relates to the economy of the press as both an industry and a service. In turn this reflects the unequal competition prevailing throughout the modern industrial economies, where the trend to monopoly and multi-national capital has resulted in a central contradiction between the ideology of free competition serving the public interest, and a lack of freedom for the smaller, less-established, independent press to challenge capital's domination of the media. Thus, as elsewhere, the general and specific cases are inter-related.

In practice, the general case for public intervention in the press is political, while the specific case is economic. The general case is political not in the sense that one political ideology should prevail, but that in practice it does prevail and should not. The notional balance between capital and labour, either as factors of production or as social and economic classes, as illustrated in Figure 1 (p. 95) is but a notion. In Figures 3-4 (pp. 97, 99) and in the related argument, capital dominates both intellectual and manual labour in the press, as in other areas of what remains a capitalist economy. Yet the press has a special role within the system since, through its reproduction and reinforcement of the dominant ideology, it has a critical influence on the remaining estates of a nominally pluralistic system, exerting a key role in the power fulcrum between the political and institutional superstructure and the economic and social substructure (see Figure 7, p. 104).

Intervention to offset the abuse of a dominant position has been sanctified in the United States since the trust-busting legislation of the 1890s. In practice, the anti-trust authorities in the United States now consider any merger affecting more than 15 per cent of the market as *prima facie* liable to monopoly abuse. The British press is already this concentrated, with more than two-thirds of daily newspapers in the control of four groups. The local press is even more dramatically concentrated, with 100 per cent monopoly in some areas by such groups as Westminster now a common phenomenon. Such concentration is much higher than in comparable developed economies.[11] In the United States, following Rockefeller's notorious domination of local press in mining and oil localities, big business has tended to keep clearer of the media – at least in terms of direct press control – than in Britain.

One reason, of course, was the fact that Rockefeller's empire, as a result of his unprincipled expansion, was actually broken up early this century by the anti-trust authorities. On the other hand, this was the last of the major cases of breaking up and divesting conglomerate groups in the United States. The anti-trust authorities undoubtedly have iron teeth, but lack the information on which to bite. Similarly in Britain, the Monopolies Commission – despite staffing by some excellent individuals – has not been able to stem a monopoly trend which in services such as personal banking has meant the domination of the market by three groups, and in manufacturing has meant an increase in the share of product and employment of the top 100 companies from a fifth to around a half since 1950.[12] Entrusting the problem of press monopoly to the Monopolies Commission on reference from the Secretary of State for Prices and Consumer Affairs, as recommended by the latest Royal Commission, would be an inadequate response to the special problems posed by press power.

None the less, there is a strong case for maintaining that the monopoly trend in the press, with increased dependence on multinational and conglomerate interests, should not only be stemmed, but actually reversed. This is the case for *divestiture* of some papers from some ownership groups in order to create a more plural and consumer-responsive press structure. Though this is a major policy proposal, it is radical rather than in itself left-wing. There is no reason why it should be considered more draconian than the round of tough anti-trust action taken with the break-up of Standard Oil. Its rationale might well be perceived in liberal terms within an anti-monopoly framework. Not, of course, that one would expect this to be the considered perception of the press barons, who no doubt would protest about the end of all our liberty because their own unequal access to the media was restrained. But this is a political issue whose feasibility depends partly on the counter-publicity which could be mobilised against press monopoly power.

There are two central issues in such a strategy of divestiture; which papers, and who divests them. The two issues are clearly related. It is important that a particular government should not be in a position to discriminate against individual press ownership groups and favour others on grounds of editorial policy as such. This is not to say that editorial policy is genuinely independent or unbiased. The reverse has already been argued here and elsewhere with considerable force. The point is that no individual government should be empowered to divest any particular press. The problem is a general problem of the structure of ownership and control in a monopoly framework. Its solutions, or counter-vailance, should be on lines which are general rather than specific. This is feasible if such powers are entrusted to an Independent Press Authority (I.P.A.). Its responsibilities and structure could be similar in essence to the Independent Broadcasting Authority. In the case of divestiture the specific remit from legislation through parliament would be different from that of that of the original I.T.A., i.e. the redistribution of press power rather than the constitution of media power in the form of regionalised television companies. But the principles and feasible autonomy of its action need be no different. In other words, it should have a strategic remit, of which divestiture is part, with the tactics of implementa-tion its own. Target criteria for divestiture by a given time period could be established by government, subject to review.

Such a divestiture role was proposed for an I.P.A. by Professor Jeremy Tunstall in his evidence to the Royal Commission. Specifically he suggested a reduction of the Thomson group's four daily papers in Scotland; that Associated Northcliffe's three dailies monopolising evening sales in Humberside and Lincoln should be reduced by selling the Hull *Daily Mail;* that United Newspapers, who own the dailies in Leeds, Sheffield and Doncaster should divest the Leeds *Yorkshire Post* and *Evening Post*; that the Westminster Press domination in the South-east should be reduced (they own about seventy weekly titles); that Pearson should sell both its Westminster Press interest in the *Birmingham Post,* and its 50 per cent interest in *The Economist,* and that I.P.C. should be required to reduce its market share in certain industrial and other journals to 40 per cent.[13]

The Royal Commission claimed that Tunstall's evidence arrived too late for serious consideration – fortunately, one might imagine in all charity, for some of the Commissioners. In fact, only his last recommendation takes the form of a target market share of the kind which a strategic remit to an I.P.A. in the previously suggested sense might take. He also proposes other roles for an I.P.A., such as power to operate a levy on excess profits; a fund of perhaps £1.5 millions a year on grants and loans for new launches; liaison with the B.B.C., the I.B.A., the Press Council, etc., and general advice to the government on press matters.

Tunstall's evidence has the merit of directly confronting the problem of press concentration and naming names, even if only in

the form of examples. The case for such an Independent Press
Authority has been strong, is strong and will get stronger as the
continued concentration of the press occurs. The proposal for an
advertising levy has its advocates and its critics. The more striking
factor is the modesty of the sum proposed by Tunstall for grants,
loans and new launches. Relative to the massive general subsidy of
the private sector by government, or the start-up costs for
large-scale ventures, it is very small.

However, there is one special respect in which an Independent
Press Authority could extensively countervail the abuse of
dominant press power. This would be an obligation on the press to
represent or seek *to represent a balanced view* in news, comment,
current affairs and other representation. Such an obligation, as
obtaining on the B.B.C. and the independent television companies
is far from perfect. On the other hand, the measure does mean
that not only editor *A* and commentator *X* have the right to vent
themselves in public on television. Commentators *Y* and *Z* will
normally be prevailed on – willingly enough – to appear. Moreover, it does not matter so much that television editors and
producers appear to categorise outside contributors by quite crude
criteria. The point is that such an obligation is a powerful enough
constraint on editors to consider seriously whether they have
represented more than one side of a case, and are thus a vehicle
for opinion rather than prejudice.

Another question is who would buy the divested press, and in
what manner one would assure a reduced dependence of the press
in general on private capital and its editorial control. There are
also related questions of the access of new ventures to plant and
equipment and, crucially, distribution. Apart from which, there is
the issue of the powers of the Press Council.

The Royal Commission ducked one of the strongest single
measures which could strengthen the Press Council: that is, the
legal *right to reply* in cases of factual misrepresentation, as already
operated in West Germany. It states that since this system 'has
worked for a number of years in West Germany we see no
practical reason why it could not do so here. The right provides a
prompt remedy, acts as a sanction, and promotes accuracy of
reporting'. But it goes on to argue that it has 'objections' on
grounds of principle . . . we believe that the press should not be
subject to a special regime of law, and that it neither should have

special privileges nor labour under special disadvantages compared with the ordinary citizen'.[14] But this is neither the intent nor
the practice of the West German provisions on right of reply. In
practice, according to the author's information, the remedy
provided by such a provision can be far from prompt. It can take
weeks or months before a reply is assured. But the principle of the
measure in West Germany not only assures the right of reply, but
in the same format, page, page position and type (including
headlines) as the original misrepresentation. It appears to act as a
very considerable sanction against misrepresentation either of
particular groups or, more importantly, individuals. Its introduction in a similar form in Britain need not involve the courts rather
than the Press Council. The difference would be that the Press
Council, with reformed powers, would have the capacity to
instruct a paper to publish a reply, with the content approved by
itself, rather than advise it to do so.

The question of operating plant and equipment as a barrier to
new entry or a key cost causing premature exit from the industry,
may in due course be solved by technical progress. None the less,
in this respect, the minority report's proposal for a National
Printing Corporation is worthwhile, and should be incorporated in
any government legislation on press reform. These three
institutions, embodying two new agencies and the strengthening of
the third, are illustrated in the form of an Independent Press
Authority, a National Printing Corporation and the Press Council
in Figure 9. Both a new I.P.A. and a reformed Press Council
would have real powers in relation to the structure and content of
the press, while the National Printing Corporation and its facilities
would be available to that underprivileged section of the press
which could demonstrate a need for its support.

However, this leaves two key issues in the specific economics of
unequal competition and press reform, i.e. who buys the divested
press (which is an aspect of access to finance), and the further
question of access to and facility in distribution of papers.

The domination of both wholesale and retail press distribution
by a few firms is well known. In the public view there is virtually
one major distributor, W. H. Smith. In practice, there are three:
W. H. Smith, Menzies, and Surridge Dawson control nearly 70 per
cent of wholesale distribution of national dailies and periodicals.
The minority buyer knows well enough that he or she cannot buy

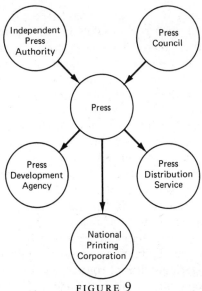

FIGURE 9

Private Eye from Smith's, and also will tend to find similar difficulty with the broad range of the minority press.

One measure which could change this situation would be *removal of a general liability on distributors* for damages relating to press content. While this would not cope with the problem of fly-by-night scandal sheets, such as may worry – or have worried – those concerned with the framing of the law, it would cover most papers most of the time, and certainly cover those which contribute substantially to exposure of business and political corruption, such as *Private Eye*. It also would cover those papers, news sheets or whatever which wished to stay in business for any length of time.

The more specific problem of the economics of press distribution could be countervailed through the establishment of a new Press Distribution Service. As with a National Printing Corporation, such a service could require evidence of qualification for its assistance, based on circulation figures and evidence of unwillingness to carry minority press in the private commercial wholesale and retail trade. While the day-to-day operations of such a service should be its own responsibility, it could be responsible overall to the Independent Press Authority, which would have power to oblige it to handle the distribution of particular papers in disputed cases. If the Press Distribution Service were to open retail outlets in only central sites in some localities (rather than the wider range of the commercial newsagents), this would represent a considerable advance in 'on the counter' assessibility for minority press and newspapers, thereby helping them break the Catch 22 circle of low sales because of low distribution because of low sales.

Similarly, the Catch 22 of short production because of low finance, or failure to break through beyond a critical starting period, could be countervailed by the intervention of a Press Development Agency on an extensive basis in press ownership and finance. Such an agency, granted public endowment funds, could take minority equity holdings in papers and press ventures, leaving majority control to the editorial board. With a distinction between voting and non-voting shares, there is no reason in principle why its finance on the capital funding side should not exceed half without endangering editorial content and control. Performance criteria could be built into ongoing finance for ventures, based on reasonable commercial criteria.

Under present circumstances, with unequal competition, high start-up costs, lack of access for new ventures to distributors, and difficulties in access to advertising and printing plant, such an agency would be no more likely to succeed than the *Scottish Daily News*. Its effectiveness would very much depend on the parallel introduction of a National Printing Corporation and a Press Distribution Service on the lines previously described. But between them, as illustrated in Figure 9, these three new institutions covering printing, distribution and finance could create a framework for the kind of pluralism in the structure of supply which could make a reality of the present myth of consumer or reader sovereignty. Not least, such a Press Development Agency could provide the public finance to purchase the share capital of papers divested by the Independent Press Authority, to which it would be responsible.

The costs of those three new agencies, in printing, distribution and finance, clearly would run into millions. If the P.D.A. in particular were to fulfil the remit both of helping the survival of papers with significant circulation but financial difficulties, and of aiding the birth, infancy and adolescence of new papers, it could incur sizeable losses in particular cases, even when new ventures or struggling enterprises were backed also by the N.P.C. and the P.D.A.

On the other hand, unlike a general subsidy to the press such as on newsprint, such new institutions would have the merit of intervening positively to offset the unequal competition and monopoly trend in the press. If their facilities were available only to ventures with revealed need, by specified criteria, they could be withdrawn after a particular threshold of performance had been achieved. Thus, depending on their nature and the social and class composition of their readership, they could be assessed directly by the corporation (in the case of the N.P.C.) or the agencies (in the case of the P.D.A. and P.D.S.), as well as indirectly by the Independent Press Authority. Diminished support could be granted on sliding scales of rate of return and readership or an adjusted index of both, as papers either were regenerated or grew from adolescence into adulthood, and an established position of consumer/reader support. Inversely, new ventures which failed to break through after a given start-up period could be foreclosed.

One of the key points in such public assistance through new institutions to the press would be the public character of the agencies, relative to the concentration of private capital. To the extent that they provided an ongoing public subsidy of some sections of the press, it would at least be within a framework for the feasible determination of the public interest by public institutions, rather than private subsidy in – essentially – private interest.

Another key point is the origin and nature of public subsidy, and its relation to other forms of public intervention in the economy. It is a false perception, reflecting the dominant capitalist ideology, to maintain that public funds are paid by the people at large, while private funds are not. In the case of the direct form of payment, the case has some merit. In terms of indirect payment, it lacks it. Income, either to the exchequer through taxation, or to private companies through sales, both come from the public. In practice, with even relatively progressive income tax, public funds are provided more by some sections of the community than others, just as private funds are provided by those who purchase particular goods or services, rather than those who do not. In other words, no private subsidy of the press is purely private. It stems from the reallocation of income derived from the public through other enterprise. In the same way, public subsidy to the press would be provided through a reallocation of tax receipts in favour of some press rather than others.

Besides which, private capital does not complain of public subsidy where this is notably less efficient, or allegedly in the public interest: that is through the form of subsidy of profit in the private sector through the previously analysed range of investment grants, depreciation allowances, tax reliefs on stock appreciation and so forth. If the proposed public intervention to subsidise some sections of the press could total millions, general public subsidy of the private sector today is in the billions, i.e. thousands of millions, each year. An annual press subsidy of £75 millions, for example, would only be equivalent to the sum which the government in 1977 granted to the Ford Motor Company to set up an engine plant in South Wales which will create only 1300 jobs overall (through the contraction of other Ford operations in the U.K.). Such a sum is not only fifty times greater than Professor Tunstall's proposed public subsidy of the press through grants and loans, but also several times greater than any sum likely to be necessary to ensure effective public support of a more plural press in the public interest. This is with the further difference that selective support of the press for a fraction of the sum granted to Ford would be likely to sustain or create more jobs, in journalism, production and distribution. Total funds of £10 million a year in press support would represent less than one tenth of one per cent of total annual public support of private enterprise.

Such arguments are neither likely nor intended to finalise the issue of public support of the press. They might contribute to putting press support into perspective. However, if such examples may give proportion to the case for support of some sections of the press, the mechanisms suggested for support do not cover the issue of press content and what press we get for our money, whether directly as consumers or indirectly as taxpayers. In terms of countervailance, the issue of editorial control is as crucial as the private economic power which at present constrains editors.

The subject of internal democracy and the press is treated elsewhere in this volume by Neal Ascherson. None the less, in this context it is important to relate it to the structures of private capitalist power and editorial control. Put simply, and as argued earlier, we do not have the news or comment in the press which journalists chose to give us. Whatever the merit and relative independence of individual editors – and in some cases not excluding the *Sunday Times* and *Guardian* it has been substantial– we in general have the content given us as approved by those editors whom private enterprise boards chose to endorse and allow. At most, this is not a 'free' press in any real sense of the term. It is the press which capital feels it can afford, on its terms and by its general criteria.

A fuller press freedom would be one which more genuinely represented a framework in which journalists were free to say what they wished, when, where, how and by what means within the constraints of right of reply, overall editorial balance and standard legislation on libel. In other words, it would mean a press which gave the powers at present in the hands of capital (see Figure 4, p. 99) to the journalists themselves. Such fuller and more effective press freedom cannot be fulfilled without journalist's control over the content of both news and commentary in the press. In other words, it cannot be fulfilled without an increase in internal or industrial democracy sufficient to ensure that journalists have the power to hire and fire their own editors. In turn this means not only an advance on the relative autonomy from capital which may be exercised by editors of exceptional calibre, but real autonomy for journalists in terms of the character and calibre of the press for which they work.

The approach to industrial democracy within the press, on such terms, would mean *inter alia* the power to describe reality as they saw it, rather than to refract the real world in terms of the criteria of the owners or find themselves unpublished when they challenged such criteria. It would not mean a licence to publish precisely what they wanted, as they wished, at any time. But it would mean a framework whereby they could ensure that the general lines of their comment on any of the principal power groups or estates within society – politics, the state, capital or labour – saw the dark of print against the light of the page. Institutionally, such power would mean not only the right to take part in the election of an editor – as has recently been the case in the *Guardian* – but also to re-elect an editor and also editorial staff. If the N.U.J. reasonably enough chose to maintain that editors once appointed should have rights to a given period of tenure, to prove or disprove themselves, this would not qualify the power of the journalists collectively to assess, confirm or dismiss particular individuals after given periods of time.

For illustrative purposes, such a power of control by journalists over editors has been extended to the question of composition of the controlling board (Figure 10). It also has been related there to the other proposed new institutions whereby public intervention could countervail the private monopoly trend in the press. The right for non-journalist labour to take part in the election to the board of papers could be relative. It should not extend to control of content, any more than journalists' control should extend to the work process of production. None the less, the contrast with Figures 3 and 4 (see pp. 97, 99) is intentionally clear.

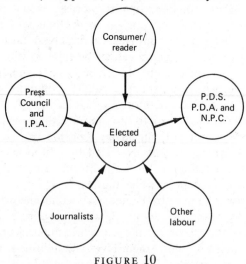

FIGURE 10

The introduction of any such internal democracy within the press could be achieved by government on an 'open door' basis. In other words, legislation could be introduced in the context of general reform of the press which gave journalists the right to elect, re-elect and dismiss both editors and management if they so wished by a declared majority vote. Such a 'trigger' mechanism, similar to that proposed for lesser forms of industrial participation in the Bullock Report, no doubt would be represented by some of the capitalist press as a pistol to the head of freedom but in fact would extend industrial democracy, not state control.

It will be up to journalists themselves to decide whether they wish to make an issue of such internal democracy, and take issue with those of the editorial élite who fear the decline of their own freedom to determine what press we have. Similarly, the response of journalists and print unions to such proposals as argued earlier for public intervention in the press should play an important role in the pace, scale and pattern of such intervention.

What we cannot support, any longer, is no public intervention in the structure and finance of press power. Indefinite further delay will give us not just a monopolistic press, but a literal monopoly press. The irony of competition in the past, through its unequal contest between the strong and weak, has been the emergence of a private press power which none of us can afford if we are interested in the future of press freedom.

Chapter 6

Newspapers and Internal Democracy

Neal Ascherson

The press cannot function as a weapon of democracy without itself practising democracy. That is the contention of this chapter. It rests on the assumption that we are advancing towards – or being passively towed into – a general political condition which is that of Chancellor Erhard's 'formierte Gesellschaft': a regulated society in which economic and political forces increasingly impose a single, monotonous harmony on the voices which lament, praise or chronicle what is taking place about us. The pluralism and variety of expression which was so characteristic of the press in the earlier phases of industrial society is being steadily subdued. If this process is at least to be fought against, only those who work in the media can lead the fight. The power of choosing what to say and how to say it must somehow be devolved. This can only mean granting and entrenching some degree of 'home rule' to the teams who write and put together each individual newspaper or broadcast programme.

The phrase 'internal press freedom' was first used, to my best knowledge, in discussions which began in Germany during the Weimar Republic. In those days, the thought was a relatively simple one: the protection of the editor's sovereignty against the pressure of a politically-minded proprietor, and the defence of a journalist's right not to be forced to write against his or her conscience. This was the sense of the draft agreement drawn up in 1920 by the Reichsverband der deutschen Presse, a remarkable and prescient document in its day.[1] Since then, however, many new and more subtle forces for conformity have begun to play on the newspaper offices of the industrialised countries. The economic weakness of the newspaper industry, particularly in Britain, has made almost inevitable the intervention of the state and public funds. However benevolent the political intention to preserve a variety of titles and types of content or opinion, state patronage requires some counterweight or safeguard which is not merely a flimsy charter of 'press freedom' but a living institution embodying the will of media workers to resist external influence. New techniques of information storage, the coming of data banks, highways and terminals, again reduce the autonomy of the individual newspaper, whether the information monopolists are commercial companies or public bodies. The British system of training journalists through the proprietor-steered National Council for the Training of Journalists was once a joke: now its insistence on technical proficiency (shorthand speed plus manipulation of a list of stock characters and screenplays which would impoverish a Punch and Judy show) at the expense of critical intelligence is becoming a menace to the mental resources of the press. Above all, however, the concentration of press ownership and the new types of concentration which are appearing return us more urgently to the old concern of the Reichsverband: the independence of editors.

Editorial independence, the old image of the captain of the ship, is obsolescent. I want to describe in more detail later in this chapter the successive morphisms of newspaper ownership and their impact on the editorial function. The central point is that the editor's formal sovereignty as an individual is being transformed into his fatal weakness. By himself, the editor is less and less able to defend the contents of a newspaper against the direct or indirect pressure of the ownership, itself often under forms of economic pressure which were not apparent fifty years ago. His relative independence, today, can only be protected by making editorial content the collective responsibility of the whole staff. And this, in turn, means transforming the authoritarian structures of newspaper offices into more democratic institutions where major decisions are the decisions of the collective.

The Royal Commission on the Press, in a fascinating shimmy between insight and inhibition, at once recognises the force of this sort of analysis and reels away from this sort of solution. The text to look at is Chapter 16, on 'Editorial Contracts'. Paragraph 16.3, on page 154, summarises much of the Commission's thinking: 'We believe it to be essential that an editor's rights should be guaranteed by his employers. We have recorded and take very seriously the possible dangers to diversity of opinion and expression which accompany the growth in concentration of ownership of newspapers. It can generate pressures which only editors can resist . . .' Three other passages in the same chapter are important. In paragraph 16.1, the Commission proposes that the 'unique role' of the editor must be protected against the closed shop (that is, the pressure or will of his colleagues) by exemption from union membership. The same point is made again in paragraph 16.5: 'Similarly, we stress the need to secure the independence of editors from their fellow journalists'. In the final paragraph, the report makes a surprising concession: 'we recommend that journalists working on a publication should be involved in the appointment of editors . . . we acknowledge the strength of the N.P.A.'s [Newspaper Publishers' Association] assessment of the support which an editor draws from his colleagues, and we believe that this must be stronger where members of his staff have been involved in his appointment. We do not make detailed recommendations . . . '

The Report is saying four things, perhaps three-and-a-half:

1. Yes, concentration of newspaper ownership is a menace to the editorial function. This simple admission of what most journalists have known for fifty years represents a tremulous but long stride forward in the mental development of Commissions on the press. It would have been nice to hear that some types of conglomerate were more dangerous than others, and to have a discussion of diversified jackdaw empires like Thomson's or Trafalgar House in that respect. But a small step for press workers, a big step for the Establishment, has none the less been taken.

2. Yes, an editor's relative sovereignty does largely depend on the support of his colleagues. Here the commissioners' long-range patrols could plainly see the outskirts of the concept of internal press democracy. But their reports confused and worried

headquarters. The closed shop dispute, which has been so calamitous for clear thinking about the future of journalism, has left the impression that the National Union of Journalists wishes by absorbing the editor to dictate policy to him from N.U.J. headquarters. The involvement of journalists in helping the editor to resist those 'pressures' was accordingly unthinkable to the commissioners. Such involvement could only be subversive and diminish the editorial function.

3. But journalists should be involved somehow, all the same. So they should have some part, some right to be consulted, in the appointment of an editor. This concession partly contradicts the crucial last sentence in paragraph 16.3, which ought really to have been worded: 'it can generate pressures *which an editor alone cannot resist*'.

4. The report is therefore reduced to seeking a contractual solution. Publishers and editors should meet and work out a form of contract which would 'publicly and explicitly guarantee editorial independence, in the context of concentration, chain ownership and monopoly' (paragraph 16.5). The only firm recommendation is that on large newspapers, an editor's contract should ensure at least twelve months' notice.

The general effect of these reflections and proposals in the report is to legitimate the existing system. The crucial perception – that the new pressures which the Commission has identified mean that the old fashioned editor is *less* able to withstand pressure from above, and that the only real guarantee of the editorial function is to spread responsibility into the collective responsibility of the editorial staff – is only a glimpse. By itself, the vague involvement of journalists in the selection of editors will only reinforce the present problem: the editor may have a better relationship with his colleagues, but his allegiance is not transferred from proprietor to staff. The journalists have no way of supporting the editor in his day-to-day efforts to strike out and maintain his own line.

The effect of the closed shop dispute on the commissioners is all too apparent. In Chapter 17 ('Closed Shop in Journalism'), we find a very revealing use of words. The two sides in the dispute are assessed thus:

> For the N.U.J., the first priority is the freedom to improve the earnings and conditions of work of its members and to deploy

its maximum strength for collective bargaining . . . For those on the other side, what matters most is to secure the freedom of the press because they cannot 'conceive of a civilised society that does not regard as its first priority the right of a man to express what he believes in whatever form he thinks appropriate, subject to the control of the law'. (paragraph 17.9)

Like a short-sighted bream, the commission here bolts the whole clumsy lure floated by the proprietors. It is accepted that the central concern of the proprietors is classical press freedom, or indeed (in the paragraph's quotation from Lord Goodman's evidence) the right of free speech itself. It is not. The proprietors are as concerned to 'deploy their maximum strength for collective bargaining' as the N.U.J. Freedom of the press is about a paper's economic freedom to survive, and the chance of founding fresh publications, about resisting the pressure of concentration on editors, about open government, about advertising. It is not about the owner's power in wage haggles, nor – other than marginally – about how staff journalists are recruited. But what is most painful about that paragraph is the assumption that by the nature of things it is the proprietors who care about freedom of expression and the journalists who do not. There are Milton, Swift, Wilkes and Lord Goodman on one side. There on the other are Jack and Jeanette Bloggs, malignant little inkies whose horizons extend no further than the next wage claim, T.V. allowances and zapping non-union rugby contributors.

How could the commissioners have swallowed a view so cheekily inverting the truth, so crudely fabricated? To suppose that James Ballantyne, publisher, might have been knighted for his services to the novel and to romantic literature while Parliament was invited by a Royal Commission to suppress the clamours for payment emanating from the scribbler W. Scott on the grounds that they threatened freedom of publication . . . too silly even to be funny. However, swallow it they did. The apparent ease of the performance only shows how effectively the ideas of 'internal press freedom' have been blotted from Establishment awareness in the space of a few years.

In Britain, the topic of internal media democracy won wide attention in the early 1970s, principally through the propaganda activities of the Free Communications Group. This was, of course, an aspect of the European movement for 'participation' which began to seize professional and white-collar elements of society in the late 1960s. For Britain, the staff takeover of R.T.F. during the Paris May in 1968 was the direct inspiration of the F.C.G., and the subsequent French and West German movements to set up elected editorial councils (*conseils de redaction* or the *Statutenbewegung*) provided models and lessons in the few years which followed.

Since then, the theme has been obscured. The main reasons would seem to be four:

1. The subsiding of the whole 'participation' excitement, and the adoption of some of its less challenging forms into moderate and officially sponsored schemes for 'industrial democracy'. I should also mention the disillusion of the contemporary intellectual left with the solutions of the late 1960s as 'élitist'. This is not the place to handle that particular contention, but there is of course a strength in the argument that radical social change is not brought about by granting professional journalists the right to decide what they put into newspapers which continue to constitute a 'bourgeois press'. The 'internal press freedom' idea, indeed, does hold a strong trace of what Trotskyites like to call 'impossibilism', meaning in this case that the journalists will find that a truly democratic and independent press cannot be attained under present conditions but will draw rich political lessons from the experiment's own limits.

2. The ferocious struggles between managements and the National Union of Journalists over the last three or four years. In the course of these struggles, the term 'press freedom' – which had just been successfully enlarged to include notions of internal democracy within the industry – was perverted and reduced by the proprietors' faction to imply merely a ban on N.U.J. closed shops. The whole course of the row, which became a national political issue, obscured the distinction between an editorial staff and an N.U.J. chapel, and eventually came to suggest that 'journalists' power' in whatever degree can only be a euphemism for direct control of editorial content by the national executive of the N.U.J.

3. The tendency of the T.U.C. and its component members, in attempting to resist the fall of living standards in recent years, to become suspicious (they were never free from suspicion) of ideas offering trade unionists 'power instead of pay'. Internal press freedom, as a proposal, has never in fact made power and pay into

alternatives. And the idea of democratising editorial departments is not simply the press industry's equivalent of *Mitbestimmung,* limited worker participation on company boards, but has deeper implications. Confusion, none the less, exists.

4. The instant and total hostility of newspaper managements – in most cases, though not all – when they have grasped what internal democracy proposals mean. The newspaper proprietors in the early 1970s provided here a foretaste of the general reaction of British industrialists to the Bullock Report on industrial democracy. (It is worth mentioning that the management campaign against Michael Foot over the N.U.J. closed shop, to the accompaniment of a heart-rending requiem for press freedom, had a second and subsidiary motive, which was to make out the preliminary case for the exemption of newspapers from any future legislation on industrial democracy.) The determination of individual journalists and chapels often faltered in the face of this hostility, which seemed to endanger the success of conventional negotiations on pay and conditions.

The Bullock Report itself provides a good example of the obscurity which has descended on the subject of internal democracy for the press. Even the proprietors' argument for exemption seems not to have been appreciated. One section mentions vaguely that 'press and broadcasting', as well as banking, shipping, construction, hotels and catering, were interests which had suggested that they should be excluded from any general scheme of industrial democracy and worker participation,[2] and the list of submissions reveals that the Newspaper Society (representing English provincial proprietors) gave evidence. The case for media exemption is actually quite powerful and could have rested on a West German analogy where the media are excluded on the grounds of *Tendenzschutz* (defence of opinion) from the provisions of the industrial democracy legislation. But either the Newspaper Society did not realise this, or Bullock did not: possibly neither was aware of the precedent. Bullock merely enumerates five grounds for exemption brought up in evidence before the Commission, none of which really bears on the newspaper industry, and benevolently concludes: 'Generally speaking, we are opposed to exemption for particular groups or classes of companies or particular sectors of industry or community activity . . .'

But in spite of this decline in interest, the original justifications for internal press democracy brought forward nine years ago have grown stronger, and new arguments have made their appearance. There remains, first of all, the argument based upon the effects of ownership concentration. Fewer titles have disappeared in the past seven years than prophets in 1970 expected. But the concentration of control has persisted, and new forms of concentration have developed much further. The history of newspaper ownership, obviously parallel to that of industrial ownership in general, has moved from the owner–editor to the tycoon controlling many editors to the multi-media concern with interests in several branches of communications. Since the end of the 1960s, we have seen the transfer of much newspaper ownership to highly diversified corporations with industrial and financial interests of all imaginable kinds. Nothing happens overnight: it is now three years since the last owner–editor, David Astor, retired from Fleet Street and the *Observer*. But the trend is clear. Newspapers are becoming one division of a diverse portfolio, and often the least profitable division. The most interesting recent development in this line has been the entry of oil revenues from the North Sea or further afield into newspaper financing, whether into Thomson's or into the *Observer* itself, now under the protection of Atlantic Richfield.

This form of concentration has four common consequences:

1. The further diminution of the effective 'sovereignty' of editors. They become divisional managers, responsible to boards which may have little understanding or sentiment to spare for newspapers which are not profitable. The old tycoon, the sometimes crazy plutocrat who ran newspapers and only newspapers, was a more reliable master. Time will tell whether the boards of Trafalgar House (the *Daily Express*) or of Mr Jimmy Goldsmith's empire, if he finally acquires a paper, will prove as romantic.

2. The increase of potential 'no go' areas for critical reporting, areas in which central management is financially involved. Companies with North Sea oil interests will be worth monitoring in this respect, in a few years' time.

3. The possibility of the sudden sale or closure of a newspaper over the heads of both editor and staff, to say nothing of sudden transformations in 'weight' and style (see again the *Daily Express*).

4. Related to the points above, the temptation for editors and

senior editorial staff to play safe, to avoid subjects which upset the advertiser and so to ensure a healthy balance book for the board.

All of these tendencies can be curbed, sometimes even prevented, by the formation of elected editorial committees with certain statutory rights. An editor, lacking the personal support of a tycoon or direct proprietor (never a very reliable prop at the best of times), requires the collective support of colleagues who may well have elected him to his job in order to preserve his own freedom of manoeuvre. Such a committee would have control, or at least a veto right, over major appointments, a right to be consulted over any proposed sale, access to the true financial position of the paper and an entrenched guarantee that the general character or slant of the paper will not be changed without their agreement. In the event of a sale or closure, this committee and the collective it represents should be offered by law the chance to take the publication over and either run it as a co-operative or seek a new proprietor.

There is also the argument of quality. In spite of the efforts of the N.C.T.J., the level of education and responsibility among journalists is rising. A paper produced by a genuine team, as opposed to an assemblage of people stratified in the manner of a Dad's Army platoon, is more likely to be a good paper. Immediate authority is indispensable in a daily newspaper office, but there is no reason why an editor or news editor whose power rests on consent should not have authority (senior appointments would be by contract, rather than revocable from one day to the next). Authoritarianism, by contrast, is the recipe for wasting talent.

The approach, indeed the presence already, of state intervention provides another justification. Public financing and public or monopoly-provided facilities – whether we are talking about subsidies, state-owned plant, the redistribution of advertising revenue by statutory arrangement, the allocation of satellite time or the procuring of electronically-communicated data – are going to invade the economy of the press decisively in the next few years. This has two kinds of implication. One is that the dependency of journalism on external goodwill and provision will increase by a whole dimension. The collective defence of a paper's identity and editorial independence becomes correspondingly more urgent. Secondly, it can be foreseen that governments rendering assistance to the press will find it politically uncomfortable to hand over unconditionally cash or technical facilities to Mr Rupert Murdoch or to the D.C. Thomson patriarchy in Dundee. Conditions are going to be set. Assistance is going to be made conditional on certain structural changes,[3] and some degree of internal democratisation is quite likely to be one of those changes. This challenge is obviously more likely to come from a Labour Government, since it does not at present seem likely that a Tory administration would venture into the field of state assistance to the press.

It is time to look in more detail at the degrees and forms of internal press democracy which should be considered. The combinations are of course endless: I list the most obvious headings in a sort of ascending democratic order.

1. Newsroom democracy. This is no more than the setting-up of self-contained news teams, each responsible for an area of the paper and each including its own sub-editors. It would replace the present vertical structure of command.

2. Consultation. Written agreement to hold regular and frequent meetings at which journalists meet editor and management and discuss openly the running and content of the paper.

3. The right to know. Access to information about major appointments and dismissals, financial information, the revealing in advance of editorial and managerial plans.

4. A share in control. This can either be through a series of veto rights (no major appointment or no change in editorial policy without, say, the two-thirds majority approval of the journalists), or through positive control, in which an elected editorial committee makes such appointments and takes the strategic decisions.

5. Shared or outright ownership. Various patterns exist for the co-operative ownership of a newspaper by its staff (for instance *Le Monde*), which allow for external investment without conceding any rights of control over content to the investor.

Most of these forms rest upon the institution of an elected editorial committee. Such a committee should ideally be chosen by all members of the editorial staff, whatever their union affiliation. This full assembly should elect a committee or council to negotiate an agreement with management in which some or all of the above rights are anchored. This would almost certainly have to be done against the background of parliamentary legislation, specifying the outlines of the system but leaving it to individual houses to decide on their own forms within the act, if any.

Where does the N.U.J. chapel come in? There is no dodging the fact that in most cases those who dominate the chapel will dominate the committee. In some cases, unquestionably, and especially in small publications, journalists will want their chapel committee also to serve as the editorial committee. This has to be accepted. The N.U.J. is and always has been ineffective against the collective will of a chapel, and I see no danger that union headquarters at Acorn House would attempt to use the machinery to nominate the *Daily Express* editor or turn the *Telegraph* Labour. No chapel would accept any such instruction unless it already intended to take such a course.

Would 'journalists' power' swing the content of the papers to the left? I think this may be so, to some limited extent, but I do not think it matters very much. The imbalance to the right remains famous. Moreover, only an unhinged editorial council would try to offer the enormous *Telegraph* readership columns of unbroken socialism. The existence and opulence of the conservative readership will ensure that editorial committees will be found to serve their taste and guarantee their principles in print, and that choice will survive.

These power-sharing models, and the institutions behind them, correspond to the range of experiments in press democracy which have arisen over the last decade in several European countries, most spectacularly in West Germany and France. Britain, so disinclined to codify abstract principles or to admit that trees have grown on the graves of the nineteenth-century entrepreneur and the great editor who shared a table at his club, is different. There have, none the less, been experiments. The most remarkable, though now evidently defunct, began when the *New Statesman* N.U.J. chapel secured a right to interview and select editorial candidates. Movements in the same direction at the *Guardian,* on several occasions, were not a lasting success. The staff of the *Observer,* conceded a right to participate in the choosing of a new editor, were not united enough to make their right very effective. Gravest of all was the failure of the *Scottish Daily News (S.D.N.),* the establishment on the ruins of the *Scottish Daily Express* of what was intended to be a newspaper under the democratic control and ownership of all its workers, printers and journalists alike. A desperate financial situation was the main cause of collapse, but under the strain the journalists did not always or all live up to the commitment of the manual workers.

The *S.D.N.* disaster has unquestionably set back the cause of internal democracy, spreading disillusion among both politicians and press workers. But the list above does not include many minor and successful agreements concluded in the press, mostly at the 'statutory consultation' level, and the awareness of the arguments for internal press democracy survives in the Labour movement as a whole.

There are, all the same, problems special to Britain which confront any renewal of these experiments. It seems to me both inevitable and necessary, as pressures on press freedom intensify, that the contradiction between an increasingly critical and disaffected corps of journalists and a more remote and less 'journalistic' pattern of ownership will explode with far greater force in the near future. A fresh wave of experiments in 'internal press freedom' will then break over us. To be prepared for that eventuality, it is necessary to be aware of some of the obstacles and dangers to a democratic transformation of the press which are particular to this country. I list some of these peculiarly British problems in conclusion:

1. Bad industrial relations in British journalism. The low pay, low social status and high degree of union organisation and often militancy on pay issues which are typical of British journalists mark them off from the splendidly-salaried Herr Dr Redaktionsrat of West Germany, or from his privileged colleague in Italy. Journalism in those countries, where editorial committees flourish, is a profession: trade union organisation among West German journalists, for example, is relatively slight. Most British journalists, in contrast, are treated as white-collar workers and correctly regard themselves as such.

Eight years after first putting forward proposals for internal democracy in the British press, it now seems to me that such experiments are not going to fulfil their ultimate purpose until the battle over pay and conditions between journalists and employers has been fought to some sort of finish. Winning an adequate salary structure and some kind of job security will – rightly – remain the priorities for the immediate future. An editorial committee set up now and endowed with its rights would probably become one more participant in the central struggle against the various proprietor groupings, an ally to the N.U.J. chapel. And yet this is no reason to delay the setting up of individual editorial committees. The cause of internal democracy and the certainty of greater state intervention are allies – in the short term. But it would be better if legislation, when it came, merely regulated the existence of a large number of editorial councils which had fought their own way into existence.

2. Failure is still failure, in Britain. With newspaper finances as they are, a workers' co-operative taking up an option to buy a failing paper whose proprietor has abandoned it will be lucky to survive. The threat of collapse is at once the usual stimulus to a takeover and the warrant that the takeover will probably fail. This is not just a matter of money. While the best printing workers will still be there when Lord X bolts for the Bahamas, the best journalists will have taken to the lifeboats already and found other jobs. See the miserable editorial quality of the *Scottish Daily News*. No amount of money from Mr Benn could make mediocre journalists into good ones.

3. Printing workers. Members of the print unions will not willingly support new structures which give journalists a share in control over a newspaper and exclude the printers. To say that the new technology will dispose of them anyhow is no answer, although it is true that the powers of an editorial committee in a paper produced as well as written by journalists would be much greater. I can see no sign that journalists, except for a small minority, would accept that printing workers had equal rights over editorial content or appointments. (The question of so-called 'censorship' by printers, like the incidents over pro-Grunwick advertisements, relates to the conviction that the proprietors are implacably hostile to the trade union movement and are throwing a low punch in the endless sparring match. A democratic editorial structure may well be one of the few institutional changes which might dissolve or modify such patterns of behaviour.) Neither, however, do most printers want rights of that kind. They would watch with interest as the journalists made their bid for power, and if it came off, they would probably ask for certain rights of a comparable kind over management – but not over editorial matters. With scepticism and reservations, print workers have seen themselves and the journalists as two sides of a triangle facing

the third – management. For the print chapels to conclude that an editorial-democracy settlement meant that management and the journalists were now facing *them,* in a reversal of alliances, would be a disaster.

If some such scheme as Bullock's ultimately went through, the press (in so far as the staff still included many N.G.A. and NATSOPA members) might well look to Yugoslav practice. There the problem is avoided by simply separating printing and editorial into two distinct and quite independent enterprises. Physically on the same site, their relationship is limited to a commercial agreement to print the paper between the two workers' councils, as if the newsroom were in one city and the presses under quite different ownership in another.

Part 3

The Making of News

Chapter 7

All the World's a Stage, or What's Wrong with the National Press

Philip Elliott

A Free Press or a Respectable Press?

The fact that the third Royal Commission on the Press produced two reports has occasioned little comment, except in traditional terms pro and con government interference in the free press. Such comment obscures the fundamentally different approach adopted by the majority and the minority. This difference is not to be found in the approach the two reports take to government intervention but in the view each takes on the best strategy to improve the press. The majority put their trust in standards and responsibility, the minority opt for diversity to increase variety. This fundamental difference is blurred by concentrating on government interference and also by the tendency of each side to pay lip service to the values of the other. The majority genuflect at the altar of diversity before going on to discuss press performance in terms of accuracy and responsibility, the minority give these values more than a passing nod (perish the thought that anyone should advocate an irresponsible press) but then discuss means of achieving greater diversity.

That this is the fundamental difference, however, shows from the way it illuminates the internal consistency of each report. Their different strategies follow from the identification of different abuses and lead to the advocacy of different remedies. The majority is concerned about press misconduct, citing such abuses as inaccuracy, 'the basing of contentious opinion on inaccurate information' (10, Add 5) and invasion of privacy which they regard as 'one of the worst aspects of the performance of the press' (10.133),[1] They look forward to a more effective and vigilant Press Council, emphasise that its primary function should be to deal with complaints against the press and give their views on the standards of responsible journalism which the Council should encourage.

The minority identify the problem as one-sided political bias, a problem which in their view the majority pass over because of complacency and inadequate research. They accept the majority's proposals on the Press Council as a step towards improved press performance but argue 'that when drawn together the matrix of these proposals and recommendations, as well as the analysis, only go to emphasise the need for further reforms [to improve] the character of the press and [encourage] the expansion in its diversity' (Minority, 4). In their view diversity is the key to genuine freedom of the press. They quote approvingly a sentence from the Commission Working Paper No. 2 which takes the Miltonian line that 'the more diversity, the more competition, the more likely that the best ideas will find a home in people's minds and be disseminated most widely and quickly.'[2]

It is a nice irony that David Basnett and Geoffrey Goodman, the authors of the minority report, should have been pilloried as advocates of state intervention for setting out an up-dated version of the classic liberal doctrine of press freedom through diversity and competition. The majority meanwhile are heirs to another classic British tradition, the concern for standards, appearances and respectability. Hailed as the guardians of the free press they turn out on examination to be little more than protectors of the authority and values of the British establishment. A further irony is that while the case against government assistance to increase diversity on the grounds that it leads to interference is at least unproven (Anthony Smith argues elsewhere in this volume that it is contradicted by overseas experience) the case against respectability is clear from the timid, uninformative character of the contemporary national press.

This is the case which I shall develop in this paper. In the course of this century it has become more and more doubtful whether the national press should be considered as information media, selecting, presenting and commenting on different versions of events for their readers. This observation has become common-place since the *Sun* set out to be more entertaining than the *Daily Mirror*. But it is a point which has much more general relevance and one which cannot be met just by substituting entertainment for information. It is not enough to ask whether we are amused when the entertainments impose their own version of people and events on the world. Instead of acting as informants, the national press acts like a group of theatrical managers, sorting through their stock of props, scripts and costumes to find those which will best serve to create the effect they are after. This analysis explains press reaction to the majority and minority reports. The irony of the misplaced labels follows simply from the press responding to the cue of government intervention. The role of the press might be termed that of self-appointed script writer to the national morale. The analogy overstates the power and autonomy of the press, but it does underline the point that the criteria for selecting a particular scenario or caricature have as much to do with creating the appropriate impression as with goodness of fit on the people and events concerned.

The material to illustrate this charge may usefully be drawn from a review of the reporting of Northern Ireland. The Annan Committee on the Future of Broadcasting saw fit to treat the broadcast reporting of Northern Ireland as a special case, atypical of the general run of news and current affairs on radio and television.[3] The McGregor Commission did not deal with press performance at all in this area. The only thing to be said for McGregor's approach is that it did not simply pigeon-hole Northern Ireland as a special case. Covering Northern Ireland may be difficult and demanding but the story is not special in the sense of being exceptional, being treated differently from other stories.

Northern Ireland does need to be treated differently in the national press and, in that, it is typical, not exceptional. One reason why it provides such a useful critical case is because of the significance of the story in conventional news terms. The current wave of 'troubles' has been running for nearly a decade and claimed nearly 2000 victims. Moreover, Ulster and Ireland are clearly subjects on which British governments and people need to be better informed. The Irish problem is no recent phenomenon. Even the Northern Irish state was in existence for half a century.

The standard the press has achieved covering Northern Ireland is not consistently bettered on other subjects. The approach the press has adopted is characteristic of that which it uses everywhere, on most types of story at home and abroad.

It is necessary to construct such an indictment to underline the need for change in the British press. On the basis of its research into newspaper content, the McGregor Commission concluded that news values introduced bias into news reporting. This research was mainly concerned with content as items of information. In this chapter I shall attempt to provide a complementary analysis of style, an account of the consistent and repetitive ways in which British newspapers tend to write up all stories according to a few limited scenarios. The foundations of this style may be traced to the organisation of British journalism, the training of British journalists and to the British approach to information management. Concentrating on the distorting effects of news values suggests that to improve output it is enough to do something about the press. Analysis of the style of British journalism has the peculiar advantage that it shows that this is not the only strategy necessary. Indeed, such attempts are quite likely to make matters worse. Some of the blame for the repeated use of the same worn-out scripts and costumes can be laid at the door of the press itself. But many of the failings of contemporary British journalism can be traced to the conditions in which the press as a whole operates. These conditions have to do with the legal, political and social restrictions which have been retained by successive governments and with the general ambience of British society in which newspapers are tolerated providing they keep their place.

Looked at in this light, McGregor's proposals to improve press standards by fiddling about with the Press Council can be seen for what they are; proposals to impose British social mores more effectively on the press and so to keep it more firmly in its place. Such proposals will not improve the performance of the press though they may help to make its behaviour more respectable. In making such proposals the third press Commission has followed closely in its predecessors' footsteps. The first Commission set out to investigate accuracy and truth and ended up recommending a General Council of the Press to foster the responsibility and respectability of journalists. A responsible and respectable press has obvious attractions for the leadership of the society but only the failings of the present newspapers have made it acceptable to everyone else. The press has few friends in any quarter of the political spectrum. It could be argued that newspapers have only themselves to blame if new restrictions are introduced following the major debacles and minor errors which have filled their pages in recent years. To accept such an argument, however, is to accept remedies which can only make press performance even less distinguished, making newspapers resemble entertainments even more closely.

The British Style of Journalism

The first point to be made about the news from Northern Ireland is that there is remarkably little of it. Currently, coverage is down to a story a day in the heavy papers, a story a week in the populars and as little as possible in the *Sun*. This level of coverage is one which Northern Ireland shares with many other locations in the world, a fact which reflects both on the curious way Ulster is classified as a quasi-foreign story and on the low priority which British newspapers give to foreign news in general. At the beginning of the troubles Northern Ireland was treated more as a domestic story and, for long periods, was front page news. At that time the stock plots and characters of the British press still looked fresh when applied to Ulster. There was plenty of mileage to be had (a phrase which is revealing in itself) out of figures like Ian Paisley and James Chichester-Clark, a turbulent priest and a country squire of historical caricature, and Bernadette Devlin and Brian Faulkner, a swinging student and a tricky politician of more recent vintage. Frustrated in their search for a successful politician who, like O'Neill, might embody the cause of compromise and moderation, there was always the counterplot that the Stormont government had no one but itself to blame if Britain took over and sorted out the mess.

Once that had happened, however, it became more and more difficult to account for the lack of progress. For a time it was enough to assure readers that our lads were doing a grand job under difficult circumstances. Then the provisional I.R.A. obliged by filling the role of villainous enemy. Since then another trend has become apparent. As the British government has become more involved in the routine affairs of the province, so the press has become less interested, or at least printed fewer stories. To put the point more succinctly and paradoxically, press attention has declined with British involvement. With the reduction of the Northern Irish story to quasi-foreign news, Ulster has become another of those far off countries about which we know little and care less; the source of occasional entertainments when some particularly striking scenario is acted out and recognised by the British press as one of its stock plots. It is hard to resist the conclusion that this was what the authorities intended, that in this case the fault lies not with the British style of journalism but with the British approach to information management.

The British army is still putting considerable effort into its information services, employing nearly 150 press officers and other staff on the work. But much of the novelty has gone from the scripts the army has to sell. 'Imminent victory', 'heroic bravery' and 'atrocious suffering' have all become tarnished through over use. Occasionally a familiar scenario from the province will be given another run on the British front pages. Sudden death cannot but be a personal tragedy for any victim, whether or not it is embroidered by the newspapers, as in the case of the man, killed after leaving his wife and returning to Ulster, who was billed as a tragic separated lover. New candidates may be found for the role of villain, for example 'Grandma Venom' (Maire Drumm) or the 'bully boy' (Ian Paisley). Generally, however, Ulster-related stories are only given prominence now if they happen on the British mainland, not in the province itself. In the course of three weeks in 1974 in which twelve people died in Northern Ireland and five in the Guildford pub bombs, the British press (Ulster editions) devoted two-thirds of their coverage of Ulster-related violence to the violence which happened in England.[4]

On the mainland each cameo is more likely to be a self-contained unit leading from initial disaster to a dramatic climax in which the forces of law and order can be seen to triumph – after the Balcombe Street siege, the Balcombe Street siege trial. In Northern Ireland, on the other hand, it is simply one damned thing after another. The remorseless catalogue of incidents is hardly interrupted by the death or defeat of any individual the press has marked out as a villain. Moreover, as there is little to single out one incident from another, there is little to be gained from following up the arrest and conviction of those responsible, even should it occur. As the McGregor Commission points out, in the context of industrial relations, disputes are reported, solutions pass unnoticed. Continuity is not one of the strong points of the British press. But then to report the resolution of disputes would be to show trade unions in a different light from that in which the Royal Commission concedes they regularly appear in all papers, 'as organisations involved in conflict' (10.48), 'as bodies concerned with starting but not ending disputes (10.49), as 'bad news' with a 'preponderance of references to discord and to hardship for the public at large' (10.52).

The appeal of self-contained cameos in which right triumphs and the choice of which triumphs to trumpet abroad are both particularly revealing about the British style of journalism. British newspapers are at their best, or at least at their most vigorous, when faced with events moving quickly towards a dramatic climax, a sequence epitomised in recent years by the raid on Entebbe. A routine hijack of an Air France airbus which initially promised no more than that it might involve a girl friend of Carlos Ramirez, turned into a classic tale in which plucky Israeli rescuers bearded the wicked Amin in his den. There is more to the attraction of such events than their drama. The dénouement must be politically right. Almost invariably this means right wing in a populist sense. It is no accident that the organisers of the distribution of Grunwick's mail up and down the country hailed newspaper accounts of their 'Pony Express operation' as the greatest story since Entebbe. There was a time when there was room for some left-wing populism in the national press, particularly through the medium of Hugh Cudlipp's *Daily Mirror.* The Royal Commission noticed the editorial gap left by the *News Chronicle* and the *Daily Herald,* and the implication of those closures and other changes in the structure of the press for the news values painstakingly identified in the content analysis. This conclusion might have been extended into a general analysis of the bias of the press had not the Commission set its face resolutely against it. On the evidence of its recommendations to counter anti-union bias the Commission ignored the problem because it would neither have known nor agreed on what to do about it. 'We do not feel able to pronounce on whether there is political bias at work in drawing up the agenda for discussion and comment', they declare. 'This would require difficult value judgements . . .' (10.126). The national press, however, shows no such empirical reticence about the making of value judgements.

The reason for this lack of reticence is that the national press devotes most of its resources to writing up and processing stories rather than to finding out what happened or is likely to happen. Less than half of the editorial staff working for national newspapers are reporters, correspondents or photographers, people whose job involves covering beats and assignments. Those who do are pre-eminently generalists, brought up in the tradition of British journalism which prizes skill in dealing with incidents of all shapes and sizes, involving all classes and conditions of men. Arthur Christiansen, long-serving editor of the *Daily Express,* praised the general reporters, 'the old contemptibles of our craft', for meeting his ideal for a newspaperman.[5] 'I wanted film critics who could cover shipping disasters and general reporters who could interview film stars', he wrote commenting on an incident in which a film critic, deprived of the opportunity to interview some film stars aboard a grounded transatlantic liner, went home without reporting the disaster. The virtue of this system is that a reporter can be sent anywhere to cover anything in the sure and certain knowledge that he will write some copy. The disadvantage is that today's copy will look remarkably like that of yesterday and the day before. Getting a good familiar story takes precedence over getting the subject matter right and in its proper context. Assigned to a story or a beat, the reporter's problem is simply to recognise which script he is dealing with as each story comes up. He is unlikely to have either the time or the knowledge to set about writing new scripts.

The Royal Commission recognised that one of the main criticisms of the press is people's feeling 'that the treatment by newspapers of the subjects about which they are knowledgeable is lacking in background information and understanding' (18.2), a feeling which has been widely voiced at home and abroad. In Northern Ireland it has long been the one thing on which everyone has been agreed, no matter what their religion or political sympathies. Some newspapers have tried to reorganise their reporting staff to allow for more specialisation, for continuity of interest and expertise. Such developments run counter to the need for editorial economy, but the traditional fire brigade technique of sending off reporters when the fire has started may itself be wasteful of resources. The paper may get multiple coverage of the surface features of the incident or it may get nothing at all if it turns out to be a false alarm. In such a case, the brigade may arrive and find there is little to do, as for example the men the national press sent to cover the Orange Parades of 1970. Simon Winchester relates that in the case of the *Guardian* eleven men covered the parades while only two dealt with the Falls Road curfew that preceded them.[6] The parades were predictable and visible but there is little doubt that the curfew was the more significant for the future.

Like other strangers on a foreign shore, reporters sent off to cover some far-off fire are to be found sticking together for companionship and convenience. The technology of modern communications requires correspondents to have a base which is well served with facilities to keep in touch with head office and to get copy out. Justified as a way of safeguarding the output, the habit of sticking together soon becomes a method of ensuring the imput. Those who have an interest in getting their views and accounts into the media know where to seek the journalists out, and journalists can keep an eye on others of their kind to make sure they are not scooped. In Northern Ireland the Europa Hotel, the place where most journalists have gathered, has acquired a certain notoriety both as a bomb target and as a symbol of the failings of British journalism.[7] A few correspondents have disassociated themselves from the practice of covering the story from the hotel bar, a practice which shows itself in ignorance of the local situation, dependence on secondhand accounts, failure to check those accounts, especially those which come from apparently reliable sources, and a general propensity to make the same mistakes as everyone else. Reporting with the herd makes for collective decisions on which particular plot and costume is most appropriate for use today.

When the events happen in England there is no need to go through this process of setting up a foreign base. Another reason for the concentration on events on the mainland is simply that they are closer to hand for hard-pressed reporters and sub-editors. It is the sub-editors particularly who benefit. They do not have to rely too closely on the men on the spot for the details of the particular story. Given a surfeit of material from their own reporters and the Press Association, sub-editors can take their own decisions on costume and plot. In the case of the Balcombe Street Siege trial, there was extensive coverage of the verdict and sentences in all the papers. This brought into play the full range of traditional Irish stereotypes and contemporary references to the media culture.[8] Mr and Mrs Matthews, the hostages in the siege, were variously reported as being angry and bitter or forgiving but uncomprehending, depending on which version of the basic plot the paper had chosen to emphasise. Such inconsistencies cannot simply be explained as differences between papers. The four accused in the trial who were denigrated in some stories as 'so-called' or 'self-styled' soldiers' were also credited in the same papers with being 'the I.R.A.'s crack unit'. The latter phrase apparently came from the Metropolitan police. At the end of the siege, the Metropolitan Commissioner, Sir Robert Mark, had minimised the importance of the captives as 'unpleasant people', 'ordinary, vulgar criminals', 'low-class terrorists'. The national press does not always write its own scripts. It is open to offers from reputable sources trying to create similar effects.

The British press rarely shows itself aware of such inaccuracies and inconsistencies, much less does it correct the mistakes it made yesterday, today. After studying six weeks of Northern Irish news in the daily press of London, Dublin and Belfast, I found only one paper which published a correction of its own mistake, and that was an Irish one. The correction was significant of a more general difference between the press in the two countries. This was not that the press in the Republic made more mistakes. In the two periods studied, there were several assassinations which were wrongly or ambiguously attributed in the British press, so much so that the two loyalist groups responsible had to declare their hands after a time to let the world know that they and not the I.R.A. had done the deeds. The difference was that the Irish papers were much more open about the process whereby they had obtained their information. Papers in the Republic tended to make clear who was saying what about each particular incident and what their interest was in saying that. In some cases the journalist went on to indicate who he believed and why. It is rare to find a British journalist who is prepared to take his readers into his confidence in this way. Instead, the British press likes to iron out the ambiguities and pretend that it is dealing in established fact. Life in the national daily press is conducted in black and white, not in many shades of grey. But then those who might have seen the shades of grey do not control the output. There is a traditional distinction between writers' papers, the quality papers, papers in which the reporter stands a good chance of seeing what he wrote printed as he wrote it under his own by-line, and popular papers, sub-editors' papers, in which copy is rewritten on the desk. The Economist Intelligence Unit survey of 1965 revealed that on average the proportion of sub-editors to reporters was actually higher in the quality press than in the populars.[9] The McGregor Commission has yet to make such detailed figures available but a crude comparison based on the total number of editorial staff in the daily press shows that the overall proportion of sub-editors increased from 16 per cent to 23 per cent between 1965 and 1975.[10] Unless the reporter's material is likely to reach the paper there is little incentive for him to work on a story by himself or to try to reveal to the reader his own assessment of the situation. The chances are the desk men will ignore his copy and find more convenient pegs for their clichés and caricatures in the copy which comes in from the Press Association.

For all the Royal Commission laboured the obvious content distinctions between the quality and popular papers, the report missed completely this point about who writes the stories. McGregor also missed the point about the Press Association. The charge against the agency is not that considered by the Commission that its output is inaccurate – quite the reverse. It is boring and unadventurous. Finicking accuracy about surface details provides the foundation on which the national press can set about erecting a familiar story from the range of models available in their construction kit. Stereotypes and scenarios might be excused as an aid to public understanding if they were inventive and apposite. The charge against the current selection is that they are repetitive and derivative. 'Mission Impossible', for example, is currently a favourite model at the *Daily Mirror,* epitomising for that paper both the Israeli raid on Entebbe and the activities of the four Irishmen convicted for the Balcombe Street siege.

The ubiquity of these models as well as such precise details as the names, ages and occupations of those involved reveals a third point which the Commission missed, the importance of style as the setting for items of content. It explains how McGregor was able to come to the contradictory conclusion that press reporting was both factual and unreal. On the basis of the content analysis, the Commission concludes:

> These studies show that news coverage . . . is *highly factual* in the sense of being both directly attributed and devoid of any overt bias. On the other hand, perhaps inevitably, the choice of items and the angle from which they are written ensure that bad news and conflict predominate, especially with distant or unfamiliar countries. News angles also mean that the images of institutions reflected in newspapers *do not correspond with reality* (10.71, emphasis added).

The analysis of the national press set out in this chapter shows that this contradictory description is quite accurate. The British national press is precisely in the business of producing unreal but highly factual images. The Commission, having missed the point, sets out to achieve its goal of a respectable press by recommending even greater attention to accuracy ('factualness', to use its own jargon). The point of the contradiction, however, is that the bias is in the unreality, not the facts.

The British Approach to Information Management

So far in this chapter references to information management have taken the form of examples of official sources 'working the system' by making information available. Indeed, if the press act like a group of theatrical managers, some official sources, the army and the police in cases cited above, have become adept at playing the role of casting director. It is not just that they have told journalists who was involved but that they have dreamed up the nicknames which have caricatured participants in the public consciousness. One of the most striking of recent cases was Donald Nielson, who, after his arrest in the Lesley Whittle case, devoted a good deal of his energy to denying that he was the 'black panther', not in the sense that he was the wrong man, but in the sense that he was not like the label. More significant than such individual cases, however, is the example of mugging. In the 1970s a new type of crime and criminal was introduced into British society, with the heavy implication that the country needed its traditional police force to protect itself from the alien threat.[11]

There is more to information management than making

information available. If the carrots of hospitality and handouts do not work, there is no shortage of possible sticks. In Northern Ireland the army has not been above strong arm tactics, freezing out or harassing journalists whom it considered hostile to its cause. The *Guardian* correspondents, Simon Winchester and Simon Hoggart, both record army attempts to bring them into line by cutting them off from the regular flow of information.[12] In the case of *The Times* correspondent, Robert Fisk, the process went further with threats of legal action.[13] In other recent cases against Mark Hosenball and Duncan Campbell the threats have been translated into action, though it is impossible to be absolutely certain that it was their activities related to Northern Ireland which prompted the action. The third and most effective technique of information management, secrecy, has been brought fully into play.

Not all the blame for the secrecy which pervades British society can be laid at the door of those who refuse to make information available. Newspapers themselves hide much away by sticking to a black and white view of the world in which heroes and heroines contest with villains. Some grey does creep into the up-market Sundays. They have more time for reflection and credit their readers with the ability to cope with some of the complexities of life. Soon after the death of Magella O'Hare, for example, readers of the *Sunday Times* were told that there was something not quite right about the army version that she had died in the line of fire between a soldier and a gunman. Months later there was another reference to the incident as a case of black propaganda such as the army no longer engaged in. Whether this was black propaganda in the relatively familiar sense of putting out a misleading account or in the much more sinister sense of an attempt to manufacture an atrocity to follow the death of the Maguire children, the incident which led to the foundation of the peace movement, has yet to be revealed. Suffice it to say that it is unlikely that any but avid news consumers, compulsive readers of the small print or people with access to the Irish papers know that a soldier has since been charged with Magella O'Hare's murder.

It is safe to assume that this is known to many British journalists, whether from published or unpublished sources. It provides an example of another feature of journalism which, if not peculiar to the British case, is found there in exaggerated form.

For all the public protestations about being the reader's representative, the eyes and ears of the British public, journalists appear to get much more satisfaction from being 'in the know' themselves, from hobnobbing with the great and famous, than from passing their information on to those on whose behalf they are supposed to collect it. To criticise this tendency is not simply to denigrate another man's pleasures. There is clear evidence, as for example in the operation of the lobby system, that 'in-group journalism' actively obstructs the right to know. Indeed one wonders whether British journalists would be prepared to recognise that the public, as opposed to themselves as a specially privileged group, enjoy such a right. The phrase is one which speaks not only to the greater openness of American government, but also to the greater democracy of American society. In the United States particular groups set less store by their privileged access to information as a sign of their position in the national pecking order. If, as in Britain, information has such a value, then it is natural that there should be a tendency to husband and hoard it, rather than scatter it abroad. The extension of the analogy is that seeds kept in barns grow few crops. In-group journalism is impotent journalism, so far as the democratic process is concerned.

Journalists' jealousy of their status is not the only reason why the public's right to know in Britain amounts to little more than a public right to be patronised. There are plenty of other groups jealously keeping guard over the little bits of information they have at their disposal. Some, such as the professions and the local authorities, have the backing of occupational sanctions; others such as the courts, the government and the civil service have been able to make use of the full resources of the law. Members of Parliament are in the peculiar position of having their own quasi-legal procedure to fall back on in the form of contempt of the House. Such sanctions are symbolic of the British approach to information management which can be summed up in two all-pervasive principles: when in doubt say nothing; and an appeal to the press (or the public) is a confession of weakness. Against this background it is hardly surprising that British journalists are inclined to play their cards very close to their chests. Such sources as there are have to be protected even at the cost of allowing them to contradict, in public, statements which were apparently made in private – the situation which arose in the recent lobby debacle over Sir Peter Ramsbottom and Peter Jay.

The practice becomes a good deal more questionable, however, when the source produces stories, not statements. The margarine industry's recent creation, 'the killer cow', may be acceptable as just another addition to the stock of public entertainments. Even so, it took time and close attention to realise that behind the headline was another campaign to wean the housewife off butter and on to margarine. Army stories designed to make a political point and show the need for a tougher security policy in Ulster, such as appeared towards the end of Merlyn Rees' time as Secretary of State, need much closer evaluation. In such cases the story is not the leaks but the leaking. As things stand, the British press is all too likely to be grateful it has a story to print. Because the supply is so limited, there is little hope that stories will be scrutinised rather than used; but because it is limited, information which does come out is particularly likely to need scrutinising to reveal the source's motives and interests.

An information policy founded on secrecy implies there is something to hide. In all probability there is, but the stock in trade of the national press is simply to put on a fit of pique when confronted by some small cog in the system, a headmaster or a hospital administrator who dares say nothing but knows little anyway. It is a pity more journalists do not follow Claud Cockburn's advice: 'never believe anything until it has been officially denied'.[14] As it is, much of the reporter's job is simply to act as a recorder of what the official sources are willing to tell him. Even the McGregor Commission was struck by the 'heavy reliance on official sources and spokesmen' (10.71) it found in the press. Several British correspondents in Ulster have recorded their surprise at finding they have been fooled by the official sources in the province. None have put it more engagingly than Andrew Stephen, who wrote in the *Observer* 'the sad experience for most British journalists once they start working in Northern Ireland is that the word of the authorities cannot automatically be relied upon'.[15]

For many correspondents, Ulster has been their first big story. The experience of passing almost directly from the provincial press to such a sensitive assignment has shown up some of the weaknesses of the on-the-job training which the provincial press provides. This training puts a premium on craft skills such as the speed and accuracy necessary to become a recorder rather than a reporter of events. It also enables the budding journalist to find out what his paper will print. There may be praise for getting down correctly what the authorities in the area say, for summarising it neatly and providing it with the right angle, but there is little for questioning whether it is true, little time to investigate any suspicions and no space to publish any results. The priorities of the British style of journalism are effectively taught in the provincial papers. It is *par excellence* the training ground of the general reporter, in which he learns how to produce the goods for the men on the desk, the sub-editors, to work over. Work on the provincial press does introduce trainees to the creative aspect of British journalism, to recognise and manipulate the stock plots and characters in which information, laboriously collected, can be packaged. It is no wonder that those who have come up through the system share a sense of in-group camaraderie and go in awe of the value of the experience. Nor is it any wonder that reporters trained to be recorders treat authorities with respect.

As Dave Murphy makes clear in the next chapter, the respect which the provincial press shows towards community leaders follows both from its involvement with them in the local social elite and from the power that elite is able to exercise. The same analysis holds at the national level. I have already discussed the tendency for journalists to be incorporated into the ranks of the establishment. The point about power is best demonstrated by considering the easy targets at which the national press commonly aims.

In many of the popular scenarios the villains are unrepresented and powerless. Indeed, they may be unrepresentable like vandals, soccer hooligans or the provisional I.R.A., in the sense that anyone would find it difficult to make a case for their behaviour. Putting such villains in the pillory makes an amusing public entertainment in the short run, but makes for public incomprehension and anger in the long run when the same villains still appear year after year. Far from acting as a watchdog against the abuses of power by the authorities, the press acts as the champion of authority as the necessary source of stability.

Journalists must be among the last people, outside of the pantomime, who still pretend to a belief in the forces of evil. This in spite of the fact that they often preside over the costume changes which make yesterday's villain tomorrow's hero, or at least a comprehensible human being by comparison with the villain of today. The following diatribe against the I.R.A. by Paul Johnson, one of two journalists who were members of the Royal Commission and the only one to sign the majority report, graphically illustrates the point.

> In Britain, as well as in Ulster, we face in the I.R.A. not a nationalist movement, not a league of patriots, not 'guerillas' or 'freedom fighters', or anything which can be dignified with a political name, but an organisation of psychopathic murderers who delight in maiming and slaughtering the innocent and whose sole object and satisfaction in life is the destruction of human flesh. The misguided patriots who joined the I.R.A. in the heady days of 1968 and after have melted away and have been replaced by men and women who have far more in common with Ian Brady and Myra Hindley than with old-style terrorists like Michael Collins and De Valera.[16]

Remembering what the British press had to say about Michael Collins and De Valera in their day, the only conclusion is that labelling is no substitute for an analysis of motivation. The dramas of the national press, however, have not developed much beyond the style of morality plays.

Most targets offer the press some advantages in terms of the political alliances which can be forged in the attack. Vandals and hooligans can be laid at the door of liberal law enforcement or progressive education. Scroungers can be used to excuse public expenditure cuts and to undermine the welfare state. The threat from the left, infiltrators or individual ministers continually throws doubt on the credibility of the Labour Party. Any stick will do to beat a nationalised industry, as was shown by the *Daily Mail* in the Leyland affair. The case provided a clear illustration of the different legitimacy the press is prepared to grant to the business practices of companies owned by the government as against those in private hands. David English's defence that the *Daily Mail* dealt with all-comers even-handedly would have been more plausible if he had been able to cite his paper's record on Lonrho, Slater-Walker, Poulson or the secondary banking system. As it was, the best he could do was point to a campaign to have VAT removed from children's clothes. VAT, incidentally, in the form of the VAT-man who cometh far into the night or early in the morning, is well on the way to being turned into another left-wing bogey. The political alliances which support the press in attacks such as these not only provide reassurance that its place among the establishment is secure, but provide it with a source of copy. Regular coverage of parliamentary affairs is as rare in the press as foreign news, but no campaign is complete without a member of parliament like Ian Sproat on scrounging or Rhodes Boyson on education to orchestrate the follow-up in the Commons.

In summary, the national press are the camp followers of the establishment. Occasionally, they may go on ahead, as at the time of the civil rights demonstrations in Belfast and Derry, to see if the leaders of British society need to move their tents. Once the authorities have pitched camp, however, they soon make clear that they expect to hear nothing more from them. Most of the time the job of the press is simply to put on the entertainments. These include public condemnations of anyone found disturbing the campsite, presiding over such public revelries as Her Majesty's Jubilee and celebrating the defeat of Her Majesty's enemies, as at the Balcombe Street Siege trial.

This brings us to the last ditch defence of British newspapers, particularly beloved of provincial newspapermen whose 'successful' products face no competition. There cannot be much wrong with newspapers, they argue, if people buy them and are amused by them. One answer to this is set out by the McGregor Commission in its introductory discussion of the functions and freedom of the press. 'Of course, the press seeks to entertain as well as to instruct and we do not dismiss this aim as trivial but it is the performance of the serious functions which justifies the high importance which democracies attach to a free press' (2.1). Another is that the widespread feeling that there is nothing but bad news these days is a clear expression of public boredom with predictable entertainments. Next year, for example, promises periodic bursts of outrage against soccer hooligans at the start of the soccer season, against crime in general when the criminal statistics come out, against workers and unions for exceeding their share whether the economy becomes bouyant or continues to stagnate, against all the other familiar villains and bogeymen whenever the occasion is right. On the other hand, there is the certain prospect of a series of royal births, romances and anniversaries to celebrate and the unlikely chance of a British national sporting victory. Is it any wonder that people find their entertaining newspapers depressing?

The Case for Change

The analysis so far presented points to two major areas in which action should be taken to change the character of the national press. What is needed are changes in the British style of journalism and the British approach to information management. The second may conveniently be taken first as it is more easily dealt with. Secrecy exists as a habit of mind at all levels in the British polity. But the habit is firmly grounded in a framework of laws and legal practices. It is unlikely that any government will bring about a change simply by affirming its good intentions. Protestations by Labour and Conservative governments in recent years have not opened up the processes, only produced more official paper in different colours. What is needed is a government with the will to tackle the legal framework. The agenda for such an attack is set out by Geoffrey Robertson elsewhere in this volume. The politics of it are bedevilled by the fact that the press as it currently operates is unlikely to inspire anyone as a worthwhile cause. Indeed, the deliberations of the McGregor Commission make clear that there is more likely to be agreement on further restrictions in the form of specific standards and responsibilities for the press than there is to be support for widening press freedom. This was after all one point on which the majority and minority agreed.

To do something about the British style of journalism is an urgent precondition for the growth of a more open and democratic form of society in Britain. We have been faced with a paradoxical situation in recent years. On the one hand there has been a demand by people for more influence and power over their own lives. As the minority report puts it '. . . in all spheres of our national life the focus of change tends to be an increasing demand by people for more involvement and greater participation. For instance, the pressure for political devolution as well as industrial democracy; for educational reform, for race and sex equality, etc.

These pressure groups which have risen to become important forces in our society do not seem to be adquately reflected in the changes (or the absence of changes) in the media' (Minority, 13). On the other hand there has been a steady decline in interest in the conventional political process. The turnout of 42.6 per cent in the Ladywood by-election in August 1977 was only a particularly graphic illustration of the steady post-war trend towards political apathy and inactivity. Many factors have contributed to this process but important among them have been changes in the fourth estate; changes in the range and functions of newspapers and other information media; the development of the British style of journalism discussed above. The predictable unanimity of the press in its selection of characters and plots has stifled interest at the national level. Instead of being offered the chance to join in a debate, people are simply deafened by a repetitive, unison chorus. The result is not so much disinterest as a feeling of powerlessness. The interest and the activity is there in matters more closely concerned with daily life. In such cases people do not have to rely on intermediary channels of communication either to realise what is happening or to debate what should be done about it.

The goal of any strategy for doing something about the national press therefore should be to provide the means which will allow and encourage people to re-engage in the political and social life of the nation. Unchecked market forces would leave the field to broadcasting and the local press. Both are pre-eminently media of disengagement. Broadasting tends to discourage partisan activities, to encourage the illusion that objectivity and impartiality can be achieved without bias, rather than with a hidden, accepted bias, hidden because it is accepted. The upsurge of pressure-group activity has mostly been locally based. The failure of the media to take it on board has largely been a failure of the local press. The widespread development of 'alternative' papers bears witness to the subject matter which the commercial local press, with a few honourable exceptions, has passed over. Instead it relies on much the same agenda as the nationals with a greater emphasis on the nice – babies, animals and local achievement – and less on the nasty and salacious unless they are accepted as matters for general indignation.

The political argument for the survival of the national press and an increase in its variety and scope can be summarised very briefly.

We already have the evidence that the fourth estate is crucial for the democratic process. As newspapers have settled into the uniformities of the British style of journalism and as many of their functions have been taken over by the broadcast media, so involvement in the democratic process has declined. This is not to deny that there is more to newspapers than politics, however broadly defined. It does however underline that it is not good enough to do something about the national press simply by doing nothing. Intervention is needed not just to keep papers alive but to increase diversity. Ultimately the uniform style of British journalism will be most effectively broken up by making newspapers more various in their form of ownership, the way they are organised and the markets which they serve. The schemes of intervention necessary to bring about such changes are considered elsewhere in this volume. The conclusion of this paper has the more limited objective of considering what changes in the British style of journalism might be within the power of journalists themselves.

Changing the British Style of Journalism

Such changes may be grouped under two main headings, organisation and training. Under the first heading the main thrust of change should be to increase the responsibility of the individual journalist, under the second to ensure that training equips him to carry them out. Many of the practices which underpin the British style of journalism and which were discussed earlier in this paper reflect the collective rather than individual nature of editorial work on British newspapers. The problem is epitomised by the practice of covering the same stories in the same way from the same hotel bars. Such practices are quite adequate to produce the output when newspapers take as their main aim that they should not be beaten by the opposition. Material which is not already publicly available in the sense that it comes from regular sources is likely to appear in other papers and can be readily packaged in such a way as to make it familiar to readers, may be ruled out on the grounds that the game is not worth the candle. It is hard to measure the return on the extra risk, cost and space involved in going it alone. If it is achieved at the expense of items which other papers carry, then it is all too easy to take that as a criterion that the paper failed. The fact that collective practices produce collective failings makes them more difficult to recognise and harder for any single paper to remedy.

Organisation

Under the heading of organisation there are four main failings to be considered: information poverty, undeveloped relationships between journalists and readers and between journalists and sources, source control and lack of originality in the packaging of popular culture regardless of its content. An analysis of these failings shows that there are exceptional cases in the present British press, cases which can be cited as examples of what might be achieved. A common feature of all these exceptional cases is that they are associated with an individual journalist or executive, underlining the point that professional responsibility is individual responsibility.

The inadequacy of the information provided by the British press is probably the most familiar of these charges. Investigative reporting is the only aspect of journalism which has become a fashionable cause in recent years. Watergate has been turned into a myth celebrating the serendipitous achievements of two comparatively junior American reporters. Chance played a large part in allowing Woodward and Bernstein the time and contacts to get their story. Newspapers, like other human endeavours, cannot be organised in such a way that they always have the luck, but Harold Evans and others have been pointing out for years that this type of journalism is peculiarly restricted in Britain.[17] Newspapers tend to skimp on the necessary reporting staff and resources. Worse, they face the secrecy and the restrictions of the British approach to information management which make it unlikely they will get the story or be able to publish given the material.

So far as the newspaper itself is concerned, what is needed is enough slack to allow reporters to pursue unpredictable stories, stories which may take time and effort before they show results, or stories which may produce no results at all. The *Sunday Times* has achieved this by being a successful newspaper backed by a wealthy proprietor. Before accepting this as a universal formula, however, the question must be raised whether the conditions for newspaper success and the sources of wealth available to proprietors are limited in such a way as to restrict the range of subjects which may be investigated. As others have pointed out in this volume and elsewhere, this question is most urgent in the case of oil.[18] Oil is at the same time the most significant contemporary development in the British economy and the main source of spare wealth which proprietors may be prepared to spend on newspapers. There is a danger that the exploitation of Britain's oil reserves will become the most important story which cannot be told. Oil companies' motives for involving themselves in ailing British newspapers may not be as philanthropically disinterested as they appear, and there is no reason why the problem should stop with oil. Oil companies are multinational conglomerates with diverse interests. Unlike a country's government, a multinational corporation in control of a national newspaper may not number the national interest among its own. Nevertheless the Royal Commission was more impressed by the traditional bogey of state involvement.

Besides Harold Evans and the *Sunday Times* there are other exemplars of investigative journalism in Britain, or at least of journalists who have been able to introduce into their coverage more than was readily available from recording routine sources. So far as Northern Ireland is concerned two notable recent cases have been *The Times'* correspondent Robert Fisk and *The Guardian* correspondent Derek Brown. In the period covered by the study already referred to, Fisk's stories on Libya's involvement in the Ulster arms trade were almost the only stories in the British press which testified to journalistic endeavour. They did not simply report something which was already a matter of public record, but depended on contacts built up and exploited by the individual journalist. Such stories need not necessarily deal with matters of great moment or be featured with special prominence as the Libyan material was. In the course of the second loyalist strike, Derek Brown checked whether it was being observed by the businesses owned by some of the strike leaders. The fact that it was not made a unique point to include in his *Guardian* coverage.

Nor are such examples confined to the quality press. Both Robert Fisk and Derek Brown have moved on from Northern Ireland leaving that specialism behind them. Chapman Pincher, however, defence correspondent of the *Daily Express* has become something of a national institution, having spent most of his working life in the post. Most young journalists have to move on if they are to make their career. As Tunstall points out in his study of specialist correspondents, there is a marked uncertainty about careers and 'the relative lack of a career pattern is accompanied by a good deal of insecurity and anxiety'.[19] The pros and cons of continuous specialisation are finely balanced, resting mainly on the value of knowledge and contacts over staleness and lack of detachment. Nevertheless the system which expects young journalists working on unfamiliar subjects to make their mark early in their careers rarely produces knowledgable and original reporters, able to add to the sum of human knowledge rather than simply package what is already known.

This point about the career structure of journalism bears directly on the second failing noted above, the failure to develop the relationship between the journalist and his reader and sources. Once again Chapman Pincher provides a relatively isolated example of the way in which these relationships might be exploited. He is one of the few British journalists, other than feature writers and columnists, whose name is immediately associated with a particular style and type of story. Readers have sufficient experience of his work to be able to form their own judgement of it. Potential sources can be in no doubt that he is working in the field, a fact which helps to keep the stories coming. Without named journalists individually responsible for what appears in the paper under their name, there is little hope of them taking the reader into their confidence in the way advocated earlier. Such confidence between reader and writer is particularly important when the story is the leak and not the content of the leak. Readers need to be able to recognise and trust the cues. Given the British approach to information management, this type of journalism is bound to rely, even more here than elsewhere, on exploiting differences of opinion between different centres of power. The ability to recognise such differences, let alone exploit them, is not quickly learnt. Nor are the relationships quickly built which would encourage a disaffected power holder to trust a journalist.

The evidence that such continuous relationships deliver the journalist into the hands of his sources is much less than the evidence that general reporters, skilled in recording the facts of an event, are a pushover for the managers of information. At least this is true in the fields that matter, the politically sensitive subjects like politics, economics, defence and industrial relations, whatever may be the case with consumer oriented specialisms, those which Tunstall identifies as serving revenue goals for the newspaper.[20] The very fact of political sensitivity ensures that others in the field will both know and care if a particular correspondent regularly favours a particular line. Knowing this may allow sources to make use of it, as for example in the case of the *Daily Telegraph* defence correspondent and 'Bloody Sunday'. Brigadier Thompson missed the events in Derry while parking his car, but reported the army line. Later he was the only correspondent in Derry on the day who was allowed to attend the Ministry of Defence press conference on the Widgery report. At the conference the report was judiciously interpreted to exonerate the British army. The hope in such cases is that other journalists may be quick enough to spot it, as Simon Winchester did on that occasion,[21] or others in the administration be cross enough to draw it to their attention. These points are salutory reminders of the initial argument in favour of diversity. The public relations technique used by the Ministry of Defence was to invite only accredited defence correspondents to the conference. Not only did that rule out those journalists who had actually seen the events in Derry; it also brought together a group of correspondents with privileged access to Defence Department sources, and so an interest in maintaining that access. The question is whether such privileges act in the interest of the public, or simply of the journalists concerned. It is the question which was raised above, whether the British value access to information more for the in-group status it confers than for the information which can be obtained. Privileged access implies vulnerability. Accreditation can always be withdrawn or withdrawal threatened to encourage greater co-operation.

In-group journalism also drives a wedge between knowing gossip and public knowledge. Studying journalists at work I have often been struck by the difference between the account of an event prepared for public consumption and the account circulating in the newsroom at the level of in-group gossip. Much of this gossip deals in a different order of explanation from that allowed in public, involving the personal motives and relationships of powerful individuals rather than their avowed aims and values. Often it is unprintable because it is libellous. Nevertheless it is an important level of explanation; one which those, including the

McGregor Commission, who subscribed to the view that news should include more background and analysis could do well to remember.

The fact that such latent knowledge often exists unused belies the claim that newspapers are scandal sheets peddling gossip for no better reason than to damage the reputations of the great and the good. The cases one can point to in which gossip has eventually become public show both the length of time it has remained latent, available only to the in-group, and the way that allows rumour to fester. In the end it appears that what has been hidden must have been scandalous and a subject for censure, if only because it was hidden. John Whale's account of the way the Jeremy Thorpe affair developed in the press provides a pertinent case in point.[22] An essentially trivial matter – befriending a homosexual – became a *cause célèbre* while a topic with greater relevance to Mr Thorpe's fitness for public responsibilities – involvement in unsound financial institutions – passed by largely unnoticed. To blame the preoccupation of the press with sexual innuendo on sensationalism and audience demand is to miss the point that it derives from the values and priorities to be found in the privileged circles from whom the gossip originates. Like other types of rumour, prurience thrives on secrecy. Attempts to protect privacy are a double-edged weapon, implying double standards for public and private behaviour. The alternative, greater openness, would make newspapers more readable, put the nation in a better humour and improve the quality of our national life, not by making it more pure but less puritanical.

The final failing which follows from the collective organisation of the national press is the lack of originality in presentation and layout, the very packaging of the content which should be the strength of the British style of journalism. Continual use of the same stock plots and characters and the fact that many are derivative from other forms of popular culture bears witness to the way the processing of news reduces the content not just to what the reader will recognise but to that with which the processors are familiar. One of the few recent innovations in layout which have captured the public imagination is to be found just inside the *Sun*. The phrase 'page three' has taken on a new meaning in the language. It provides a rare example of the press contributing to popular culture rather than being parasitic on it. Other innovations like the colour supplements have just been introduced as commercial vehicles. They have not found a distinctive cultural form. The world of the colour supplements is the world of the ads they carry. The cultural initiative has shifted from editorial to advertiser. Lack of originality suggests an industry which has lost its nerve. The corollary is organisational practices which make presentation the lowest common denominator of the most familiar.

This discussion has taken us beyond the topics considered by the Royal Commission into an analysis of the editorial organisation of the press and journalistic practice. Inevitably such an analysis must be sketchy and superficial given the secrecy with which journalists surround themselves, an irony which has been noted more than once in this paper. The lessons to be drawn from it cannot be stated in more than general terms – more emphasis on the gathering of content rather than its processing, less reliance on routine sources, more scope for effort and initiative in pursuing original lines of enquiry, a greater readiness to discuss the origin and implications of stories rather than meticulous recording of irrelevant detail, less collusion between journalists themselves, more attempts to contribute to popular culture rather than feed off it, above all a greater readiness to take chances and break new ground, attracting the reader through competition by originality rather than similarity.

If these are to be more than exhortations, they point to a need to reconsider the internal organisation of newspapers, the balance of staff involved in different types of activity, the internal careers which are available to journalists within the press and the public careers which are available as reporters, correspondents, columnists and editors. A final example of journalists' secrecy about themselves is the refusal of many to take part in the survey of work and careers organised by the Royal Commission. That survey might have enabled journalists to take a look at themselves with some of these questions in mind. As it is we are left with the mythology of journalism. Just as the press paints the world in familiar shapes and colours, so it is particularly attached to its own beliefs about itself, in particular its ideas on how journalists are born and made.

Education and training

Unlike editorial organisation, the Royal Commission did consider the topic of journalism education, backed by a survey in which journalists and trainees took part. The survey shows that journalists experiencing training are least satisfied with it, while those who have passed through the experience become more satisfied the further it is behind them and the more senior the post they achieve in newspapers.[23] As always with an exploratory survey the results are open to various interpretations; nevertheless they do suggest strongly that training is regarded as a *rite de passage,* even a baptism of fire, through which recruits must pass before being admitted to the hallowed circle. Such an interpretation squares both with types of dissatisfaction expressed by junior journalists, that there was too little supervision, that they were 'not being given enough guidance' and were 'being thrown in at the deep end', and with what one knows of the awe in which experienced journalists hold the training system.

To call journalism training a *rite de passage* is to imply that it is unique to the occupation. So far as possible journalism has avoided contact with the education system, one possible vehicle for training schemes, and it has not developed a system of professional examinations such as are to be found administered by the professional associations of many other occupations. Instead it has concentrated on testing proficiency in the craft skills necessary to do the job, reluctantly accepting that some of these might be taught in technical colleges in block release or full-time pre-entry courses.

The industry's reluctance to make provision for graduates has been even greater. Though there are now two courses designed for them, one at University College, Cardiff and the other at the City University, London, graduates are still regarded with deep suspicion. The suspicion shows through the measured tones used by the Royal Commission to review its evidence. 'Much of the evidence we received and the opinion survey we undertook showed that there would be considerable reservations *in the provincial newspaper industry* about increasing substantially the ratio of graduates. It was held that such a policy would attract too many highly educated recruits for whom there were not suitable jobs and exclude candidates less well qualified by education but with particular flair or local knowledge' (18.29, emphasis added). General educational qualifications have a universal value while journalism training is unique, making the former peculiarly threatening to those who have experienced only the latter. As a result suspicion shades over into hostility, hostility which shows too in the general treatment of educational matters in the press.

The *rite de passage* is of greater value to the elders of the tribe in that it protects their own qualifications from challenge. Less educated labour is cheap labour, in the sense that it is ready to take on the job at a younger age. It is also more easily controlled, slotted into the available niches in the occupational structure. This is another way of reading the survey findings quoted above. The peculiar training system plays a part in socialising recruits into accepting their place in the occupation. Certainly this is what those in control of the provincial press appear to value. Their fear of 'too many highly educated recruits for whom there were not suitable jobs' may be read as a fear of recruits who might not be prepared to work the present system, people who might want to introduce changes or otherwise be a disturbing and disruptive influence.

It is the provincial press which effectively controls the current training system. As the Royal Commission notes, it has to bear the major cost, an arrangement which seems hardly fair when other media cream off the trainees. Nevertheless it does mean that the system is geared to the needs of provincial newspapers, needs which are relatively modest compared to the national journalism considered in this paper. Effectively the national press and other national media get a system of basic training on the cheap. It is hard to know whether their satisfaction with the system is prompted by the quality of the training or its low cost.

The Royal Commission was content to make recommendations within the context of the existing system, accepting the evidence that 'a policy of requiring higher educational standards at entry is the best means of improving standards of journalism' (18.29). My argument in this paper has been that what is needed amounts not so much to an improvement in standards as a change in style. It is much less clear whether that can be achieved within the present system. Basic training in English, law, public administration and shorthand is designed to equip journalists to work for provincial newspapers and yet these are the newspapers which even the Royal Commission noted for being uncritical and uncontroversial.

A more general indictment of the provincial press is set out by Dave Murphy in the next chapter. The unenterprising, safety first practices followed by national journalists and the national press may be traced back into the training that is given through provincial newspapers, a training in recording and packaging which leaves the journalism to take care of itself. Like other initiation rites, the hard grind of the provincial press may be good for the soul, but it does little to set the imagination free. Imagination is needed to introduce new plots and costumes, to realise the potential of the newspaper in the modern world.

Chapter 8

Control Without Censorship

Dave Murphy

In discussions of the production of news such terms as 'inaccurate', 'bias', 'factual reporting' are carelessly tossed into the fray as if their meanings were non-problematic and the identification of the states they describe were a process so simple as to require no discussion. This is because there is a 'common-sense' view as to what constitutes balance, factual reporting, accuracy and the rest. And this view is one which is broadly accepted by the current Royal Commission on the Press. My aim here is to argue that these words are constructs which have meaning in journalistic and political milieux as justifications for, and descriptions of, practices which enable journalists to be seen by themselves and by others to be playing their role according to their rules. It is these professional practices of journalism in the manufacture of news which define what is meant for the journalist by fair, balanced, true news. I want to examine in particular how in one area – interaction between newspapermen and contacts – the practice of journalism defines news. In doing this I shall look at the processes of news coverage of local politics as they are practised primarily by local weekly newspapers. But first, in order more clearly to understand the ground we shall be covering, let us consider what is meant by the notions of biased and unbiased, and factual and non-factual news.

The notion of 'bias' or 'accurate reporting' or 'balance' or 'impartiality' implies that there are two base lines from which any given statements can be seen as varying. These are the base lines of truth or neutrality. If we examine these, however, we shall see that neither is useful in the analysis of how news is produced or how it relates to other areas of activity, such as political conflict. Truth as a guideline is only available to judge whether any particular statement in a story is true. For instance, the issue of whether or not Lord Ryder wrote the famous 'slush money' letter may be amenable to a test of truth which would be acceptable to all. But in general this sort of question is not at issue. If it could be shown that all the individual statements in a news story were 'true' this would not tell us that the story was 'true'. This is because a news story is a construct: a series of 'factual' statements are placed together in a way that implies that they are connected. Other 'facts' are left out because, given that the editor is constrained by various limited resources, they are considered less important or less available for publication. The criterion of truth does not tell us what should be left out and what should be included. The same applies to the production of a newspaper. One story is used in preference to another. Prominence is given to the page one lead; the page seven story below the fold is consigned to oblivion. Clearly the notion of the reporter or editor as the blind slave of fact is absurd (despite the often quoted journalistic nostrum 'we only report the facts').

The McGregor Commission's Report on the Press confronts these issues only obliquely. Bias is raised as a problem, the superficial difficulties of definition are acknowledged; but the fundamental nature of meaning is not attended to. This leads the report into what appear to be contradictory positions: namely that the impossibility of measuring or identifying bias is recognised but attempts are still made to carry out these exercises. The value-laden nature of the concept is pointed out:

> the findings of the study of content which related to bias are not so clear as to make precise statements about the degree of bias. (p.82)

> content analysis is unable to compare the material it analyses with an unbiased version of the truth. Personal beliefs and assumptions are all-important. (p. 83)

On the other hand, a hankering for some definitive statement about such bias constantly crops up. Following the last quoted sentence, the report seems to imply that there is some identifiable, impartial story: 'Even so, content analysis can be useful by providing evidence to show . . . to what extent industrial relations contain those elements which might be expected to appear in an *"impartial" or "truthful" account'* (p. 83, my italics).

Again, in an account of the 'completeness' of industrial relations stories the range is between 73 per cent and 93 per cent – except for the *Morning Star* which scores only 59 per cent. These figures refer to the extent to which stories contain the 'key points' which are derived from a scanning of the generality of newspaper coverage of given industrial relations issues. The difference between the *Morning Star* and others is explained thus: 'This is one of the indications that the *Morning Star* stands apart from other papers by virtue of different news values: it often contained a considerable number of points not reported elsewhere. Despite its different news values, the *Morning Star* would give readers the same stories, as appeared elsewhere, even if it did not report the same "key points" ' (p. 84). 'Completeness' then is a means only of measuring one newspaper against the average performance of the rest: a score of 100 per cent could be achieved simply by including in a reported account all the 'key points' included in all other coverage. So by statistics one is able to establish the 'common-sense knowledge' that the *Morning Star* takes up a different position on strikes and trade unions than other British daily newspapers! 'Completeness' as an attempt at a quantitative assessment of newspaper content is indicative of the underlying impossibility of the exercise. One can attempt escape by the process of using averages to provide ideal-type stories – which simply sanctifies the collective conventional wisdom of newspapers as a scientific measure, and one can constantly introduce codicils recognising the difficulties of definition, and of the inevitability of value judgements being built into numerical measures.

This problem stems at least in part from a stance of apparent hypnosis in the face of numerical methods. No matter how naive the techniques or how simplistic the assumptions they are considered superior to literary qualitative accounts. For instance, in referring to analyses of newspaper organisation by Tunstall,

Seymour-Ure and Boyd-Barrett the McGregor Report confers this
faint praise:

> By its nature the work . . . cannot easily be rendered in
> summary in the same way as the basic empirical research . . .
> Here we record only that they provided useful background
> material for our deliberations. Such central issues as the
> relationship between journalists and sources, between the
> press, political parties and political institutions and between the
> press and trades unions, and the role and importance of the
> editor were illuminated and clarified by their work (p.92)

The contention in this chapter is that 'basic empirical research' is
not synonymous with statistics but is defined precisely by its
empiricism and by its relationship to 'central issues' and that
consideration of these admittedly central issues merely as
background information is hardly worth the effort of writing it
down.

These areas covered by Professor Tunstall *et al.* are it seems to
me of fundamental importance in understanding how what is news
becomes news. This process can only be understood by the analytical description of the practices of journalists which make up the
organisation of news production. In looking at the local press in
these respects, I am concerned with the general problems of
newspaper organisation, although it need hardly be stressed that
the local press in Britain is an important part of the newspaper
industry in a number of ways: first, much of the training of young
journalists takes place in the local weekly and evening papers, so
that many journalistic attitudes and practices found in Fleet Street
are taken on board in the provinces; secondly, as the successive
Royal Commissions on the press have shown the local press is
increasingly owned and controlled by large publishing enterprises
with local monopolies increasingly involved in other areas of
business; thirdly, much of the concern about the secrecy of
government relates to local government; and finally as the current
Royal Commission shows (p.89) there is dissatisfaction with the
local press among the public who feel that it is generally less
willing than the national press to criticise vested interests in the
form of advertisers.

The production of news is a social achievement. In order for something to be acceptable as news it has to be the product of certain socially approved procedures. And it may be necessary to show that these procedures have been properly undertaken. In order to prove he has done his job properly a reporter, if challenged, may have to show an editor that a story came from a reliable contact or source. Indeed the fact that news emerges from such processes makes it news, rather than any inherent quality in the events depicted in the news story. Various attempts have been made to define news in terms of the quality of events in the world: from such luminous statements as 'quickening urgency is the essence of news' to the apparently more reasonable reflection that news is something which 'breaches our expectations'. But a cursory examination of the newspapers reveals that none of the universal definitions offered covers a significant number of stories. To take for example the notion that news breaches expectations: a story of the gentle dog-loving father-of-three and doting husband who was a rapist would be news, but then, so would a violent thug terrorising women. Violent thugs are not the sort of people you would want as neighbours but they cannot be accused of breaching expectations when they terrorise women. However, when one turns to the subjects which make up much of the news in the local press, clearly even consideration of such generalised concerns as normal expectations being disrupted is inappropriate. A spring fair raises or does not raise a certain amount of money, is attended by a number of people. Local rates go up, down or stay the same. Local schools go or do not go comprehensive. It is all news: because it appears in the local newspaper and is presented by the recognised, competent news reporter. The newspaperman creates news by organising his resources around the solution to a series of practical problems.

The first problem is the need to fill the editorial part of the paper with news and pictures in such a way that the paper is recognisably a local newspaper that people will buy and advertise in. Secondly this has to be done within a strictly limited time period, and thirdly by a limited number of people and finally within defined financial limits. In order to solve these problems the newspaperman has to order a mass of conflicting versions of reality into formulated discrete happenings with each presented as a coherent set of events. But in order to do this the versions of events which the newspaper publishes have to be capable of validation according to some socially appropriate notion of proof. In effect this means that the story comes from an authoritative source; not that a story is checked out according to any deductively adduced rules of evidence. For instance a story that a road accident has occurred, involving named individuals at a given time, is accepted by an editor, not because it is checked out with all those involved – but because the information has come from the police. Similarly stories about council plans are validated by virtue of the fact that they come from the council minutes.

The first element then in the organisation of newsgathering is a system of contacts from whom the journalists obtain information. The choice of contacts reflects how the local newspaperman sees the 'local community'. All of the editors I observed at work expressed some view of the local community and had what might be described as a sociological theory about the 'structure' of local society which they used as a means of organising their working life. They assumed that 'local people' identified with a locality at various levels: the street and neighbours; their immediate district – identified by such things as community associations, bowling clubs, pubs, schools and so on; and the local town, identified with the council, the trades council, chamber of commerce, rotary club.

Contacts are chosen because of their position in relation to this perceived social order. They are headmasters, chairmen of community associations, secretaries of political parties, secretaries of bowling clubs, council officials and councillors. In American studies of local newspapers these contacts are seen as 'gate-keepers' in the sense that they control a flow of information from one part of a social network to another. The point that I am making is that they are chosen by journalists in order to provide the sort of stories which they believe will sell papers to the audiences the journalists are aiming at. The contacts are made gatekeepers by virtue of the activities of newspapermen. Even to use the word 'chosen', however, exaggerates the extent to which the process is a defined and conscious element in the organisation of news coverage. What happens is that a reporter wants information on a given story and he goes to a contact known to himself or recommended by a colleague as appropriate. This involves categorising the story as of a given type so that from the outset there is an interaction between the journalists' perception of events and the social organisation of news 'gathering'. The news is created and manufactured, not found. Indeed the very use of the word 'gathering' suggests a far more primitive organisational and economic process than that which actually takes place.

Every time a contact provides information which is usable in creating satisfactory stories his role as a 'good contact' is underlined and information which emanates from him is regarded as reliable, which in turn makes it more likely that the journalist will turn to him later on for other information. Further, where journalists are 'looking for stories' they go to a 'good contact' to see if anything is happening which can be used as a story. Each journalist will normally keep a contacts book in which he will have the names, addresses and telephone numbers of people whom he has found useful as well as those in formal positions such as the town clerk or headmasters. Contacts in formal positions are used by journalists in two ways. First they are approached for routine news of a given type. (By type of story we are referring to the source of the account on which the story is based, rather than to any inherent quality in the story.) For instance most local weekly newspapers make a daily call to the police station to see 'what's on the pad'. This is normally a formal arrangement in which publicly available information about accidents, fires or deaths is given. The contact in this case is, say, the duty sergeant purely by virtue of his rank. Secondly, such formal contacts are approached in relation to news stories which journalists see as involving them which have been discovered elsewhere. The town clerk may be called on to comment on a story which is being written on the basis of an item in the monthly council minutes. Or where a local pressure group is organising a campaign against some council policy, the same official may be asked for the 'council's side of the case'. Other sources of information are what might be regarded as non-official contacts – individuals who are seen by journalists as being able to give them 'inside information' on issues. They may either be regular contacts or a reader who writes a letter giving information about one particular. I found that journalists often refer to such informants in their mythological tales of great journalistic deeds, but in my observation of their work I found that local weekly journalists rely heavily upon official contacts and regular predictable events as the sources for stories. In explaining how they work journalists again stress the notion that they meet people in pubs who give them stories that they follow up. My experience as a journalist and as an observer of journalists has been that the people that journalists meet in pubs are other journalists.

It is not difficult to understand why this state of affairs prevails. The local journalist – editor or reporter – has to produce a given amount of news every week or every evening. The determining factor in the size of a newspaper is the amount of advertising: and the amount of news expands and contracts proportionately to match the fluctuations in this quantity. The newspaper man reports a world of events which seem to be, and are for him, the state of affairs as they exist. Reporters and editors whom I interviewed repeatedly produced the claim 'we only report the facts: we don't engage in campaigns'. In other words they portray themselves as the subjects of a tyranny – the tyranny of facts or 'truth'. But clearly the tyranny which bears most insistently on them is to fill the paper with something called news. To do this they organise the world of 'fact' into a predictable order. Events are presented as bounded entities, 'facts' are constructed together into stories and contacts are the socially organised means by which this is done.

In the area of local government coverage, the newspaper is able to rely on a regular and predictable supply of information in the shape of the meetings of the council and its committees and the minutes of these transactions produced by officials. Within this area a useful source of news are the reports by officials to their own committees. None more so than the Medical Officer of Health's Annual Report which is a mine of stories. The opening section is usually a summary of the locality's major health problem laced with stentorian and often apocalyptic comments. This is often fashionable and provides ammunition for major news stories (for a local paper), which over the past decade have varied from the dangers of cigarette smoking, to the problems of high-rise flats to various forms of pollution. At a different level of operation officer's reports are also prepared on an *ad hoc* basis to explain small policy decisions in committee – such as, for instance, the choice of a particular site for a school or the state of the local sewers.

The written material in the council minutes and the meetings themselves provide the journalist with a supply of news material which can be processed by paraphrase, summary and amplification. The journalists I observed went through a process known as 'checking' on stories in the minutes or 'digging' or 'lobbying'. However, this did not mean that the journalist checked to see if a version of events with which he was presented was true according to a set of evidential rules. What it did mean was that a reporter would ring up a contact, or approach one after a council meeting either for information or a quote about some issue, and would stop when he came to the first contact who could give him the information. Given that reporters and local government personnel are usually well known to one another the reporter usually gets to the 'right' contact first time, and rarely has to make more than two calls. There are times when journalists would interview several contacts in the course of a story but these are normally where several sides of a case are being sought. What is involved in this sort of story is the acquisition of a variety of opinions – not the substantiation of evidence.

The council then provides the newspaper with a series of events organisationally constructed within given boundaries, and all that the journalist has to do is to follow the leads provided, selecting those items which are seen as having the strongest appeal possible to the audience at which the paper is aiming. But the chief element in the organisation of events in time in the newspaper office is the office diary. The events of each day that are revealed by the mail coming in to the office or as a result of a reporters' calls on contacts are entered into the diary and allocated to a reporter and/or a photographer. The expected outcome of this news-gathering activity is then used by the editor to plan his paper. This is done with varying degrees of explicitness. In one highly organised local weekly which I observed, the chief reporter made a typed list of diary jobs with reporters initials and expected size of stories and features in column inches. From this the deputy editor then allocated these articles to various positions in the paper.

Thus on the basis of products expected in the light of experience the newspaper personnel work from the organisation of time over a week and translate that order into the spatial arrangement of the newspaper. This they may alter and vary throughout the week but all within a fairly rigid framework of expectancy of certain types of material. In as much as the editor can hypothesise a future shape for his paper this requires that the reporter can make a reasonable prediction of the sort of story he is likely to get from each news-gathering activity. What he works to then is that outcome which is satisfactory given the perceived constraints within which he works. The constraint of time on a weekly paper takes the form of the knowledge that as soon as one story is written another has to follow and that the whole paper must be filled by a deadline. If a reporter is writing a story on a house-building scheme and he obtains information from the Town Hall to the effect, say, that a new plan to rid a town of slums will cost £5 million, this will be enough, along with explanatory background material, to make a 'good story'. Once he has found the sort of story he wants, from an acceptable source, he stops looking and writes. He does not bother to check out the story to see if he can find a better angle. It is important to note this. The journalist seeks the first acceptable solution to the problem of providing news stories. The process is not one of carefully weighing alternatives. Once a story is available such alternatives are only hypothetical. A great deal of effort may be expended and nothing discovered.

The editors I spoke to stressed that their resources were limited. They had limited finances, which led to limited numbers of reporters, which led to limited time available to each reporter for each story. In such a case the efficiency of a paper is seen by the journalists as dependent on having good contacts. The maintenance of a satisfactory relationship with these contacts makes for the desired predictable flow of information. Offence caused to these contacts can breach this vital link and then obtaining information would become a demanding business in terms of time and effort.

Naïve revolutionaries often believe that advertisers exert malign influence over newspapers. This misses two vital points: first, inasmuch as 'business interests' are those of the advertisers, they are no less those of the proprietors of newspapers, and there is little reason to think that the perceived identity of interest needs any stressing – or that in general advertisers care about the paper except from the point of view of its sales to appropriate markets. Secondly, the jugular vein of the editorial department is the organised and predictable flow of news and those who have a day-to-day influence over this process are in a position in the organised structure of production to exert an influence comparable with that of striking. A number of editors made this point, comparing the attitude of the national newspaper reporter visiting an area on one story to that of the local newspaper whose journalistic livelihood is involved with the locality. In the words of one editor dealing with a delicate story involving the strip-search of school girls in the search for an allegedly stolen watch: 'We have to be dead careful, we have to go back to these people' – in this case the headmaster. 'Nationals can come in, offend people and then bugger off, knowing they will never have to see them again.'

The extent to which the entrenchment of contacts into the processes of defining and manufacturing news influences the final product is illustrated most clearly in cases where there are conflicting versions of reality from which the newspaper has to choose. Nowhere is this more strikingly exemplified than in stories which involve conflict between local government and pressure groups out to reform or to change the policy of that government. Newspapermen, eager to show themselves fearless protagonists of the little man against the bureaucratic monolith readily provide examples of stories where local government's view of reality is challenged in their newspapers. Even more, they provide examples of the anger which their activities generate among the officials and politicians in the councils whose affairs they observe and report. These claims to formidable prowess in the eternally vigilant struggle for freedom can only be understood if one examines more closely the nature of local government, pressure group and newspaper activity.

First, the general level of secrecy which surrounds the activity of government in Britain is seen at its peak in local government. Committees of councils meet now in public only because they are obliged to do so by law. And during the fifteen-year period following the 1961 'Thatcher Act' which obliged councils to admit the press to all full council meetings, many local authorities avoided implementing the Act by meeting as a General Purpose Committee with all their members minus one. At the same time as committee meetings have been made open to public scrutiny, many of the decisions which they used to take have been removed from their remit. This is due to the growth of a 'managerialist ' approach among local government officers symbolically exemplified by the growing fashion for renaming the old Town Clerk as 'Chief Executive'.

This managerialism takes the form of the removal of 'routine' business from the committees so that they can concentrate on non-routine or 'policy' matters. At the same time, as the size of local authorities has grown with the reorganisation of local government, Chief Officers operate a committee system wherein the departmental heads meet regularly to discuss interdepartmental relations, implications of present policy for the officials and new policy proposals. As this heppens, the 'routine' decision-making is moved away from the committees and moves down to the second in the department to be dealt with. What we now have are two areas of governmental activity which are not available to public scrutiny: the 'non-routine' work of the departments and the committee structure of the bureaucracy. Before the new moves to 'open' local government these activities were not usually undertaken in public but decisions taken were written into the publicly available council minutes unless it was specifically decided not to, which was something which would have been minuted.

At the party political level, Labour, Conservative or Liberal groups meet in private and adopt policies and lines and horsetrade between one another. What is left then to be transacted in public are the rubber-stamping of decisions taken elsewhere, the ceremonials and rituals of the council and the set-piece confrontations between parties about issues on which they cannot do a deal, and where the arguments are often repetitions of debates at national level. The 'routine' matters which decreasingly appear for public view are the allocation of minor contracts to firms, planning decisions small capital projects: a whole range of areas involving what in the end amounts to large amounts of the council's money, and often the payment of that money to private firms and individuals.

In the secretive sort of atmosphere which prevails in local government it is not surprising that councillors are often angry with the press. But this in itself does not indicate the press's potency: rather the excessive passion for the covert on the part of government which even the mildest revelation may upset. Inasmuch as the press report criticisms of local authority decisions they normally do so in a specific sort of context. The first type of acceptable protest is the public display of frustrated consumerism. Two of the examples I observed will indicate the sort of protest I am referring to. The first was a protest by 400 mothers in Congleton, Cheshire in order to obtain the services of a crossing warden for their children who had to cross the main road on the way to school. The second was a march to Wigan Town Hall by housewives angry that their dustbins had not been emptied for weeks on end. This type of protest takes the form that the council is not properly providing some service for which it is paid by the ratepayers – the consumers of local authority provisions. The form of the protest – marches, delivery of petitions, barricades across streets where accidents have occurred – is also significant, inasmuch as it provides a discrete event around which a story can be formulated. The method used to cover such a story would probably be a description of the protest event, with quotations by the organisers explaining their case and a reply by Town Hall officials. The story would probably be accompanied by a photograph of the protest activity.

The second type of protest which is regularly covered is more complex in terms of its organisation and in its relationship with the press and the local authority. Its aim is to change government policy in some way. The local press rely on pressure groups prosecuting such campaigns as a significant element in their coverage of local politics. These pressure groups organise themselves to deal with the local government bureaucracy in order to gain viability as negotiating partners in the bargaining involved in obtaining policy changes. This is because they are aiming to persuade government to take on an alternative policy and in order to do this their proposals have to be formulated in terms which are meaningful to the local government officials who will translate policy into administrative action. For instance, groups who wish to replace slum clearance with improvement of existing property in a given area will have to challenge official claims about unfitness of houses, cost of improvement and also will need to make themselves familiar with the housing acts and government circulars in order to present a case. For such groups, the first sign of success is the achievement of negotiating status with the local town hall departmental chiefs and committee chairman. The longer they are in existence, the more regularised these negotiating relationships became, and normally they develop a committee structure with officials who 'shadow' those of the local authority. They often have legal constitutions, general meetings, regular meetings of com- mittees and subcommittees, and in so doing engage in precisely those sort of organised and predictable activities which are recordable in the local newspaper's day book of jobs and reportable as news. The local authority may eventually recognise them as 'interested parties' to be contacted: they appear in the council committee minutes and are referred to in chief officers' reports. Relationships between the press and these bodies are negotiated through a procedure laid down by their committees who often appoint 'press officers', issue hand-outs and put on events which they believe will obtain good press coverage – given that the journalists involved are warned in advance. It is not uncommon then for journalists to include the spokesmen of such pressure groups in their calls on contacts to find out if 'there's anything doing'.

The relationship of newspaper–contact is one however which has to be achieved. The contact has to be able to provide the reporter with information which is reportable as news and about which he is acceptable as a source whose account will be a validation of truth in itself. The contact on the other hand has to believe that at least it is less trouble to talk to or contact the press than to ignore them, at most that they will obtain some benefit from the relationship. There are cases however where the aspirant contact fails to achieve this relationship and this state of affairs is the outcome of a number of factors. Journalists I interviewed explained that they can distinguish those who have genuine stories from those who are cranks, trouble-makers or paranoiacs. Where they think there is a case they investigate it, they said, and the distinction is a 'matter of judgement'.

However, I examined the reporting of a number of pressure group campaigns in and around Manchester and found that where contacts were ignored there was no investigation of their stories by the newspaper as such. In one case where a reporter went to some trouble to investigate a story he had to use the so-called 'underground press' as a vehicle for publication. This case involved a squat in houses which had been bought up by a local estate agent acting for a London property company. The council wanted to clear the area on the grounds that the houses were unfit for human habitation and that a road had to be redirected to take traffic away from a shopping area. The tenants from the squat houses were being rehoused by the council but the property company were to retain the ownership of the land and redevelop it with blocks of luxury flats and offices. The company had apparently been instituted specifically for this redevelopment scheme and had bought the houses with money borrowed from a large high street bank, and the agent had been negotiating with the council over the deal for ten years. The squatters moved fatherless families into the large empty Victorian houses in order, they claimed, to get these mothers and children rehoused. The news editor of the local paper told the reporter who covered the case that the story would only be published if they achieved their end and rehoused a family, and the background to the redevelopment scheme was not considered as a story. Even though in the end numerous fatherless families were rehoused the squat story never appeared in the local paper.

Another case concerned an ex-councillor who was subsequently re-elected to the council and who was a local estate agent. Along with an associate he bought a piece of land on which planning permission to redevelop had been repeatedly refused by the council to the previous owner. During negotiations for the purchase, council officials recommended rescinding the ban on redevelopment and shortly after the property changed hands the council lifted the ban and subsequently granted permission for the site to be redeveloped. All the reports by chief officers were 'private and confidential' and the planning committee minutes contained insufficient information to identify the owner. A number of neighbours of the property, one of whom was 'gazumped' in an attempt to buy the land himself, tried but failed to get the press to take up the story. The local government reporter they approached had had a long working relationship with officials and councillors, although not the councillor involved, and was not predisposed to believe that officials or council members were anything but honest and regular in their dealings. I investigated the case and found that documents emanating from the council over the case contained inaccuracies and were internally contradictory, and that the factual allegations of the pro-testers were supported by documentary evidence. What was not clear was whether the individual involved had malign motives. Even a report on the affair conducted by the town clerk, which was also private and confidential but was referred to at a council meeting, received no coverage by the local newspapers in the area.

A third case involved members of a housing action group who

were regarded by at least some of the local council officers as trouble-makers. They discovered that a member of the council was a property management agent, a builder and on the management of a large number of housing associations. One of these housing associations was involved with the council in rehousing applicants on the council waiting list and the council member's building firm was receiving contracts from the housing association to be paid out of loans from public funds. As a result of questions from a councillor, town hall officials produced a report on the policy of co-operating with housing associations in rehousing. This report – which was published – contained a detailed factual index which revealed that advances already made for work to be undertaken by this council member's building firm totalled over £230,000 out of a total of more than £380,000 which had been approved. Altogether the association were engaged in joint schemes totalling one and a half million pounds which would generate over £11,000 a year in estimated management fees for the property management firm of which the council member was a director. He had scrupulously declared his interest in schemes at all stages but the one local newspaper which mentioned the issue of conflict of interest between public and private council activities still did not mention that a council member was financially involved in the joint rehousing policy. Other newspapers relied entirely on the council debate and the rest of the official report which was a general summary of the nature of housing associations. The appendix to the officer's report and the issue of conflict of interest which occupied much of the debate were ignored.

There is no suggestion offered here that in some sense the 'truth' was left out and a false version of events published. The aim is to show that the version of events proferred by actors who are not established as newspaper contacts do not get an airing in the established press. The fact that these versions do not get manufactured into stories is due to a variety of factors: investigation of a contentious version of events may take weeks; the outcome may be that the account proferred is paranoid fantasy; the final story may become libellous. But in terms of understanding the day-to-day process of reporting, the relationship between the contact and the newspaperman cannot be stressed too highly, since it is this relationship and this system of relationships which is the cornerstone of the organisational apparatus by which the newspaper makes the world of reality reportable as news. In the local political and governmental world these contacts tend to be those in positions of authority since they organise and timetable the events which the newspaper reports as news; in other areas also contacts tend to be high-status individuals such as headmasters or vicars. Even in sports clubs and allotment associations the contact is likely to be the secretary or the chairman. This is not to say that the bar room 'snout' with his tales of governmental murk does not exist and is not used by journalists. He does and he is. But he is not the *characteristic source of news,* and out of the ten to fifteen stories a local weekly newspaper may write in a week it is unlikely that any will come regularly from such a source. The one quality he does not have and which only high status individuals do have is that they are by their nature self-validating sources of information. If the town clerk prepares a report on a new shopping centre the journalist only has to summarise it and attribute the contents to the town clerk. If a snout presents him with a scandal he is faced with the need for rigorous checking and no certainty of outcome.

I have tried to describe as dispassionately as possible how news is manufactured although it is probably apparent that I think this leaves much to be desired. What I would desire is a greater variety of news coverage including open accounts of departmental affairs and of councillors' business interests, however innocent or murky. And this is what the press should be doing according to their own definition of themselves through all of the press organisations: the journalist's union, the editor's guild, the proprietors' association. They all claim to be watchful guardians of the public weal. And whenever criticised they turn to odd cases of revelation to show their vigilance. In radio discussions with editors in their own behalf I have been belaboured with the Poulson case, for instance, *as an example of press vigilance.* I find this level of complacency eloquent of the state of the British local press.

My research and experience as a reporter leads me to believe that whatever claims the interested participants in the world of newspapers make for themselves as guardians of democracy, at the local level at least reporters and editors spend most of their time solving immediate organisational problems of news production and little or none on democracy. If you accept the inevitability of the entertainment function which Philip Elliott shows the press perform for most of the time even on a serious national issue, then the present state of things is satisfactory and the absurdly inflated claims which journalists make for themselves may simply serve as additional light relief.

If however an attempt is to be made to provide something more serious and more vital then we need to ask fundamental questions about the nature of news and what we expect the press to do. Because I do not believe that news is simply 'factual' or that it is possible for individuals to be 'impartial' it seems to me that we are faced with a fairly limited range of real choice. Although it is not possible to produce final and for all time 'true' versions of events, or some ideal-type complete range of opinion in mythical balance, it is possible to try to maximise the publication of different versions of events to give an increased range of views of the best ways to organise our political life. The way in which our local press operates now results in tendencies which are the reverse of these aims. The organised production of news puts those with a vested interest in the political and commercial *status quo* in a position of being the defining authorities of truth, and the originators of news values.

This seems to me to spring from the nature of the daily activities of news production, with its pressure on continuous and fast production, and from a legal and political system which values statements from some individuals as worthy of quoting or even privileged from legal attack, while others are ignored, without regard to any inherent quality of the statements themselves. This leads to conservatism and a passive reliance on established contacts and procedures in newspaper reporting. Such a state of affairs both reinforces the perceived power of the privileged and underlines the exclusion from allegedly democratic processes of those without ideological resources.

To propose changes of ownership which, like traditional nationalisation simply replace a corporate ownership with a state bureaucracy would solve nothing, since the limitations I have identified are part of the working processes of individual practitioners. The attitudes and perceptions of these practitioners especially towards officials and politicians need to be changed: they need to be liberated from the organisational reflexes which are part of a newspaper industry based upon private ownership and the formal absolute power of the editor. Thus freeing the press from control would require both reforms of the newspaper industry itself and of the government and commercial information control systems.

Within the newspaper office the reporter needs more control over what he does. In his dealings with the local government bureaucracy and with business undertakings the journalist needs to have access to the documents which are visible to officials and others concerned with issues which can sensibly be seen as being matters of public interest. In order to achieve this a number of other aims which primarily involve intangibles need to be achieved. The first concerns the training of young journalists. They should be encouraged to regard statements from all sources in the same light, to be judged in relation to their inherent logic and in relation to how they stand up to some agreed rules of evidence, so that local government hand-outs are not automatically sanctified as news and claims by trouble-makers automatically rejected. On this the McGregor Report is singularly unforthcoming. The account on the Selection and Training of Journalists (Appendix G, pp. 144–9) relies heavily on the formal qualifications of journalists, pointing to the increasing numbers of young entrants to the profession with 'O', 'A' levels and degrees, but pays no attention to the qualitative nature of the training they receive. Lecturers, senior and junior journalists were asked to assess the journalists' proficiency certificate as a 'fair measure of skill' (p. 159), but no indication is given of what sort of skills the respondents had in mind: investigative, literary, spelling, typing or shorthand. Words such as practical and academic are used. But whether the sifting of versions of events for contradictions and inconsistencies would be seen as academic or practical or even whether it enters the minds of respondents as an issue is unclear.

It is hard to believe that radical changes are likely to be achieved within the present context of ownership and organisation in the newspaper industry. Local newspapers in which most young journalists are trained are increasingly owned by large business undertakings geared if not to profit maximisation then at least to the minimisation of costs.

There seem to be two ways of achieving the sort of organisational reforms required to encourage autonomy among journalists. The first is the growth of various forms of workers' control sanctioned by law or agreement; the other is some form of co-operative ownership of newspapers made possible by the fact that publications using contract printers with modern technology can be lanched with minimal outlay. Neither of these solutions seems to offer more than limited hope of success. With the first there is always the danger of control being manifested corporately over the general 'line' or policy of a paper, and of the operation of an 'iron law of oligarchy' which puts the control in the hands of a committee, rather than providing the individual reporter with greater autonomy of working practice. The second, the 'underground press' really only provides for small circulation weeklies with small staffs and often padded with pages of 'what's on' guides to catch readers. None the less, both provide for improvements on what we have now. The first makes for greater choice for journalists; the second provides a mouthpiece for readers whose views would not otherwise be heard.

An invaluable help in altering the attitude of journalists to government would be its de-mystification by giving the reporter legal rights to examine political processes. This could be done by laying the liability on government always to show why transactions should be carried on in private, rather than as at present with the law prescribing those areas of activity which are public. This could be done by two methods. First, all meetings which involve decision-making over policy, whether of officials or councillors, could be open to public scrutiny. This could also involve an opening up of the consultancy procedures with interested parties which could be conducted on the lines of a public tribunal rather than behind closed doors.

Secondly councils would be compelled to publish documents prepared by officers on which committees and councils act. Only where compelling reasons could be given would the council be allowed to return to its endemic covert ways. What the local press also needs is the right to challenge secrecy decisions cheaply and quickly in a local court. Now although none of these reforms would work in the strict sense that councils would still find ways of avoiding publicity where they did not wish it, they might produce a new attitude among journalists who would be obtaining information by right and not as a result of a grace-and-favour relationship with some favourite contact.

A further aid to active journalism would be the extension of such agencies as the Registry of Companies and the Registry of

Friendly Societies, both in terms of making more information available with strict penalties for avoidance, and in terms of making this information more readily available at less expense. The Land Registry could also be made available for public scrutiny. A registry of councillors' interests, and those of chief officers would also encourage the freer coverage of local affairs and perhaps make the personnel of local government more circumspect in their treatment of the local press.

Finally the libel laws could usefully be reformed with the introduction of the American doctrine of the separation of the public from the private, so that while individuals' private affairs are protected, ligitation against statements about public activities only succeed where malice is shown. For a fuller discussion of these issues, see Geoffrey Robertson's article on law for the press in this volume.

These reforms are proffered in the knowledge that their proneness to failure would be high. This is because the interests which are stacked against the publicising of the background to local politics in this country are deep and entrenched, and because the newspapers over the past century have become conditioned to the response of these interests. Although the Poulson affair must have come as no shock to anyone familiar with local government, local newspapers or the building industry, this sort of corruption is probably not the prime cause of our furtive local government system. It is more probably the profound belief among officials and politicians that they can get on with their job better unencumbered by the press and the public interfering and 'getting the wrong end of the stick'. The present and past operation of the local press has assisted in this and even taken part in the moral justification for, and the mystification of the system. Whether it could ever change from being a lap-dog to being a guard-dog remains doubtful.

Chapter 9

The Making of Foreign News

Harold Jackson

Since it is always the simple points that are forgotten it is as well to state them clearly from time to time. News is a commodity: it is packaged, seasoned and retailed just as much as baked beans. Some like it spicy, some bland, but virtually everyone wants it hot. But, unlike baked beans, its shelf-life is a matter of hours rather than months. That is the dominant fact that governs the way that the national newspapers react to foreign news.

There have been two simultaneous though divergent influences changing the pattern of foreign reporting in the British press in the past decade. The first has been the enormous capital investment that television companies around the world have sunk into satellite technology. Though the impetus for this did not stem from a thirst for faster and more accurate information – the Olympic Games and the Eurovision Song Contest seem to have been the larger influence – the very existence of the facility carried its own momentum. The siege of the Israeli athletes at Munich, Richard Nixon's resignation broadcast, the American moon landings, all were beamed round the world simultaneously to Marshall McCluhan's global village. The antiquated technology of the newspaper industry was wiped out of the competition so far as *reporting* the events was concerned.

At the same time, particularly in the case of Fleet Street, the economic recession made imperative a reappraisal of the resources devoted to overseas news coverage. In terms of true cost per column inch – salaries, expenses and transmission costs so far as the correspondent was concerned, and the administrative costs of an overseas bureau and the back-up facilities falling to the home office – the product was rapidly pricing itself out of the market. Through the cold eye of the accountant the logic of foreign news coverage was insane. If you could fill a column with domestic news at a true cost of something like £75 how could you possibly justify the expenditure of something nearer £350 for reports which are in any case reckoned to be of minority interest? A disaster in Worthing might well cover most of the front page and a lot of the inside pages. The same event in Wagga Wagga rates three lines in the news in brief, but it could cost almost as much to put it there.

So foreign news, in strictly economic terms, is a loss leader. It's there because it has to be seen to be there, but it is under severe pressure most of the time in most of the national papers. Behind that generalisation, however, there are notable exceptions. A British pop star's matrimonial disasters in California can lead to the expenditure of collossal resources, as can a riot by British soccer fans in, say, Germany or Spain. But this is because these events have moved out of the category of 'foreign news', which happens to foreigners, and into the cost-effective area of reader-identity stories. It is what people will be talking about over the breakfast table or in the works canteen: it is likely to make them buy newspapers, or so the received mythology proclaims.

And mythology is an important ingredient in any consideration of news gathering and presentation. Just as journalists subscribe to a whole range of unresearched beliefs about their industry and their customers, so the readers invest the national newspapers with largely fantastical qualities. Ten seconds rational reflection would suggest to any reasonable person that the production processes of a Fleet Street newspaper are not the ideal way of arriving at or transmitting the ultimate truth about anything. With large squads of academics poring over tons of first-hand evidence, there are still endless disputes about what really happened during the Second World War. Does it really seem credible that a few reporters working against the clock are likely to get it right on the night?

In the case of domestic news coverage there are built-in

correctives. In a general sense the reader is likely to have a certain level of basic information from his own resources: he knows that the inhabitants of Penzance don't go round in grass skirts and live in mud huts, he knows that Scotland is north of England and is not run by a military junta. But what does he know about Mali? If he reads a report that three oilfield workers there have been killed by a man-eating tiger it is unsafe to assume that he knows that Mali has neither oil nor tigers. The report is not inherently incredible: it comes well within the range of what he is prepared to believe.

So here is the first hurdle that the national newspapers hit, and few of them clear even this. For the proper reception of overseas news the reader requires a level of pre-knowledge that is simply not available. So far as Western Europe goes the increase of cheap holiday travel to selected countries has expanded the horizons of a proportion of the newspaper public. To put it at its lowest level, they now have a clearer idea of the geography of, say, Spain or Yugoslavia. But it does not go much deeper than that and this increased knowledge certainly does not apply to the further-flung parts of the world.

What is required is a continuous reporting of the processes of overseas societies so that the events that occur in them can be more readily placed into their context. But this implies a network of overseas bureaus staffed by reporters qualified both linguistically and professionally to present the complexities of the local scene. Since 1965 the number of staff correspondents based abroad by the national papers has dropped from 111 to 73,[1] a 35 per cent cut in manpower during a period when the significance of international relations has impinged far more deeply on most people's consciousness, if only in the aftermath of the OPEC action on oil prices and its ripple effect through the industrialised economies. The most successful paper commercially during that period, Rupert Murdoch's *Sun,* does not think it necessary to employ any foreign staff reporters.

The cutback, of course, is a direct consequence of the economic problems of Fleet Street which are, in turn, partly a reflection of the broader plight of the country. So the irony is that the more severe the impact of events abroad the less the specialist coverage accorded them. The survey carried out by Professor Denis McQuail for the Royal Commission[2] showed that the proportion of news space given to foreign news ranged from 9 per cent in the

Daily Mirror to 27 per cent in the *Guardian*. This can generally be accepted as the difference in value judgements between the popular and the quality papers. Events abroad are governed by a perverse logic at the popular end of the market. If something happens in a foreign country it is not of itself interesting or exciting: if it is interesting or exciting then it is not consigned to the foreign news ghetto. The barriers confronting 'regular' news from abroad are far higher than those facing domestic news.

More complex still are the judgements of what areas of the world are 'interesting'. Fleet Street's seventy-three overseas staff men are based in:[3]

North America	26
Western Europe	34
Africa	4
Middle East	5
Far East	4

There are none at all in the Soviet Union, Eastern Europe, South America or Australasia and the Pacific. To some extent this gap is offset by stringers, or part-time correspondents, for the four quality papers. The largest numbers are the thirty-four in the Far East and the twenty-six in Africa. But there are only four in Eastern Europe and eight in Latin America. Again, there is no one directly representing the national papers in Moscow. To a degree this is a situation imposed on the papers by the constraints of reporting from the Communist countries and the costs of maintaining offices there. But these factors do not, for example, hinder the major American papers from basing staff correspondents there.

The inadequacies of this staff coverage are offset primarily by the international news agencies – Reuters of Britain, and Associated Press and United Press International of the United States. These agencies have built their reputation and their commercial success on the fast transmission of accurate information to a wide range of customers, some of whom are newspapers but many who are not. Their raw material is thus processed to what must be regarded as a basic diet which can be used by anyone from Tokyo to Taunton. It tends to be long on 'facts' and rather shorter on interpretation and it is also heavily biased towards the areas covered by the majority of staff correspondents – North

America and Western Europe, which accounted for something over a third of the output monitored by Oliver Boyd-Barrett of the Open University.

But the impact of the agencies is often crucial in the way that news will be treated by the people whose job it is to carry out the heavy sifting of items thought suitable for publication. In the vast majority of cases the agency account is the first that the office-bound journalist will have of some event. Almost unconsciously it becomes the yardstick against which he measures all later information. Given the competition between the agencies to be first with the news the chances of some degree of error are inevitably high in the early despatches. They may well be modified subsequently and, assuming there is time, the problem disappears. But given the geographical bias of Fleet Street's news coverage, time is the one commodity it has sacrificed in its concern for North American coverage. Early evening in New York is when editions are running off the presses in London: the pressure is not to get it right but get it written.

One staff man sitting in his office in New York or Washington has an uphill job competing with the agency version of an event in San Francisco. He, after all, is as far away from whatever is going on as he is from the man he is talking to on the transatlantic line to London. He may well suspect, from his own background knowledge, that the story is not quite as it is being told. But he has no direct knowledge, very limited time to improve his knowledge, and few convincing arguments to sustain his case.

It is an eccentricity of Fleet Street's pecking order that the prestige and cost of an overseas posting usually dictates that it goes to a fairly senior man. But the decisions about the treatment of his copy, particularly late at night, can often be made by relatively junior and inexperienced sub-editors. Given the inability of most readers to exercise an informed judgement about the details of what is presented to them, the spiral of error can be considerable. Where there is not even a staff man and where agency information is being used as raw material to be condensed into extremely limited space, the room for innocent but effective distortion is unlimited.

And the distortion is mostly, though not invariably, innocent. It springs from haste, misunderstanding and inexperience rather than malice – but the end result is much the same. The problem of reporting from abroad is that there is very little come-back. The embassy of the country concerned may protest about some item but it can hardly be regarded as a disinterested party and there is no guarantee that the protest will go further than the editor's wastepaper basket. Where the home news reporter is subject to a readership likely to include some ratio of informed critics who are on his doorstep, the foreign correspondent is operating largely in a vaccum. He has little contact either with his reader or his editors. He may well not see the published version of his story until days after it has appeared, by which time his protests about rewriting or other maltreatment of his copy will probably be drowned in the sea of new material flooding across the foreign editor's desk.

At its worst this produces a dispirited and isolated malcontent who settles for the easiest life he can get away with. Since no one apparently either knows or cares if he has got it right he is content to pick up his information from the easiest available sources – the local news media, routine press briefings, public relations hand-outs, other correspondents and anyone else easily accessible. This of course is the popular stereotype and he is as typical as any other stereotype: you cannot deny his existence but it needs some pretty assiduous searching to find him.

The much commoner frustration is that of the serious and professional reporter hemmed in by the structural shortcomings of his calling. In the first place he is expected to cover a territory which may be umpteen times the size of Britain: where a national paper may well have five staff men covering Westminster Palace it will have one coping with the whole of South-east Asia. Secondly, he is competing with the rest of the world for space: his carefully researched piece on some aspect of his patch may well get into one edition only, to be tossed out because of a trivial but eye-catching event thousands of miles away – but also 'abroad'. Thirdly, he can assume nothing but ignorance among his readers: they don't know who the president is, they can't remember what happened last, they don't necessarily even know where the country is. So inches of precious space goes on tedious repetition of salient facts and you get the shorthand stereotype phrases – 'oil-rich Kuwait', 'poverty-stricken Bangladesh', 'strife-torn Lebanon'. They are not much of a help to understanding, generating as they do a Pavlovian reaction in the reader which usually serves only to reinforce his preconceptions. As a small example, most people assume a war to be a bloodbath from one end of the country to another. They haven't actually thought the proposition through: it is a generalised impression formed partly by the fact that that is all they are currently reading about the country and that newspaper cartographers are fond of large sweeping arrows to delineate the opposing forces. Every war correspondent knows this to be nonsense, that wars are confined to very limited spaces and are in reality an extremely inefficient method of disposing of the enemy, short of a nuclear strike. A fairly large shell, from my personal experience, can explode twenty yards away without causing injury. So 'war-torn' is an indication of a state of mind rather than a factual description. But that is not what is conveyed to the reader.

Much more difficult is the cultural gulf implicit in the very language of a report. A correspondent based in, say, south-east Asia who writes about 'houses' is triggering a concept in his English reader which is totally inappropriate. What he is referring to is not a hovel, nor a shack but it is most certainly not a house as carried in the mind's eye of his audience. The same applies to 'job': in many cases this is little more than the state in which subsistence becomes feasible. It has little to do with hours and wages and conditions as it has in a European context.

Nor, of course, is the reporter free of his own cultural imprinting. 'Efficiency' – or more usually inefficiency – is a common yardstick applied to Third World countries. But it is not an absolute value, it is a subjective assessment founded in a largely north-west European ethic. By our standards, for instance, it is extremely inefficient to build a trunk road with shovels and wheelbarrows. By local standards it is probably an extremely efficient way to distribute resources through a wide section of an impoverished rural community. In other words, the road is not an end in itself, as it would appear to European eyes, but a mechanism in the economic chain wholly appropriate to the circumstances.

The famous Green Revolution, widely lauded by British newspapers of all political shades as the answer to chronic starvation, is another example. Certainly crop yields were increased dramatically, but only so long as the seed was treated with high-cost agricultural chemicals. These were not available in sufficient quantities locally and thus had to be imported at the expense of foreign exchange balances. The educational standards of peasant farmers were such that many were forced off their land by their low productivity, the distributive system was distorted and so was the broader economy. All in all it probably did as much harm as good. But to this day the project is firmly in the newspaper memory-bank – writers' and readers' – as a Good Thing.

Even within the Anglo-Saxon world there are enormous problems. For all the weight of reporting from North America it cannot really be argued that the newspaper public knows or understands what is happening. The Federal system, as an example, remains largely baffling to an English audience. It cannot grasp why, if the President says Concorde can land, and the Secretary for Transportation says it can, and the Federal courts sustain that judgement, a man running the New York docks can say it cannot and carry the day. The most frequent phrase the homecoming foreign correspondent hears is 'Why don't they . . .' It tells him that he has failed in his job. The reason 'they' do not do whatever-it-may-be is because 'they' don't choose to. The reason 'they' don't choose to is what he should have conveyed clearly and convincingly to his readers. That repetition of 'Why don't they . . . ' is the greatest single cause of books by foreign correspondents: the last great cry of anguish is let forth in hard cover.

And that, really, is the nub of the problem. The speed of television satellite communication and the spurious 'reality' of colour moving pictures has forced Fleet Street to compete for hot news where it is not equipped to do so. The pressure of cost and space has inevitably taken its toll: there are fewer staff correspondents abroad and, except in the quality papers to some degree, their ability to provide a coherent coverage of their area is capriciously circumscribed. There are technical answers to some of this. It is, for example, perfectly possible for a reporter sitting at a keyboard in Lagos to set type in London and for it to be on the street within twenty minutes. But the state of industrial relations in Fleet Street puts that into the realms of wonderland.

But even if we suppose this miracle to have come about, is the net result any better? The newspapers may provide a competitive service within their own terms, but they will remain what they have always been – a mass product for a mass audience. At some stage of the calculation the eccentricities of the readership must be added in. If the man on the Clapham omnibus goes into Woolworths he doesn't expect to see them selling gold plate: he goes to Aspreys for that. Yet for some strange reason he anticipates that something that is manufactured from scratch every night of the week, every week of the year, which has little or no control over its raw material, which is produced by the million, distributed throughout the country within three or four hours, and has no value within twelve hours – that this improbable vehicle should be the distilled essence of reality and truth. He does not define either quality, he does not agree with many other people when he does try to define it, but he expects the newspaper industry to meet his definition.

The newspapers, of course, collude in this fantasy: what they are selling is authority, reassurance, a tidy concept of a disorderly world. They are reinforced by everyone from governments to educationalists to solemn academic studies. Why will no one accept what is so plainly obvious? Newspapers are shoddy goods sold cheap and should be read accordingly.

Part 4

External Constraints on the Press

Chapter 10

Law for the Press

Geoffrey Robertson

British law is the enemy of the British press. It circumscribes press virtues, and comforts press vices. The blind Goddess of Justice raises her sword against the investigative journalist while her other hand fondles the Sunday muckraker. The values of open government and public accountability she traduces by punishing the most anodyne disclosures of public service decisions and functions. She suppresses the truth about crooked financiers, disreputable companies and hypocritical politicians on the pretexts of contempt of court, breach of confidence and infringement of copyright. She offers a tax-free bonus to assuage the *amour propre* of wealthy libelled litigants. This Goddess not only minds the information store, but pursues journalists rash enough to put its spoils on show in the market place. Yet on hearing the step of the pandar, she dons her blindfold and points permissively to her toothless pimp, the Press Council. She brings the watchdog to heel and unleashes the lapdog, exterminates the ferret and pets the skunk. Her scales of justice balance badly – but they can always be tipped. The law *can* be made to work for the press, instead of against it.

The jurisprudence of other countries demonstrates this. In an age when crucial decisions are increasingly made by administrative and corporate priesthoods – whose power is otherwise inscrutable

– the law can be radically restructured to permit the press to fulfil its public responsibility. There are four accepted political principles, readily translatable into British law, which would free investigative journalism while restraining the worst excesses of sensationalism.

The first is the principle that in a democracy the public have a right to know the basis upon which all decisions which affect the common good are made. That value is given statutory support in America and Scandinavia by Freedom of Information legislation. This provides citizens with a legal right of access to documents produced by government bodies. It also imposes legal obligations upon companies to disclose details of their operations.

The second doctrine is that the press can only serve the public interest, once it has obtained information, if it remains free from injunctions and other forms of pre-censorship. This value finds its most absolute expression in the doctrine against 'prior restraint' adopted by the Supreme Court in its interpretation of the First Amendment. The American press may publish and be damned, because damnation comes after, and not before, publication has taken place.

The third principle is simply that of equality: individuals whose actions or reputations are mishandled by newspapers should have equal access to a speedy redress for mis-statements of fact, without the delays, uncertainties and expense of libel proceedings. In some European countries this is achieved by a 'Press Ombudsman', a judge empowered to investigate and order appropriate retraction of any demonstrably false report.

The fourth value is privacy: the right of an individual to enjoy a personal life free from morbid or prurient curiosity. This ethic has been secured in many jurisdictions by laws which curb invasions of intimate joys and griefs, without inhibiting revelation of the surreptitious hypocrisies of public figures.

All of these legal developments have served to promote accurate and responsible journalism, while at the same time opening up new areas of public importance for investigation and criticism. The worst excrescenses of defamation, breach of confidence and official secrecy have died unlamented, replaced by proper concern for public disclosure and protection of human rights. The law is no longer a snare for the press: instead it may be used as a battering ram against future administrators and governments who turn a duty to tell into a right to propagandise. The newspaper abandons its traditional court-room role of defendant, and enters the lists as plaintiff for the public's right to know.

Such fundamental change in the philosophy of law demands a corresponding revaluation of the role of the press. At present there seems little institutional pressure for reform: the Royal Commission remarked that 'we received little evidence on legal constraints upon the press . . . nor have we been strongly pressed to examine them.[1] This complacency does little credit to a profession which must realise that the British frontiers of press freedom are more constricted than those of its international counterparts. The routine newspaper response has been to employ teams of lawyers to sanitise its pages before publication, degutting public interest stories which might provoke court reprisals. Press lawyers are inevitably more repressive than press laws, because they will always err on the safe side, where they cannot be proved wrong. The lawyer's advice creates a broad penumbra of constraint, confining the investigative journalist not merely to the letter of the law but to an outer rim bounded by the mere possibility of legal action. Since most laws pertaining to the press are of vague or elastic definition, the working test of 'potential actionability' for press comment is exceptionally wide. The journalist is placed always on the defensive: he or she is obliged to ask, not 'what *should* I write?' but 'what *can* I write that will get past the lawyers?' Proprietor and editor can offer scant support, for the lawyer is there to protect *them*.

So long as all British newspapers are subject to the same restrictions, there is no competitive pressure for change. Greater access to government materials would call for greater skills in its analysis, for training or hiring experts at the expense of knockabout reporters. It would offer greater temptation to embarrass settled interests – interests perhaps, which are dear to the hearts of proprietors. Even journalists might cringe at the thought of how a general right of access to information might break down the comfortable monopoly of the lobby system, or how privacy protection might restrict the divine right to snoop and gossip. The Royal Commission should not have been surprised at the timidity of its witnesses: pressure for a challenging role will never come from within a protected institution. Nor will it be exerted by the protectors themselves – the lawyers who are paid to guarantee newspapers a quiet life. It can only come from readers who demand more information and higher standards of presenting it: and from a Royal Commission appointed to represent them. When the Royal Commission discovers, for example, that only 3 per cent of all social welfare stories emanate from newspapers' own investigations[2] (as distinct from official hand-outs and public speeches) then that Commission must seek ways of improving the press in spite of itself.

The Royal Commission singularly failed to recognise the capacity of law to assist and elevate the performance of the British press. It found very little wrong which could not be cured by implentation of recent Royal Commissions into Official Secrecy (Franks),[3] Defamation (Faulks),[4] Contempt (Phillimore)[5] and Privacy (Younger).[6] Its refusal to go behind these commissions was a serious abdication of responsibility, and a measure of its failure to develop any coherent philosophy about how law should serve the public by serving the press. The four reports which it found so convincing propound few major reforms. They are largely the work of lawyers and politicians and thus reflect an overweening attachment to secrecy, concealment and respectability. Moreover, their approach embodied the traditional legal philosophy that the fourth estate cannot be trusted, and that courts must therefore be vigilant to restrain its dangerous volatility. American courts see press freedom as an end in itself, a value which can only be supplanted by the weightiest burden of proof. In Britain, lawyers interpret 'press freedom' as they would an ambiguous contract – that is to say, narrowly. It is seen as a means to the end of responsible and respectable government, a freedom to be curtailed whenever it injures powerful interests. Hence the rise of the injunction in Britain at the very time when the Supreme Court has announced its demise in the United States Legal paternalism – the theory of prior restraints on an inherently untrustworthy media – is the philosophy behind those Royal Commissions whose findings are uncritically accepted by the Royal Commission on the Press. That philosophy may still appeal to politicians, lawyers and proprietors; it should not go unchallenged by a public they assume does not care. In fact, the reading public does care: over 60 per cent of recipients of Britain's two most popular dailies thought that news coverage was exaggerated and sensationalised, and about half accused the press of invading private grief and concentrating on trivia.[7] The public deserves a better press than the law at present permits.

Extracting Information

The workings of government are cocooned from public scrutiny by the criminal law, embodied in the Official Secrets Act. Section 1 prohibits the passing of any information which might indirectly assist an enemy for the purpose of prejudicing the interests of the state. The courts have permitted the state to define its own interests, thereby preventing journalists from pleading that their purpose was to serve the interests of the public. The normal burden of proof is reversed, and the prosecution is permitted to deduce the defendant's guilt from the defendant's associations – his friends, family and political beliefs. Section 1 was assumed by the Franks Committee to be directed only at spies working for foreign powers, and its use was so confined until 1977, when it was invoked against two reporters working for *Time Out* who had interviewed a former soldier. The prospect of fourteen years in prison for journalists who probe defence operations cannot but chill investigations which may be of crucial public interest: had the use of torture techniques by the British Army in Aden been exposed by the press, the use of those techniques in Ireland, and Britain's subsequent conviction at the European Court of Human Rights, might have been avoided.

Section 2 of the Act punishes journalists who receive confidential information from public servants – it is a section wide enough to cover disclosure of the brand of toilet paper used in departmental lavatories. Needless to say, it is selectively enforced, although a *Daily Mail* reporter was once jailed for two months for disclosing details of a will a few hours before its official release,[8] and a fit of Labour Cabinet pique landed a journalist and editor in the dock at the Old Bailey for publishing an army report on the Biafran war which falsified ministerial statements in Parliament.[9] Experienced journalists told the Franks Committee that the Act had a two-sided effect: it inhibits newspapers from publishing stories which have not been 'officially leaked', and it imbues Whitehall mandarins with an obsession for secrecy which makes reliable information difficult to extract against ministerial wishes.[10]

This secrecy obsession protects information which has no conceivable relationship to defence or national security, but which may lead to embarrassing revelations of incompetence, inefficiency or high-handed treatment of citizens. The Franks Committee recommended replacement of the Section 2 with a more closely defined category of secret information – a category which the Royal Commission noticed was 'still fairly wide'. By making prosecution more likely in the defined area, this 'reform' might actually lead to greater concealment of information than at present. The only satisfactory solution is to abolish Section 2 in its entirety, and to confine Section 1 to public servants who traitorously transmit defence secrets to foreign powers.

While such a reform might do something to dispel the miasma of secrecy in Whitehall, it would still permit the government to manage the news by selective leaks to favoured newspapers. The press might find public servants more approachable, but they would not necessarily be more forthcoming. Only positive legislation will secure a legal right of access to information of legitimate community concern. It must be for a judge, and not a minister or public servant, to decide whether information sought should be protected from disclosure. Such legislation is essential to any democracy which pays lip service to 'the public right to know', but in which ministerial involvement in departmental decisions occurs only at levels of high policy. Ministers neither control nor are answerable for thousands of decisions made by middle-ranking departmental officers – decisions which may vitally affect individuals and communities. A new system of control must be developed if executive accountability is to be made a reality. The press and the public must be given the power to inspect the information acted upon by administrators. The creation of such a power would engender community involvement in decision-making by breaking down the secrecy barrier between governors and governed. Public participation in government would lead to better government: as the *Sunday Times* has pointed out, 'Secrecy should be radically re-examined not so that errors can be exposed – although that is important – but because in a system where disclosure is more nearly the norm, errors are less likely to occur . . . Many events of recent history might have turned out not merely different but better if public opinion had been allowed to play upon them'.[11] Freedom of information legislation would challenge the prevailing mentality of bureaucratic secrecy. Establish a presumption in favour of disclosure, back it with a legal right enforceable in court, and it becomes a socially-subscribed value which public servants will ignore at their peril. Such legislation would require Whitehall to issue annual indexes of documents prepared and received, which would be available for public inspection subject to exemptions. Cabinet minutes, documents relating to defence, foreign policy, economic or political security of the state and law enforcement operations would not have to be produced if disclosure would seriously damage the national interest. This decision would be made by a High Court judge, after inspecting the document in question and weighing against the government's claim the interest of the public in scrutinising executive actions and expenditures. Privilege might readily be accorded to information supplied in confidence by foreign governments, or papers pertaining to secret codes, military installations and defence strategies, or containing information which could endanger life. With all other classes of information, the government should be required to prove that suppression would be in the public interest.

The benefits of freedom of information legislation are apparent in the quality and range of media investigations stimulated by disclosures made under the Act. These have included manuals used by tax inspectors; the Parole Board's guidelines and decisions; military rulings on internal discipline; criteria used by law enforcement agencies in deciding whether to prosecute; environmental impact statements and other submissions by corporations; internal policy directives on immigration control; contracts between government departments and private contractors; guidelines and manuals on drug analysis, highway management and supervision of social security benefits; and reports by the government analysts on food additives, pesticides and vitamin pills.[12] Documents disclosed under the Act have revealed radio-active contamination of state water supplies; an increasing incidence of cancer among workers in nuclear plants; risks inherent in the use of silicone in cosmetic surgery; and potentially corrupt connections between public servants and big business.[13] The Freedom of Information Act has assisted spectacular press revelations of illegal and ignoble activities by government agencies.[14] It provided evidence of the perverted mind of J. Edgar

Hoover, who bugged Martin Luther King's bedroom and gloatingly played the tapes to his cronies. It exposed the C.I.A. programme of L.S.D. experiments on unsuspecting citizens (one of whom died as a result) and C.I.A. plots to assassinate Castro, Trujillo and other Third World political leaders. The army report on the My Lai massacre has been disclosed, as have reports by staff scientists in the Atomic Energy Commission that a nuclear reactor accident could kill 45,000 people. The public was informed for the first time of their government's interpretation of the Vietnam peace agreements when a judge ordered the legal opinion to be released pursuant to the Act. The F.B.I.'s programme of illegal harassment and disruption of dissidents and left-wing groups came to public attention when courts ordered production of Bureau documents. Press comment on such releases of information provides a safeguard against repetition of executive misbehaviour, and a hope that the warnings of concerned scientists will be taken seriously.

Reform of official secrecy must be accompanied by a thorough overhaul of the classification system. Sir Martin Furnival-Jones, former head of M.I.5, solemnly told the Franks Committee that 'It is an official secret if it is an official file'.[15] It is time to supplant this circular nonsense by classification categories which correspond to realistically apprehended injury to the national interest – reviewable in the spirit of Justice Stewart's injunction to government in the *Pentagon Papers* case:

> The very first principle [of a wise security system would be] an insistence upon avoiding secrecy for its own sake. For when everything is classified, then nothing is classified, and the system becomes one to be disregarded by the cynical or the careless, and to be manipulated by those intent on self-protection or self-promotion. I should suppose, in short, that the hallmark of a truly effective internal security system would be the maximum possible disclosure, recognising that secrecy can best be preserved only when credibility is truly maintained.[16]

A wise classification system would have a 'top secret' category imposed only with ministerial approval, and reviewed regularly by an independent arbiter conscious that the security stamp can cover, perhaps for decades, the footprints of a nervous bureaucrat or a wary executive.[17] National security, as Richard Nixon and his co-conspirators discovered, can be used as an all-purpose cloak for dishonourable activities. While it may genuinely protect military codes, advanced weaponry design and NATO strategies, it can equally be used to withhold information vital to public debate over the future of weapons policy and nuclear power. C. Wright Mills notes that 'The entire sequence of decisions concerning the production and the use of atomic weaponry has been made without any genuine public debate, and the facts needed to engage in that debate intelligently have been officially hidden, distorted and even lied about.'[18]

Once the public service is opened to press scrutiny, then other repositories of power might be similarly unlocked. The rule limiting public access to cabinet minutes and documents can be reduced to ten years, now that the Lord Chief Justice has held that Richard Crossman's account of cabinet arguments and voting patterns may be inflicted upon the public after the passage of a decade.[19] Local authorities, which could hardly claim a national security value for their files, could be forced to open them for public inspection. All large companies could be obliged to place on public file their submissions to government and to statutory authorities, and to make annual 'environmental impact' statements detailing the safeguards against pollution at their industrial plants. A right to inspect auditors' working papers used in preparation of balance sheets would provide the press with more data upon which to calculate the true performance of public companies than is offered by self-serving annual reports. Multi-nationals, private firms, partnerships, trusts and nominee companies should disclose more details than the law at present requires about their shareholders, beneficiaries and interests. Coverage of the City is the shoddiest aspect of British journalism, bedevilled by lack of expertise and conflicts of interest. Very few major collapses have been predicted, and even fewer have been satisfactorily analysed. At a time when vast quantities of public money are being ploughed into nationalised industries, and the private sector increasingly depends upon subsidies and tax relief, the press should have special access to corporate information and documentation which would not reveal secret processes or assist competitors. Informed comment on big business is rarely the product of investigative journalism: more often is it inspired by an individual 'whistle-blower' who may have private reasons for maligning and distorting. Industry, like government, provides a host of public relations officials whose function is 'press promotion', that is to encourage the press to act as promoters rather than critics. 'The public's right to know' becomes the public's unfortunate lot to be told glowing half-truths. Laws obliging a greater measure of public disclosure would be one safeguard against both administrative incompetence and anti-social corporate profiteering.

Prior Restraint

Once the journalist has extracted information of public importance, and convinced the editor and the editor's lawyers that it deserves publication, he or she must still run the gamut of legal action by some aggrieved party which will prevent the story hitting the streets. At any hour of the day or night a High Court judge may issue an injunction against publication if it is suggested that a forthcoming article is based on confidential information, copyrighted documents, or else passes comment on pending litigation. This power to restrain publication is in effect a power to censor – upon hearing claims which may never subsequently be justified. It has been used in recent times to suppress material as diverse as the background to thalidomide manufacture, the financial manipulations of James Slater and the sex life of the Rolling Stones. Aggrieved parties have the right to sue for damages if published material injures them in an unconscionable way, so why should they have the right to persuade an idosyncratic judge, late at night, to kill a major story for readers on the morrow? The law provokes bad press practice, because newspapers which decide to publish a contentious story hesitate to ask for comments prior to publication, for fear that any forewarning will prompt a restraining order. The *Sunday Times* endeavoured to be fair by sending Distillers the Thalidomide article for comment prior to publication – a kindness reciprocated by an avalanche of writs. After that experience, the press is understandably chary of seeking advance comment to balance its big exposées. The *Daily Mail* failed to put its Leyland bribes allegations to Lord Ryder, doubtless fearing that he would rush to a secret court and suppress the whole story. Had advance comment been sought, the newspaper would have been alerted to the false aspect of its scoop in time to alter them. Legal remedies should never lead to a practice which is in the interests of neither newspapers nor their targets, by inhibiting balanced treatment of matters of public interest.

The U.S. Supreme Court ruled prior restraint impermissible in its historic *Pentagon Papers* decision. The government got wind of the *New York Times* plan to publish a set of army research papers on the history of American involvement in Vietnam. It sought to injunct the newspaper on the ground that the papers contained military and diplomatic secrets, disclosure of which would substantially damage the national interest. The Supreme Court refused to allow any restraint on publication, on the principle that

> the only effective restraint upon executive policy and power in the areas of national defense and international affairs may be in an enlightened citizenry – an informed and critical public opinion which alone can here protect the values of democratic Government. For this reason, it is perhaps here that a press that is alert, aware and free most vitally serves the basic purpose of the first amendment. For without an informed and free press there cannot be an enlightened people.[20]

The importance of this principle was emphasised by those Justices who accepted that disclosure would substantially harm the national interest, and that publication might even render the newspaper liable to subsequent criminal action under the Espionage Act. None the less, they ruled that only when the government could prove that disclosure would cause 'grave and irreparable injury to the public interest' (examples given were details of troop deployments in wartime, or information which might trigger a nuclear holocaust) was a court entitled to stop the presses. The Supreme Court's protection of the rights of the press makes wistful reading when compared with the judgement of the Lord Chief Justice in the Crossman Diaries case. Lord Widgery was happy to gag the press whenever national security, as defined by the government, was alleged to be at stake. In other cases, prior restraint was in order whenever a newspaper article was based upon information obtained in breach of confidence, and the court divined that the public interest justified suppression. Crossman's diary escaped the judicial axe only because its secrets were stale: a newspaper account of current cabinet manoeuvres could be injuncted on the theory of 'premature disclosure'. Lord Widgery clearly would have had no hesitation in banning a story of the *Pentagon Papers* variety. His decision gives a new lease of life to a doctrine developed in circumstances far removed from great public issues. The action for breach of confidence was established to protect trade secrets and patents. It was used once in the nineteenth century to restrain an artist from selling private etchings of the Prince of Wales,[21] and once to prevent the Duchess of Argyll from telling her sordid story of life in the Duke's bed.[22] On the strength of these two rather silly cases of lese-majesty, the *Sunday Times* has been taken to court for its attempts to reveal cabinet machinations and was for two years restrained by court order from publishing Charles Raw's account of the collapse of Slater–Walker.

The other broad area of prior restraint concerns the doctrine of contempt of court. Injunctions will be granted against newspapers which desire to publish material tending to prejudge any question which is at issue in likely or current civil litigation, or in a dispute which is the subject of negotiation with a view to settlement. There is much to be said in favour of curbing press comment on issues involved in current criminal proceedings, where jurors might be swayed by what they read. But there can be no justification for prohibition of public debate on issues arising in civil cases, which are tried by judges alone – persons supposed to have sufficient fortitude to decide cases on the evidence heard in their court, not outside on Fleet Street. None the less, the *Sunday Times* was injuncted from telling the full Thalidomide story on the pretext that writs for damages had been issued against Distillers over the previous decade, and some had not yet been settled. The House of Lords justified its ruling by the popular judicial assumption that British people overwhelmingly deplore 'trial by newspaper'. 'If we were to ask the ordinary man' pontificated one Law Lord, 'or even the lawyer in his leisure moments why he has that feeling [i.e. that trial by media is a "horror" which is "wrong and should be prevented"] I suspect that the first reply would be – well, look at what happens in other countries where that is permitted'.[23] Leaving aside what happens in some countries where it is *not* permitted, it is at least possible that the ordinary man has a good deal more respect for the press which uncovered Watergate than for the press which for two years ignored the Poulson bankruptcy. And it is distinctly probable that he is enured to 'trial by newspaper' because his Sunday reading is devoted to little else, although the victims of Rupert Murdoch's Kangaroo Courts do not normally have Distillers' pre-tax profits of £73 million. 'Lawyers in their leisure moments', of course, abhor trials by newspaper, because they sometimes cast aspersions on lawyers in their professional moments. The Law Lords were openly paternalistic: 'If people are led to think that it is easy to find the truth, disrespect for the processes of the law could follow and, if mass media are allowed to judge, unpopular people and unpopular causes will fare very badly.'[24] The corollary – that if the mass media are not allowed to judge, bad people may remain undeservedly popular – did not seem to trouble them. Nor did the naïvety of the view that truth will ultimately emerge, butterfly-like, from the cocoon of litigation. How much 'truth' has emerged from legal actions against Distillers?

One problem unresolved by the Thalidomide case is whether the press are entitled to publish morally justified editorial criticism of one party's stand in litigation. The problem was epitomised in an analogy which should haunt Distillers for the rest of its corporate life: would it have been contempt for the *Venetian Times* to editorialise that Shylock, by persisting in his legally valid claim, was acting reprehensibly? Lords Diplock and Simon thought such 'public obloquy' was manifestly criminal contempt. Lords Reid and Cross disagreed, so long as the language used was 'fair and temperate'. (They would presumably convict the Rialto canal press for describing Shylock as an 'inexecrable dog' or a 'capitalist pig'.) The casting vote on this crucial question resided with Lord Morris. He condemned 'public advocacy in favour of one particular side' which might involve that side in 'the flurries of pre-trial publicity', and limited his approval to 'inviting Distillers to consider' whether they should increase their offer. He carefully refrained from approving press criticism of Distillers' moral position. In this unsatisfactory state of the law, the press finds itself inhibited from tough analysis of the well-heeled litigant who uses the courts to mount a private crusade. Goldsmith, Gouriet, McWhirter, Blackburn and Whitehouse have all been treated with kid gloves by Fleet Street, even when their litigious pre-occupations might be thought to jeopardise press freedom. There is urgent need to reform the law of contempt, in the interests not only of press comment on matters of public importance, but in the interest of knowing with some degree of certainty what the law of contempt really is.

The Libel Industry

London has become the libel capital of the world. Recent lavish handouts to Lords Bernstein and Wigg, Telly Savalas, Robert Wagner, Natalie Wood and Princess Elizabeth of Toro serve to underline the absurdity of a form of compensation available only to the wealthy for transient stings which leave no permanent mark. At a time when other countries are abandoning metaphysical valuations of dignity in favour of protecting privacy and encouraging press professionalism, our libel law is serving little purpose beyond inhibiting journalism and lining legal pockets. Libel trials may occasionally provide good courtroom theatre and some sensational front-page copy – witness the 1975 case of the 'spanking colonel'. But they all proceed on the assumption that the law must afford protection from 'words which tend to lower the plaintiff in the estimation of right thinking members of society' – a relevant belief, perhaps, in an age when social and political life was lived in gentlemen's clubs, when escutcheons could be blotted and society scandals resolved by writs of slander. But are we justified today in spending scarce legal resources to preserve the sense of dignity of those rich enough to wait years for the hearing, and to gamble massive legal fees on the outcome? Libel has broken down: it is too protracted, too unpredictable and out of the financial reach of the people who really need its protection.

Libel law has become hideously complex in volume, protracted in length and unpredictable in result. When the Telly Savalas jury plucked £34,000 out of thin air, as compensation for a gossip columnist's passing remark about the difficulties of working with the actor, its foreman wrote to *The Times*: 'where a jury has to decide, as men and women of the world, "how much", the degree of uncertainty is so great that a random answer, consistent only with a total lack of any sort of yardstick, can be expected. Their Lordships would do as well to use an Electronic Random Number Indicating Machine.'[25] Immediate cries went up for trial by judges alone. But judges have dispensed the same capricious largesse:

they heartily approved a £33,000 award to Lord Bernstein and £40,000 to the captain of the ill-fated P.G. 17 for an author's suggestion that he was responsible for that war-time debacle. Judges distrust the press and lean to titled or establishment litigants, while juries are impressed by showbusiness personalities and think that newspapers make large profits. Each case which goes to trial is an elaborate gamble: how much should be paid into court, and when? If the defendant makes a payment, the plaintiff may seize it and call quits. If he presses on and wins, but is awarded less than the payment, he must foot the entire legal bill. When the spanking colonel won a derisory ½p, the *Sunday People* were saddled with costs which could have been avoided by 'paying in' the lowest coin in the realm. But when Dr Dering, an Auschwitz prison doctor criticised in '*Exodus*', was awarded his halfpenny he became liable for all legal costs because Leon Uris and his publishers had the foresight to pay in £2. In circumstances like these, the temple of law becomes a casino.

It is necessary to find a procedure which enjoins the speedy public correction of false statements: the libel law merely offers a balance of money and reputation long after the falsehood has been published. There is need for a procedure to evaluate the truth of defamatory statements, but the adversary system of trial, in which each side exaggerates its own case and history is hamstrung by rules of evidence, is rarely satisfactory. The truth about Dr Dering's activities in Auschwitz cannot be extrapolated from his jury verdict. The evidence which Reginald Maudling gave to the Poulson bankruptcy trustee could not be used by 'World in Action' when he sued them for slander. The laws of libel serve neither the needs of the present nor the records of the past. They require radical reappraisal, so that defamatory statements can be swiftly investigated by an independent and respected tribunal which can set the record straight, if need be, by ordering a retraction, and compensation if actual damage has been done. The most recent Royal Commission on libel laws reported that cases were 'unduly long and unnecessarily costly' and that their results 'both as to liability and damages are unpredictable'.[26] But that Commission was top heavy with lawyers – libel lawyers, at that – and its proposals opted for revision rather than reform. It even recommended extension of liability to defamation of the dead, and rejected Lord Shawcross's suggestion that newspapers should be protected from suits on matters of public interest where all reasonable care had been taken to establish the truth of the facts stated. This reform, the committee maintained, 'would seriously alter the balance of the law of defamation against the defamed plaintiff. Such a shift is intrinsically undesirable'. Why intrinsically? Because the committee failed to study the social consequences of libel law: it looked only at the symmetry of its principles.

Again we must look to the jurisprudence of other countries for a proper balance between the claims of personal dignity and press freedom. Sweden has established a 'Press Ombudsman' empowered to investigate allegations of false derogatory statements, and to order offending newspapers to publish appropriate retractions. In Britain, the law of civil libel could be replaced by a tribunal with staff and the statutory power to investigate defamatory statements and to order appropriate redress. In most cases this would take the form of a public retraction, given prominence equal to that of the original libel. In rare cases it might mean a fine or suspension for a journalist who has deliberately or recklessly filed inaccurate copy. Publishers could be ordered to pay damages to complainants who have suffered in some measurable way (for example by loss of work) from the effect of any false statement. Such a system would provide speedy and certain redress for victims of inaccurate reporting, free journalists from the inhibiting effect of 'gagging' writs and liberate their proprietors from the nuisance of gold-digging claims. The Royal Commission largely supports these views, although oddly it deals with them in its chapter on the Press Council rather than in the course of its comments on defamation law. It was impressed by the 'obvious independence and public standing' of the Swedish Ombudsman, and advocated the introduction of a 'legal right of reply' to correct factual misstatements. This system works well in Europe, and 'we see no practical reason why it could not do so here. The right provides a prompt remedy, acts as a sanction and promotes accuracy of reporting.'[27] Its introduction would make the present English law of defamation redundant in relation to the press.

There are convincing reasons for reforming the law of criminal libel. Truth is no defence, and the requirement of a tendency to disturb the peace is unacceptably vague as a standard for criminal sanctions. Yet there is scope for an offence of knowingly publishing a deliberate falsehood with the intention of injuring another. A national newspaper editor who publishes, on the eve of a general election, a deliberate lie about a party leader in order to bias the electorate against him deserves to be punished. But as the law stands even an editor who quite innocently publishes a serious libel can be jailed for up to twelve months – at least if his victim is sufficiently wealthy to launch a private prosecution.

Reported libel cases are merely the tip of the iceberg. Commercial considerations usually dictate settlements which avoid prohibitive legal costs, even if this means abandoning authors' beliefs in the accuracy of their words. Books, scripts and newspaper articles on topical subjects are frequently degutted by libel lawyers who tend to err on the safe side, where they can never be proved wrong. The libel laws offer no protection to the privacy of the ordinary person: they function to confer a tax-free bonus on wealthy public figures. Throw your hat into the ring, and you can collect unearned income whenever it is accidentally trampled. If truth will out, there must be a better way of extracting it.

Privacy

'The shortest and most satisfactory definition of privacy' Sir Harold Wilson has suggested, 'would be a clause which said "Newspapers will accord to the general public the same rights of privacy they accord to their own proprietors, or even the proprietors of other newspapers".'[28] His cynicism was immediately justified by the refusal of journalists and editors to participate in a confidential Royal Commission survey of their earnings and political ties.[29] Even the editor of the *News of the World* had the effrontery to complain that the survey invaded his privacy! The Royal Commission found ample evidence, in the operations of the *News of the World* and its ilk, of unsavoury snooping, deception, 'flagrant breaches of acceptable standards' and 'inexcusable intrusions into privacy'.[30] It castigated the Press Council for failure to maintain proper ethical standards and pointed out that no satisfactory form of discipline or redress exists to combat wanton violation of a basic human right. The importance of these findings is not confined to the public; they suggest that journalists are being forced to degrade themselves and their profession by editors prepared to sacrifice common decency on the altar of circulation.

It is perhaps not surprising that in no area of public concern is press comment more muted and defensive than when confronted with media invasions of privacy. The most specious of excuses are formulated to justify prying into private lives. Marital problems of ordinary people are presented as a mirror of modern society; detailed accounts of the sex lives of vicars, schoolteachers and policemen are excused by the canting refrain that the press is merely guarding the guardians, and of course nobody who is related to, or has relations with, a 'public figure' has any right to privacy at all. Abuses occur at all levels: the *News of the World* sends its attractive female reporters to answer contact advertisements, deceive the advertisers, secretly tape admissions about their sex lives, secretly photograph them and then 'make an excuse and leave' in time to meet next Sunday's deadline. The *Daily Mail* makes a sniggering innuendo about the domestic life of Ms Maureen Colquhoun M.P., is thrashed with the Press Council's feather, and then deliberately misreports the adjudication so as to give currency to the original innuendo. Another Labour M.P., Tom Litterick, leaves his wife for a *Times* journalist. His local paper followed by the national press (with the exception, *pace* Harold Wilson, of *The Times*) titillates its readers with the details. The local editor lowers sanctimony to new depths: 'To me his credibility as an M.P. was then in question. I ask, on behalf of his constituents and my readers, is his credibility questionable through over-commitment publicly or privately?'[31]

Hypocrisy, truly, is the key-note not only in press response to calls for legislative protection of privacy but to rational criteria for separating fair comment from prurient curiosity. Vicars who preach sermons against adultery, and then rush off with other men's wives, might have a case to answer – but only if they preach that sort of sermon. Policemen deserve protection from prying into their love lives but not from surveillance of corrupt deals with criminals. Mr Litterick, unlike some other M.P.s, is not given to moral exhortations, and his affair of the heart could not conceivably affect either his credibility or his constituency duties. Lord Lambton's sexual performance in Norma Levy's bed was unrelated to his performance as a Minister of the Crown: his hypocrisy deserved disclosure because it lay in effortlessly breaking the law against cannabis which his government was eagerly enforcing against its less exalted subjects. Chronic alcholism, conflicts of interest and betrayal of party ideals are proper areas for press exposure of public figures – labour politicians who send their children to private schools or take advantage of private medical treatment must remain fair game. The American press which is so quick to expose all the President's Men maintains a moratorium on all the President's women, at least until that President's departure from office. Of course, the scope of private matters which do not bear upon public performance is necessarily limited. The bankrupt financier living it up in casinos, or the dowager who charters an airliner to fly her pet dogs to a tax haven, cannot expect to escape notice. What people do with their money or their credit is always a matter for the public domain, but what they do to each other in the privacy of their own homes deserves some veil of tolerance. There are exceptions, even here: social butterflies can hardly complain if their activities provoke gossip – there is a difference between snooping and recording the obvious. Lord Shawcross is partly if partially correct when as Chairman of the Press Council he writes that 'those who . . . seek to cultivate public support or even become public idols must accept that the public may be properly concerned to know about some aspects of their lives which they themselves might prefer to protect from public appraisal, possibly because they do not feel that these aspects would enhance the kind of reputation which they seek to cultivate'.[32]

It is easy to state the principle, but more difficult to find an appropriate remedy for its breach. The Royal Commission thought that Press Council rulings on the subject were conflicting and sometimes unduly partisan. Some countries favour a legal right to privacy, enforcable in the courts, which may compensate victims by awards of damages.[33] This solution has many drawbacks. Ordinary people whose private lives are inexcusably 'exposed' often lack either the money or the knowledge to sue. Trials can be counter-productive, in that they give dramatic publicity to the original wrong. Judges and juries may have difficulty in weighing the competing claims of privacy and public interest, and court procedures and awards are inevitably dilatory and unpredictable. How can a money value be placed on privacy any more than on reputation? The existence of a generalised legal right, arbitrarily enforceble, would do little to raise newspaper standards or contribute to press professionalism.

A more satisfactory answer is to permit a 'Press Ombudsman' to enforce privacy principles by disciplinary action against editors and journalists who inexcusably breach the Press Council code which should be incorporated into the N.U.J. code of conduct. The code requires that

> The public interest relied on as the justification for publication or inquiries which conflict with a claim to privacy must be a legitimate and proper public interest and not only a prurient or morbid curiosity. 'Of interest to the public' is not synonymous with 'in the public interest'. It should be recognised that entry into public life does not disqualify an individual from his right to privacy about his private affairs, save when the circumstances relating to the private life of an individual occupying a public position may be likely to affect the performance of his duties or public confidence in himself or his office . . . Invasions of privacy by deception, eavesdropping or technological methods which are not in themselves unlawful can however only be justified when it is in pursuit of information which ought to be published in the public interest and there is no other reasonably practicable method of obtaining or confirming it . . . Reporters and photographers should do nothing to cause pain or humiliation to bereaved or distressed people unless it is clear that the publication of the news or pictures will serve a legitimate public interest.[34]

This is a satisfactory statement of principle: the need now is for an authoritative tribunal which can build up through its rulings on individual cases a practical guide for working journalists. This authority must have the power to monitor all newspapers, and call for explanations of invasions of privacy whether they have been complained of or not. It must have a statutory power to reprimand, order published apologies, and in bad cases to fine and even to suspend repeated offenders from work for short periods. Only in this way can a code of conduct pass from the airy realm of the counsel of perfection and become a practical rule of thumb. Disciplinary procedures are necessary in all professions whose work affects the public in privileged ways: in this respect, journalism is no different from law or medicine. The Press Council has devised standards, and the Royal Commission has gathered evidence that they are sometimes traduced without civil penalty or disciplinary action. A code of professional discipline is not only an essential protection for the ordinary citizen, but a long overdue protection for the ordinary reporter from pressures to obtain an easy story by cruel intrusions into the private lives of powerless people.

Political Censorship

The Royal Commission owed its existence to a fervent belief in Labour circles that their politicians and policies received unfair media treatment. The Commission turned up some evidence which supported this view: 71 per cent of newspaper editorials are biased towards the Conservative Party, the trade unions are generally portrayed as the initiators of industrial conflict, being 'connected with bad news . . . discord and hardship for the public at large'.[35] Proprietorial business interests link most major newspapers with commercial concerns whose financial prospects would be threatened by socialism. The near monopolies which prevail in wholesale distribution (W. H. Smith, John Menzies and Surridge Dawson cover 70 per cent of the British market, and John Menzies has a monopoly in Scotland) create difficulties for publishers of left-wing magazines refused display space in chain newsagents. This picture is sufficiently clear to justify fears that left-wing viewpoints are not given the hearing to which they are entitled. As the Chairman of *Times* newspaper put it in his 1976 Haldane Lecture, 'there is a gap at the point where there ought to be serious newspaper coverage of the news from a left-wing standpoint'.[36] It is a gap which the Commission declined to fill, contenting itself with pious hopes that the trade union movement would launch its own national daily, and that left-wing publishers would build up their own distribution system. Such self-help is obviously inadequate when ranged against hostile and established market forces. Is there any assistance that law can render to ensure the availability of radical views in the public arena?

One solution canvassed before the Commission was to impose a legal obligation upon major distributors to supply any periodical requested by a customer. This was naturally opposed by the distributors in question, who maintained their divine right 'not to handle publications which they find abhorrent even though lawful'.[37] This claim to censor the reading wishes of the public may be allowed in the case of a sole trader, but is an assumption of breathtaking arrogance in the mouth of a monopolist. 'Getting into Smith's' spells survival for most periodicals, and provides the large distributor with a political power over the press which is incompatible with the public's right to receive the information it desires. The distributor's position can only be supported on two grounds, which both derive from legal anomalies. Local police forces are empowered by the Obscene Publications Act to raid newsagents and seize stocks of popular periodicals, which may then be destroyed by local justices – a fate which frequently befalls 'adult' magazines in benighted jurisdictions.[38] No distributor can be obliged to carry a publication which could attract police to his premises. The short answer to this objection is to provide that national magazines may only be censored after a jury trial in London. The other anomaly is the law of libel, which fixes distributors with liability for defamatory statements in any publication theoretically 'of a character likely to contain a libel'. This anomaly was exploited to the hilt by Sir James Goldsmith in his vendetta against *Private Eye*. He sued all distributors, forcing some of the them to settle on such terms that they would never again stock the magazine.[39] Since most left-wing periodicals could be characterised as potentially libellous, distributors have a ready excuse for refusing to handle them. Both the Court of Appeal and the Royal Commission have criticised this aspect of the libel law: its abolition would pave the way for an obligation on all major distributors to handle publications requested by their customers.

A thornier problem of political censorship is presented by the conflict between editorial freedom and the right of journalists to have their version of news or opinion presented without varnish. Given that proprietors have declared political predilections, editors are under the same pressure to conform by rejecting or cutting articles, however competently written, which present the other side of the story. Lord Goodman, in his evidence to the Commission, fervently championed 'the right to write', maintaining that society must 'regard as its first priority the right of a man to express what he believes in whatever form he thinks appropriate, subject to the control of the law'.[40] In the context, Lord Goodman was inveighing against 'closed shops', but his argument applies with equal force to the right of a reputable journalist to have work published without editorial suppression or distortion. The Royal Commission seemed unaware of this conflict: it recommended a Press Charter which would include both 'Freedom of a journalist to act, write and speak in accordance with conscience', and 'Freedom of an editor . . . to accept or reject any contribution . . . so long as this freedom is not abused'.[41] It did not venture to define 'abuse', nor did it suggest an appeals mechanism whereby a journalist might ventilate a grievance against editorial discretion exercised on political grounds. It would be too onerous to require editors to justify rejection of unsolicited contributions, but the principle of 'journalistic conscience' can only be effected by providing some complaints procedure for those whose articles, submitted to daily newspapers in the course of their employment or else specially commissioned, are tampered with or twisted for apparently political motives, as distinct from reasons of space or readability. Complaints would doubtless be rare, but the possibility that they might be raised and publicised would discourage distortion, and provide the professional journalist both with a sense of integrity and a right to vindicate it.

Conclusion

'We define freedom of the press' said the Royal Commission 'as that degree of freedom from restraint which is essential to enable proprietors, editors and journalists to advance the public interest by publishing the facts and opinions without which a democratic electorate cannot make responsible judgements.'[42] This degree of freedom is unobtainable in Britain, and the major fault lies not in prejudiced proprietors, circulation-crazed editors or incompetent journalists, but in a web of vague legal doctrines which catch facts and opinions essential for informed scrutiny of social power. It is a mesh for the most part woven by judges out of the common law – that infinitely elastic formula which by-passes Parliamentary scrutiny and seems to expand effortlessly whenever the *Sunday Times* has an embarrassing scoop (it has been the ironical achievement of that courageous but unsuccessful litigant to have done more damage to press freedom in the course of its court-room battles than its investigative journalism could ever redress). Had the Royal Commission on the Press the foresight to put its recommendations where its mouth is, the electorate might soon be making responsible judgements: as it is, the Committee's conclusions about law will do little to achieve its professed ideals. Instead of tinkering with a system of restraints as haphazard as they are oppressive, there must be a radical realignment of legal power in a way which places it squarely behind media efforts to extract information which the public is entitled to possess. This shift of legal weight must be balanced by an effective and independent disciplinary system which secures retractions of errors and restricts invasions of privacy. This equilibrium could be achieved by:

Abolition of Section 2 of the Official Secrets Act.

Restricting the scope of Section 1 of the Official Secrets Act to betrayal of defence secrets to a potential enemy.

Legislation of a Freedom of Information Act, providng a legal right of access to documents in all government departments, with a High Court judge to investigate and determine government claims to privilege.

Additional duties of disclosure on public and private companies and their auditors, and on partnerships and trusts.

A reformed classification system for government documents, and release of cabinet materials as a matter of course after ten years.

'Prior restraint' by court injunction to apply solely to information which would seriously damage the national interest: only remedy for breach of confidence and copyright (other than patents) to be provided by money damages assessed after publication.

Abolition of the doctrine of contempt of court in cases to be tried by judge without a jury.

Abolition of the libel law in relation to newspapers and periodicals and replacement by a tribunal with power to order the press to publish appropriate retractions of errors of fact, and to order compensation when actual damage has been proven.

Replacement of the present offence of criminal libel by a law against publishing a deliberate falsehood with intent to injure.

Establishment of a disciplinary tribunal with power to investigate invasions of privacy and other contraventions of the code of press conduct, and to reprimand, fine or suspend offenders.

Legal obligation on all large distributors to supply customers with any British newspaper or periodical on request.

Abolition of Section 3 of the Obscene Publications Act, doing away with the right of police officers to enter news-agencies to seize and destroy periodicals without jury trial.

A complaints tribunal to hear and adjudicate on allegations by professional journalists that their copy has been cut or censored on political grounds.

Implementation of these reforms would produce a law which works for the press, and not against it. It would be a law which acknowledges that members of the public have a right to full information about decisions made by public or private bodies which may affect their lives. It would emphasise that press freedom, in servicing that interest, is a value in its own right which should receive positive protection – at the expense only of the very highest level of national security and the right of ordinary citizens to personal integrity. The reforms require new legislation as well as abolition of some existing procedures, but this radical restructuring would not place any additional strains on the courts, nor leave existing wrongs without appropriate redress. The changes would not work an overnight improvement in newspaper functioning, but they would certainly produce higher standards, greater accuracy and the reception of a wider range of comment and information. Members of the public would be permitted to monitor government decision-making more effectively and the role of the journalist in analysing and passing on that information would be correspondingly enhanced.

Law cannot open closed minds, but it can open closed doors and influence community values. A recent opinion poll revealed that only 2 per cent of the public would place their trust in journalists. Proposals to increase public esteem, to force the British press to raise its eyes from the gutter and peer instead into cabinet offices and board rooms, deserve to be taken seriously, even if the press itself is happy to wallow in official hand-outs and calculated leaks. The issue becomes more urgent with every development of the nuclear economy, as more and more decisions of vital import for the quality of life are taken without the public knowledge or participation. How long can we afford to live with a system that places an editor on trial for exposing government lies over the Nigeria/Biafra war, and with a press which reserves its highest accolades for the man who traced Norma Levy's wedding photograph?

(

Chapter 11

Advertising and the Press

James Curran

Introduction*

'More nonsense is talked about the influence of advertising', writes Charles Wintour, 'than about any other area of newspaper activity . . . It is my opinion that in general advertising influence is negligible and even where it is not, that it is harmless'.[1] This considered judgement, based on a lifetime's distinguished service in Fleet Street, is broadly endorsed by all authoritative public enquiries into the British press that have considered advertising influence on the press.

The first of these, the Ross Commission, investigated every substantive allegation of undue advertising influence that it received. Not one serious complaint was upheld.[2] Many allegations, including one from a former Fleet Street editor who has since become Deputy Prime Minister, were pointedly dismissed as being based on misconception.[3]

The conclusion of the Ross Commission was profoundly reassuring. 'As long as newspapers are sold to the public for less than they cost to produce, they will need a supplementary source

* I would like to thank the German Marshall Fund for financing a content analysis part of which is reported in this article, and also Angus Douglas and Garry Whannel for carrying out the content analysis with such ability.

of income. Of the various possible sources of income, the sale of their space to advertisers seems to us to be one of the least harmful . . . its receipt creates a relationship both remote and impersonal.'[4]

Its successor, the Shawcross Commission, was rather more qualified in tone, stressing the difficulty of establishing conclusive 'proof either way' of undue advertising influence. After a somewhat limited enquiry, it was content to reproduce verbatim the conclusions of the Ross Commission published thirteen years before.[5]

The McGregor Commission was also circumspect, stressing the difficulty of investigating advertising abuse. It found no concrete example of undue influence, however, and concluded that the influence of advertising on the press was limited.[6]

Yet, despite the comforting unanimity of these official enquiries, there are good grounds for questioning their verdict. Their analysis rests primarily on a stimulus–response model of advertising influence in which attention is focussed upon overt attempts by advertisers to secure favourable coverage for their products and interests. Their conclusion that 'such attempts appear to be infrequent and unsuccessful' is the main basis on which the charge of advertising influence is rejected.[7] While the McGregor Commission also considered, in a general way, the influence of advertising on the press, its examination was, as we shall see, so perfunctory and superficial that it scarcely constituted an attempt to go beyond the traditional model of advertising influence inherited from its predecessors.

This model prescribes its own remedy. By posing the problem raised by advertising in simplified ethical terms – newspapermen are subject to as much influence from advertising as they will let themselves be – all three Commissions unconsciously define their response. For a simple moral problem calls for a simple moral response – greater moral integrity. As far as all three Press Commissions are concerned, the problems raised by advertising can be best dealt with by calling for greater responsibility on the part of everyone concerned.[8]

In this chapter, we will outline an alternative way of viewing the impact of advertising on the press. The complacent conclusions of successive Royal Commissions on the Press, it will be argued, reflect their failure to identify adequately the different ways in which advertising shapes and influences the press. This failure of diagnosis resulted, in turn, in an entirely inadequate response to the problems caused by advertising finance of the press.

Overt Advertising Pressure

It is not in the interests of either publishers or advertisers to proclaim publicly that one is greatly influenced by the other. It is therefore unlikely that the procedure pursued by Royal Commissions on the Press of asking simple-minded questions of interested parties, whether they be advertisers, advertising agents, or publishers, is likely to elicit very useful information. Certainly there seem to be discrepancies between the testimony given by some witnesses and the internal records of the companies they represented. For instance, the chairman of a leading advertising agency, the London Press Exchange Ltd, told the Ross Commission that the press only accepted a story 'wholly on its merits',[9] whereas executives from the same agency frequently claimed in letters and memoranda to clients that advertising helped to secure favourable editorial treatment for their products or services.[10]

This example relates to the past not the present. It highlights the difficulty of pinning down overt influence rather than demonstrating its existence, on any significant scale, in the contemporary press. While confident assertions in this area are difficult, an impression has been obtained that overt attempts by advertisers to suppress criticism or secure favourable coverage either through blackmailing threats of withdrawing advertisements or through promises of additional patronage are indeed rare (though not as rare as successive Press Commissions suggest) and are generally resisted. The extent of overt advertising pressure varies, however, between different sections of the press. Overt advertising pressure on the main news sections of the national press is negligible. It is greater in specialised magazines, because major advertisers are also often major sources and topics of news, and in the local press, where social contact between advertisers and newspaper executives is more common than in the national newspaper press.

Overt advertising pressure on the editorial contents of the press is probably less than it used to be. The rise of the advertising agency as an intermediary between advertisers and the press, preparing advertising media schedules largely on the basis of technical criteria, has acted as a break on the manipulation of advertising patronage as a means of securing favourable editorial coverage. Attitudes hostile to the crude manipulation of advertising power to secure editorial promotion have also hardened in the advertising industry since the 1930s.[11]

Indeed, the conventional preoccupation with overt advertising pressure on the contents of the press, reflected in the reports of three Royal Commissions, has served merely to deflect attention from the ways in which advertising really does influence the contents of the press. For this process of influence is essentially an impersonal one that is inherent in the system of advertising finance of press rather than an 'abuse' that can be attributed to 'rogue' advertisers. The image of the predatory advertiser threatening the editorial integrity of the press is itself profoundly misleading. For advertising influence is not imposed upon the press so much as internalised by newspaper managements in strategies designed to maximise revenue. It is an integral part of the economic system in which the press serves two clients – advertisers and readers.

The Structure of the Newspaper
The McGregor Commission did consider the general influence of advertising on the contents of the newspaper press. Its negative assessment was reached on the following grounds:

> As far as newspapers are concerned, we believe that there is evidence that the overall balance of newspapers is not unduly influenced by the needs of advertisers. The analysis of newspaper content undertaken by Professor McQuail showed that there had been very little change in the contents of newspapers, measured by the proportion of space given to different subjects, between 1947 and 1975. If it were true that the influence of advertising had increased *pari passu* with the growth in consumer spending in the intervening years, then much greater change in the content of newspapers would have been expected.[12]

This is seemingly powerful evidence not only for the reason given but because a comparison is being made between two years in which the relationship of the press to advertisers was very different. In 1947, newspapers did not need to compete for advertising because newsprint rationing created a space shortage in which advertisers literally booked weeks in advance in order to place insertions in the national press.[13] In 1975, by contrast, competition for advertising had reached such suicidal proportions that some papers were accepting advertisements at bargain rates that did not cover costs.[14] If there was little change in the editorial contents of the press between these two years, the case for dismissing advertising as an influence is clearly a strong one.

In fact, the McGregor Commission's bias led it unconsciously to misrepresent its own evidence. For, contrary to what it claimed, its content analysis – which is published – does reveal major changes in the contents of the six newspapers that were examined in 1947 and 1975.[15] Because of the content categories that were used in the analysis, however, it is by no means clear what all these changes were. For instance, 'other' features were reported to have increased from 26 per cent to 42 per cent of total feature space in the *Daily Express,* and from 27 per cent to 41 per cent in the *Daily Mail,* between 1947 and 1975.[16] Since the category 'other' is a rag-bag covering anything from holiday and travel to certain types of 'human interest' feature, we are left little the wiser. But clearly important, if ill-defined, changes have occurred in the contents of the post-war press.

The limitations of content analysis as a method also need to be recognised. Content analysis can confirm or refute specific hypotheses about newspaper content using procedures that minimise the subjective element inherent in unsystematic analysis. But the results of a content analysis are necessarily defined by the questions – in the form of content categories – that are asked. Denis McQuail's historical content analysis did not attempt to investigate advertising influence: it was merely built piggy-back on top of a purely descriptive analysis designed thirty years ago. That it failed to reveal advertising influence therefore proves little since it did not use categories – that is, ask questions – likely to elicit whether advertising has influenced the content of the press or not.[17] (A similar objection applies to the McGregor Commission's not very illuminating comments on political bias in the press.[18])

An alternative content analysis was conducted, therefore, to explore further the questions left unanswered by the McGregor Commission using methods similar to those employed in the

Commission's investigation.[19] This analysis revealed, first, a remarkable growth in advertising-related editorial features – defined as editorial items covering the same product or service as advertisements on the same or facing page – during the post-war period (see Table 11.1).[20] In eight out of the nine national papers investigated, advertising-related editorial features increased as a percentage of total editorial space between 1946 and 1976. The greatest increase was significantly amongst the quality papers, which derive over half their revenue from advertising, and it was least amongst the popular papers, which are less dependent on advertising. Top of the league in 1976 was the *Sunday Times,* which devoted a third of its editorial space to features linked to advertising – a proportion nearly double that of the *Sunday Times* in 1946.

TABLE 11.1 *Editorial content linked to advertising as a percentage of total editorial space, 1946 – 76*

	1946 %	1956 %	1966 %	1976 %	1946/76 difference % points
The Times	14	18	36	30	+16
Daily Telegraph	3	11	14	22	+19
Daily Mail	6	6	10	11	+5
Daily Express	1	5	8	10	+9
Daily Mirror	2	0	3	5	+3
Sunday Times	18	23	38	33	+15
Observer	13	22	13	24	+11
Sunday Express	2	11	12	9	+7
Sunday Mirror	6	2	5	5	−1

Sample: 336 issues

This growth in advertising-sponsored features was accompanied by a major shift in the pattern of advertising in the national newspaper press during the post-war period. A growing proportion of advertisements was placed on the same or facing page as features covering the same topic. This change was most marked in the case of the *Observer,* where display advertising related to editorial content increased from 23 per cent of total display advertising space in 1946 to 44 per cent in 1976, and in the case of *The Times,* where editorially-related display advertising increased from 13 per cent to 38 per cent of total display advertising space during the same period.

This growing convergence between editorial and advertising content reflects the increasing accommodation of national newspaper managements to the selective needs of advertisers. The majority of advertisers, including even the majority of advertisers oriented towards the mass market, have been primarily concerned to reach particular target groups rather than achieve indiscriminate exposure. This has created difficulties when buying space in newspapers since newspaper audiences seldom correspond to the target groupings that advertisers want to reach. (To take a simple example, advertisements for garden sheds inserted in national newspapers reach a large number of people without gardens.)[21] The problem of hitting the target market is made more complicated by the fact that groups of readers do not look at every page in a newspaper with equal attention. Consequently advertisements can be placed in parts of a paper which gain relatively high attention among readers in general but not among the target groups that particular advertisers want to reach.

Publishers have catered for these difficulties in the way they have planned the development of newspapers in order to maximise advertising revenue. For market research has long confirmed that the attention generated by editorial features tends to spill over into adjacent advertising areas on the same and facing pages.[22] Specialised features have been introduced or expanded partly in order to segregate readers into the groups that advertisers want to reach, and to direct their attention to particular parts of a paper where they can be efficiently picked out by advertisers. The structure of the modern newspaper, particularly the so-called 'quality' newspaper, has thus evolved in a form that organises readers into market lots, packaged in suitable editorial material, for sale to advertisers.

This process is illustrated in Table 11.2, which shows the growth of sponsored features that enable advertisers to pinpoint particular sub-groups from amongst the general readership of newspapers – home-buyers, home-makers, motorists, holiday-goers, film-goers, gardeners, consumers of beauty and fashion products, book-readers, job-seekers, investors and so on. This is not to suggest

TABLE 11.2   Growth of advertising-sponsored features, 1946 – 76*

	Average issues of four national Sunday newspapers†					Average issues of five national daily newspapers†				
	1946 col cms	1956 col cms	1966 col cms	1976 col cms	1946/76 difference col cms	1946 col cms	1956 col cms	1966 col cms	1976 col cms	1946/76 difference col cms
Business/Financial										
Editorial	164	161	2974	3371	+3207	383	832	2522	3514	+3131
Advertising	40	200	3789	3978	+3938	152	538	1114	1787	+1635
Books										
Editorial	564	756	843	1088	+524	13	177	74	201	+188
Advertising	297	520	540	292	–5	9	71	58	87	+78
Travel										
Editorial	–	316	348	412	+412	–	22	10	86	+86
Advertising	–	145	498	670	+670	–	15	5	115	+115
Beauty/Fashion										
Editorial	30	277	814	601	+571	26	66	333	138	+112
Advertising	83	1003	736	582	+499	30	77	329	92	+62
Theatre and live arts										
Editorial	20	316	348	386	+366	56	78	38	196	+140
Advertising	1	145	498	629	+628	50	27	31	115	+65
Gardening										
Editorial	10	43	124	174	+164	19	34	105	81	+62
Advertising	3	93	362	301	+298	46	92	224	118	+72
Films										
Editorial	118	362	196	19	–99	31	11	20	37	+6
Advertising	189	252	50	6	–183	17	3	7	13	–4

Property										
Editorial	–	–	–	+102	102	–	–	35	51	+51
Advertising	–	–	–	+408	408	–	–	30	245	+245
Motoring										
Editorial	–	46	14	+31	31	–	45	12	69	+69
Advertising	–	56	10	+139	139	–	40	8	96	+96
Home-making										
Editorial	53	13	94	+177	230	11	48	108	159	+148
Advertising	17	5	85	+207	224	11	54	85	309	+298
Foreign countries (special features)										
Editorial	–	–	–	–	–	–	–	360	535	+535
Advertising	–	–	–	–		–	–	293	525	+525
Jobs (not in business/financial sections)										
Editorial	–	–	11	+54	54	–	–	30	36	+36
Advertising	–	–	19	+496	496	–	–	117	186	+186
Eating/Drinking										
Editorial	12	11	18	−7	5	7	10	3	56	+49
Advertising	7	16	8	+16	23	4	38	24	49	+45
Other‡										
Editorial	8	48	243	+254	262	16	78	202	210	+194
Advertising	2	25	157	+100	104	11	42	84	94	+83

* Editorial content linked to advertising has been defined as items covering the same product or service as display advertisements on the same or facing page. Display advertising linked to editorial items, also summarised in this table, has been defined on the same basis.

† Same sample of newspapers as in Table 11.1.

‡ Pets, art/museums, sport, T.V./radio, medicine.

that the sole purpose of these features is to generate advertising. But the selection of minorities that are catered for in the growing proportion of space absorbed by advertising-sponsored features has clearly been influenced by advertising considerations. Twelve out of the thirteen main categories of sponsored feature service consumers of heavily advertised products and services (the exception is film features). The introduction of some of these features has also owed more to advertising than to consumer demand: survey investigations into what people read, commissioned by newspaper publishers and advertising agencies, show that many sponsored features are among the least read features in newspapers, while survey inquiries into 'topic satisfaction' do not suggest that the majority of these features gratify an intensely felt interest.[23] The growth of these features is often very closely linked to the growth of advertising they generate. Thus, to take but one example, sponsored financial and business features accounted for only 13 per cent of all sponsored features in the *Sunday Times* in 1956, and linked financial and business advertising accounted for only 12 per cent of its editorially-linked advertising. Twenty years later its sponsored financial and business features had grown to 60 per cent of its sponsored feature space, while linked financial and business advertising had grown to 58 per cent of its tied advertising.

Advertising sponsorship is not a new phenomenon. The growing convergence between the editorial and advertising content of the press in the post-war period represents a return to 'normality' artificially interrupted by newsprint rationing during and after the war. For newsprint rationing restricted the space available for features that generated related advertising and insulated newspapers from competition for advertising. As competitive pressures mounted and space restrictions were lifted, newspaper managements sought ways of increasing the utility of their newspapers to advertisers. They reverted to the time-honoured practice of providing editorial material that enabled advertisers to pick out specialised or selected groups in a favourable editorial setting as a way of improving their service to advertisers. Advertising sponsorship crept back to pre-war levels, and in two instances – *The Times* and the *Sunday Times* – advertising-sponsored features more than doubled as a proportion of total editorial space between 1936 and 1976. A detailed comparison between newspapers in

1936 and 1976 tends also to confirm that there is a close link between the allocation of editorial content and related advertising.[24]

In short, the desire of advertisers to reach particular target groups within the large audiences reached by national newspapers has had a profound influence upon the structure of the modern newspaper, and contributed to the disproportionate growth of service features linked to advertising during the post-war period. How much space has been allocated between these different features has also depended, in part, upon the level of advertising sponsorship they have received. This process has not been resisted by publishers. On the contrary, they have positively promoted the sponsorship system, even pioneering advertising research techniques for assessing the influence of editorial content on the attention given to advertisements by different types of readers.[25] To say all this may seem merely to labour the obvious. Indeed, only a body as impressionable as the McGregor Commission could possibly have concluded that the balance of contents of the press has not been crucially influenced by the needs of advertisers.

The Wider Implications of Advertising Sponsorship

Advertising sponsorship creates problems quite unlike advertising that is not tied to the editorial contents of newspapers. For the attraction of sponsored features to some, at least, of their sponsors is not only that they organise readers into the market categories they want, but also that they provide an editorial ambience that enhances their advertisements' effectiveness. Some advertisers believe that editorial feature material can dispose readers to respond favourably or unfavourably to adjacent advertising: for instance, that features celebrating the virtues of holidays abroad can encourage a positive response to related foreign travel advertisements. When buying space, therefore, they seek a conducive 'editorial environment' for their advertisements as well as the attention of the right readers.

This generates pressures on newspaper managements, in the highly competitive market for national advertising, to publish feature material that satisfies the requirements of their sponsors. A form of self-censorship has developed in which journalists writing sponsored consumer features are positively encouraged by some newspaper managements to rely heavily upon sponsors for feature material and are discouraged from causing unnecessary offence. Press championship of consumer interests has consequently been much less vigorous than it would have been without the growth of advertising sponsorship.

There are, however, a number of countervailing pressures that prevent the total subordination of sponsored features to advertising interests.[26] Some features, such as sponsored financial sections, are relatively autonomous in that leading sponsors are sometimes sharply criticised. There is, perhaps, a tendency for commentators on the left to exaggerate the extent to which individual advertisers are immune from criticism.[27]

Advertising sponsorship raises a much wider and more important question, however, than whether individual advertisers are shielded from criticism or receive preferential treatment. For advertising sponsorship distorts the news values of the press, and consequently the images of society mediated by the press. Not only does it influence, as we have seen, what topics are covered and at what length, but it also indirectly influences the way in which these topics are covered. Sponsorship helps to set the editorial agenda of sponsored features and, perhaps more important, to define their intended audiences. In this discreet and indirect way, rather than in the more obvious sense of overt pressure, advertising sponsorship has come to colour portrayals of reality in the press.

The financial and business sections of the national press, the largest and fastest-growing category of sponsored feature, provide a good illustration of this discreet process of distortion. They reach a relatively small, but none the less highly influential, audience, the majority of whom are not exposed to an alternative source of specialised financial journalism.[28] Providing detailed coverage of the economic process, they inevitably make a contribution to the current debate about Britain's economic crisis amongst an élite stratum of British society.

At a time of runaway inflation, mass unemployment and a collapsing pound, pride of place was given in the business and financial sections of the press to tipster articles on shares similar in character to punters' features on racing form in the sporting pages (see Table 11.3).[29] More space was also given in all dailies to market prices, serving in some respects a similar function to racing results in the sport sections, than to news reports and comment on national economic affairs. Indeed, editorial content primarily concerned with investment guidance accounted for over half the content of specialised economic coverage of all but one national daily (the *Guardian)*. The second biggest category was management news and features, much of it consisting of company gossip rather than critical analysis, and in the *Daily Mail* and *Observer* to features on personal finance concerned with such topics as personal tax, insurance and mortgages. The national economy came a very poor third.

The sparse economic coverage in the main news sections of most national newspapers does not make unnecessary detailed news or analytical insight in its specialised economic coverage. Yet in most papers little attention was given to the wider crisis of capitalism of which Britain's economic crisis is only a part. There was very little recognition even that the rate of inflation or unemployment in Britain is crucially influenced by developments and events outside this country. Indeed, in five papers aspects of the international economy received less than 1 per cent of the space in their specialised economic sections. The two principal exceptions to this myopia were the *Sunday Times* and the *Guardian,* both of which devoted over 10 per cent of their business/financial sections to aspects of the international economy (see Table 11.3).

The contents of sponsored economic journalism is crucially influenced by who pays for it. The heavy concentration on the servicing of investors is because of the importance of investment advertising. This represents the most important single source of sponsorship for nine out of ten financial and business sections in the national press, and accounts for over half the advertising in five of these. The other important source of sponsorship, particularly for some quality papers, is executive job advertisements. The routine provision of management news of a narrowly defined character is an economic way of gathering job advertisements, while the heavy emphasis on servicing investors reaps a large harvest in investment advertising. The character of specialised economic journalism is thus a reflection of the pattern of advertising sponsorship (see Table 11.4).

This pattern of commercial sponsorship leads to distortion as well as trivialisation. The concentration upon editorial servicing of investors itself produces a misleading definition of the economic

TABLE 11.3 *Editorial content of national newspaper financial and business sections in 1976*

	Dailies						Sundays			
	The Times %	Daily Telegraph %	Guardian %	Daily Express %	Daily Mail %	Daily Mirror %	Sunday Times %	Observer %	Sunday Express %	Sunday Telegraph %
Market prices	37	43	19	37	16	14	12	–	–	1
Investment form	28	29	25	41	36	55	14	31	57	26
Total investors' guide	65	72	44	78	52	69	26	31	57	27
Company news	8	7	15	7	3	14	12	19	–	25
Profiles, human interest	5	4	3	1	6	–	16	9	–	4
Managing labour	3	–	5	–	–	–	2	–	–	4
Other management features	–	2	3	3	–	3	2	–	–	–
Total managment news and features	16	13	26	11	9	17	32	28	–	33
Personal finance	2	3	1	4	25	4	5	20	3	1
Miscellaneous (index, letters etc)	3	2	5	5	3	7	7	6	30	8
Total personal fi∴ance and miscellaneous	5	5	6	9	28	11	12	26	33	9
National economic and financial affairs*	9	9	12	2	11	3	14	15	10	28
International economic and financial affairs*	5	1	12	–	–	–	16	–	–	3
National and international economic and financial affairs*	14	10	24	2	11	3	30	15	10	31
Sample % issues										

TABLE 11.4   Advertising in the financial and business sections of national newspapers in 1976

	Dailies						Sundays			
	The Times %	Daily Telegraph %	Guardian %	Daily Express %	Daily Mail %	Daily Mirror %	Sunday Times %	Observer %	Sunday Express %	Sunday Telegraph %
Investment	41	28	49	44	91	56	14	66	92	92
Jobs	37	66	30	40	3	–	71	25	–	5
Business services/Products	–	2	10	1	1	–	11	2	–	1
Government information	–	1	3	–	4	44	3	7	–	–
Property	10	1	7	–	–	–	–	–	–	2
Other financial	10	1	1	11	1	–	1	–	–	–
General (non-financial)	2	1	–	4	–	–	1	–	8	–

Sample: 96 issues

process. New share issues are subjected to careful editorial scrutiny as if they were profoundly important events in British economic life. The Stock Exchange is tacitly portrayed as a nerve centre of the British economy as a consequence of the advertising-induced editorial attention that its activities receive. An impression is frequently conveyed that decisions taken by the small private investor are of central importance to the British economy.

This highlights the discreet influences of advertising sponsorship. There is little covert advertising pressure, no conspiracy, no conscious suppression of information. The mere editorial visibility purchased by sponsored advertising, and the narrow orientation to the public induced by sponsored advertising, produces its own ideological distortion. In practice, of course, the economic significance of the *small* private investor is marginal, not least because 96 per cent of personal shareholdings are owned by 5 per cent of the adult population.[30] The Stock Exchange is an institution that manipulates the value of capital rather than raises capital for industry. During the period 1971–6, for instance, new issues of ordinary share capital accounted for a mere 3 per cent of new capital funds financed for industrial and commercial companies in the United Kingdom.[31] Yet most City feature writers were too busy backing winners to notice.

The consequence of this ideological distortion is not only to reinforce myths, widely believed amongst Britain's economic élite, but to 'classify out' issues and perspectives from the realm of public debate. Even the issue of industrial investment, which is central to the level of production, inflation and employment in Britain and which representatives of the trade union movement and labour left have been attempting vainly to establish as a major national issue in speeches up and down the country for years, was barely mentioned in the specialised economic sections of national newspapers except within the investors' guide framework of what constitutes a good 'buy'. Indeed, in a number of newspapers like the *Daily Express, Daily Mail* and *Sunday Express,* less than 1 per cent of references to investment in the financial sections related to investment in a national context. The one paper where investment was least often discussed within a tipster's framework was the *Sunday Times,* where references to investment in a national context accounted for 12 per cent of all references to investment in its business section. This may not be unrelated to the fact that the *Sunday Times* carried a smaller proportion of investment advertisements in its business section than any other paper and devoted a smaller proportion of editorial space in its business section to servicing investors than any other paper.

Specialised economic coverage in the national press merely exemplifies a more general pattern of distortion induced by advertising sponsorship. Thus women's features, the category of sponsored feature most read in the national press, generally cater for readers in a form that is defined by advertising sponsorship. They tend to service women as consumers of cosmetics, fashion, foods and things for the home. The reason for this is not accidental. As Ernestine Carter, the former women's editor of the *Sunday Times,* explains in her memoirs, the growth of women's features in her reign was related to the growth of advertising that they generated.[32] The practical outcome of this product-related growth of women's features has been a tendency to define the interests and horizons of women primarily in terms of consumption, and tacitly portray the roles of women as that of mother, mannequin, and housekeeper. The problem, in short, is not so much that women's features are sychophantic to individual advertisers as that they echo the consumption values of their sponsors, and reinforce restrictive and stereotyped perspectives of women's function in society.[33]

The growing influence of advertising sponsorship on the images and range of issues presented by the press has important implications.[34] Empirical sociological research shows that newspaper influence is exerted primarily through its tacit images of the social process, its selection of issues and frameworks for understanding these issues, in what it designates as significant and what it chooses to ignore – rather than through a frontal assault on public opinion with editorials.[35] In compromising their news values, newspapers are surrendering an important part of their influence to advertisers.

Advertisers as a Licensing Authority

Although the influence of advertising sponsorship is increasing (and is a more insidious influence on magazines than it is on newspapers), it is still relatively insignificant compared with the overall impact of advertising on the market structure of the press. The overwhelming majority of commercial publications – national newspapers, regional morning and evening newspapers, local weekly newspapers, trade and technical publications, and most women's and consumer magazines (with the notable exception of publications aimed at children and young adolescents) – sell at a loss. The net return on the cover price (that is, sales receipts less distributors' discounts) is less than the cost of production.[36] The difference, and any surplus in the form of profit, is made up by advertising receipts.

This confers on advertisers almost a *de facto* power to license publication, for their support is crucial in determining whether publications in most sectors of the press are economically viable or not. The freedom to publish and the freedom to buy publications – crucial elements of any acceptable definition of press freedom – are largely vested in advertisers in a press dependent on advertising for profits.

The dependency of the press on advertising is generally recognised. It is frequently objected, however, that the licensing authority of advertisers is chimerical, since advertising reflects 'readership or willingness to buy' a publication. In reality, it is argued, the public is the real arbiter of advertising allocation since advertisers are only interested in placing their advertisements where they will be seen by the public. In short, advertisers merely follow readers' preferences.[37]

This persuasive characterisation of advertising media selection is highly misleading. For advertisers are not equally intersted in reaching all people. Some people have more disposable income or greater power over corporate spending than others, and consequently are more sought after by advertisers. The overall allocation of advertising spending inevitably reflects inequalities of income and power in society.

These inequalities are reproduced in the market structure of the press. For how advertisers spend their money decisively influences what publications are available on the market. This process is illustrated in relation to the popular and quality press in 1973, the most recent year for which all the data summarised in Table 11.5 is available.

Although there are almost as many quality as popular newspapers, the quality press has less than 20 per cent of national

TABLE 11.5   *Quality and popular national newspapers in 1973*

	Dailies		Sundays	
	Popular	Quality	Popular	Quality
Number of papers	5	4	4	3
Circulation*	12 278 00	2 306 000	19 007 000	3 088 000
Percentage of national daily/Sunday circulation	84%	16%	86%	14%
Net advertising revenue†	£67 143 000**	£48 015 000	£20 677 000	£25 032 000
Net advertising revenue‡ as percentage of total revenue	36%	70%	38%	74%
Percentage of advertising revenue not absorbed by costs	15%	45%	5%	40%
Advertising surplus per 1000 copies of average issue#	£2††	£19	£1	£62

* Audit Bureau of Circulations, reported in Royal Commission on the Press, *Interim Report,* 1976, Table E.1, Appendix E, p. 92. The *Morning Star,* which does not have an audited circulation, is not included.

† Royal Commission on the Press, *Interim Report,* 1976, Table E.7, p. 98. The figures relate to the financial rather than the calendar year.

‡ Royal Commission of the Press 1974 – 7, *Final Report,* Table 5.1, p. 32.

§ Royal Commission on the Press 1974 – 7, *Final Report,* Table 5.5, p. 39. The percentages are to the nearest 5 per cent.

Advertising surplus was estimated by calculating (*a*) the average net advertising revenue per 1000 copies of each category of newspaper, and (*b*) the proportion of this revenue not absorbed by costs. Each estimate is expressed to the nearest pound.

** Estimate includes London evenings.

†† This estimate is based on the average net advertising revenue per 1000 copies of London dailies (including evening papers on the basis of their Monday – Friday circulations). It was not possible to take into account, however, the lower proportion of advertising revenue absorbed by costs of London evening newspapers (65 per cent in 1973) since no separate figure for advertising revenue of London evenings is available.

newspaper circulation. The reason why quality newspapers are able to survive with small circulations by comparison with the popular press is not primarly because they charge high cover prices. Although the majority of quality papers sold at a cover price double that of popular papers in 1973, they still derived on average less than a third of their income from sales. Their main source of revenue was the large advertising receipts that their predominantly middle-class readers generated. The real value of these receipts was enhanced, moreover, by the high advertising rates they were able to charge per reader, thereby increasing the proportion of revenue that remained after costs. Indeed, when the costs of obtaining and publishing advertisements are taken into account, the advertising subsidy per 1000 copies was eight times higher for the quality daily press than for popular dailies and London evenings, and a remarkable 62 times higher per 1000 copies for the quality Sunday press than for popular Sunday newspapers (see Table 11.5).

This has important implications for the political culture of British society. The only minority newspapers with detailed coverage of public affairs and extensive political analysis are quality papers catering for mainly middle-class audiences occupying roughly that part of the political spectrum that extends from the Conservative Central Office to the Reform Club. Their virtual monopoly in the newspaper field – they are almost alone in the national press in devoting more than 12 per cent of their editorial space to political, economic and social affairs in Britain – ensures that they exercise a strategic influence on British political life. Their construction of reality and definition of salient issues influence the news values of broadcasters, shapes the agenda of political debate, and influences even the debate within the trade union movement.[38] For the quality press not only reflects the values and interests of its middle-class readers, it gives them force, clarity and coherence. It plays an important ideological role in amplifying and renewing the dominant political consensus.

The effect of advertising finance is thus to distort the structure of the press in a way that reflects and also reproduces inequalities in society. The advertising subsidies that middle-class audiences generate ensure that the most comprehensive and sophisticated newspaper interpretations of the external world are produced in publications that reflect the ideology of the dominant class. This is not a natural, inevitable and unalterable fact of life. The demand for serious newspaper journalism is not confined to mainly middle-class audiences. Nor has the intellectual ascendancy of the middle-class quality press been so little contested as it now is. The present depressing state of affairs has come about, as we shall see, partly as a result of the way in which the advertising licensing system has developed.

Objection may be raised, however, to the characterisation of advertising as a licensing system on the grounds that it is entirely voluntary. Publishers are free to become independent of advertising any time they want, it could be argued, by charging a higher cover price. But, as we have seen already, high cover prices for quality papers make a relatively small contribution to their finances and do not eliminate their dependency on advertising. Publishers' freedom of action is further constrained by the way in which advertising as a subsidy system has distorted the cost and revenue structure of the press. Rising advertising expenditure has subsidised a high level of editorial outlay and low retail prices. To buck the system, particularly in the field of serious newspaper journalism, requires not only cutting back sharply on the quantity and the technical quality of the editorial service offered to the public, but also charging a higher price for it, in competition with rival papers offering a more expensive service at a cheaper price. The *Morning Star,* with editorial costs pared down to a minimum, printed on only six to eight pages, selling at a high but still uneconomic price of 12p without advertising support, is a graphic illustration of what freedom from advertising means. Thus advertising subsidies, by shaping the economic structure of the press and defining public expectations in terms of both price and editorial outlay, have perpetuated dependency on advertising. This is why none of the eight national newspapers that have closed down since 1955 even attempted to solve their economic problems by charging an economic price. This said, the declining real value of advertising subsidies for the popular press has created new opportunities as well as new problems, to which we shall return.

The Licensing Authority at Work

Important changes have occurred during the last thirty years in the way advertisers spend their money. The development of formalised marketing criteria for the selection of advertising media, informed by scientifically derived data, has greatly reduced subjective bias against radical publications in advertising allocations. The growth of working class consumption has also enhanced the advertising value of publications appealing to the working class.[39]

These two trends – the professionalisation of advertising media planning and 'the growth of affluence' – have given rise to the belief that advertising subsidies have been redistributed within the national press in favour of radical and working-class papers, and consequently that radical working-class papers like the *Daily Herald* died as a result of editorial failure rather than lack of advertising support. This view finds uncompromising expression in the McGregor Commission Report, which uncritically reproduces the conclusions of experts from the press and the advertising industry:

> It was generally agreed, however, that the history of the *Daily Herald* demonstrated some of the changes in media planning, and their effects, between the 1940s and 1950s and today. While the *Daily Herald* immediately after the war had failed to attract advertising partly because of bias against a paper with its readership profile, the advent of more systematic media planning meant that in its later years it was able to attract advertising on more equal terms.

From this it was experts concluded that:

> The reasons for the failure of the *Daily Herald* were not to do with its inability to attract advertising but with its failure to meet the changing needs of readers.[40]

This is to rewrite history, apparently with the official blessing of the McGregor Commission, in a way that obscures the censorship role of advertisers. For what is said to have happened to the *Daily Herald* in this often repeated mythology is almost the opposite of what did happen.

The *Daily Herald* had not 'failed' to attract advertising immediately after the war: on the contrary, it attracted more advertising revenue per 1000 copies than other popular dailies including the *Daily Express* and *Daily Mirror* because of the redistributive effects of newsprint rationing. In its closing years, it was not able to attract advertising 'on a more equal basis': on the contrary, it received less than half the net advertising revenue per 1000 copies of either the *Daily Mail* or *Daily Express,* and less than one-sixth of the advertising revenue per 1000 copies of *The Times,* in each of its last four years.[41] The *Daily Herald* was, in fact, progressively squeezed out of advertising schedules during the post-war period.

It is clear that this contributed directly to the closure of the *Daily Herald.* Its net advertising revenue declined from £1,965,000 in 1955 to £1,592,000 in 1964 – a net reduction of 19 per cent. Since the annual volume of advertising it published increased by 10.4 per cent during the same period, it incurred higher costs for a smaller return.[42] In real terms, advertising support for the *Daily Herald* probably declined by over 25 per cent between 1955 and 1964 at a time when its total costs, in common with those of other papers, rose sharply.

This loss of advertising was only partly the result of a decline in circulation. For other papers also lost circulation heavily during part of this period without having any reduction in advertising revenue, largely because of the rapid growth of national advertising expenditure. The *Daily Mirror,* for instance, had a net loss of 204,000 circulation in a series of bad years between 1955 and 1959. Yet its net advertising revenue increased by £2.539 million – a remarkable 83 per cent increase sustained uninterruptedly over the same five-year period. In contrast, the *Daily Herald,* which lost 384,000 circulation in the same period, also lost £305,000 net advertising revenue. Indeed, the decline in the *Daily Herald's* share of advertising did not correspond to the decline in its share of circulation. In 1955, the *Daily Herald* had a 10.8 per cent share of both national daily circulation and national daily net advertising revenue. By 1964, its share of national daily circulation had declined only modestly to 8.1 per cent, whereas its share of national daily net advertising revenue had slumped catastrophically to 3.5 per cent.[43]

The *Daily Herald's* central problem was not that it appealed to fewer people but that it appealed to the wrong people. For a time this had not mattered, since the advertising space famine caused by the early strict newsprint rationing had made advertisers willing to advertise almost anywhere in the national press. But the lifting of economic controls left the *Daily Herald* highly vulnerable, its readership profile exposed in damning detail by market research. The *Daily Herald* appealed more to men than to women, more to older than to younger people (in common with all other popular text dailies) and overwhelmingly to working-class rather than to middle-class readers. These characteristics had correlates in terms of purchasing behaviour that made the *Daily Herald* a highly marginal advertising medium. For instance, the *Daily Herald* was the most expensive popular daily for reaching car-owners in 1962, despite being the cheapest daily in which to reach adults, because large numbers of *Daily Herald* readers did not have cars.[44] This marginality of the *Daily Herald* as an advertising medium forced its management to offer progressively larger discounts on its advertising rates, at a time of increasingly cut-throat competition when market leaders were keeping advertising rates per 1000 circulation artificially low, with a resulting reduction in the *Daily Herald's* advertising revenue.

But if the *Daily Herald* was lacking in appeal to advertisers it did not lack in appeal to a section of the general public. Admittedly, the *Daily Herald* suffered as a consequence of its continuing commitment to the left during the conservative consensus of the 1950s. But this is not the same as agreeing with the verdict of Sir Denis Hamilton, Editor-in-Chief of Times Newspapers, that 'the *Herald* was beset by the problem which has dogged nearly every newspaper vowed to a political idea: not enough people wanted to read it'.[45] The *Daily Herald* 'idea' may be regarded as misguided, its readers can be dismissed as being of no social consequence. But there were, as it happens, a lot of them – in fact over five times as many readers as those of *The Times,* with which Sir Denis Hamilton is associated. With 4.7 million readers in the last year, the *Daily Herald* actually had almost double the readership of *The Times,* the *Financial Times* and the *Guardian* combined. Indeed, when it was forced to close, the *Daily Herald* was probably amongst the twenty largest circulation dailies in the world. It died, not from lack of readers, but because its readers did not constitute a valuable advertising market (see Table 11.6).

Regular *Daily Herald* readers were also exceptionally devoted to their paper. Unpublished survey research shows that *Daily Herald* readers thought more highly of their paper than the regular

TABLE 11.6   *Readership of selected national newspapers,*
1963 – 4

	Total number of readers over 15 years old '000	Proportion of readers of social grades			
		AB %	C1 %	C2 %	DE %
Daily Herald	4744	3	10	48	39
Guardian	954	45	31	15	8
The Times	917	51	25	17	8
Financial Times	552	59	28	9	5

Source: *National Readership Surveys* London: Institute of Practioners in Advertising, July 1963 – June 1964) tables 1A and 18A.
Social grades were classified as follows:
AB – upper middle class and middle class
C1 – lower middle class
C2 – skilled working class
DE – semi and unskilled working class and 'those at the lowest levels of subsistence' (Appendix E, p. 139)

readers of any other popular newspaper.[46] They also read more in their paper than the readers of other popular papers despite being overwhelmingly working class – a group that generally reads newspapers less intensively than the middle class.[47]

Yet the *Daily Herald* was only one of a number of casualties of the advertising licensing system. The *News Chronicle,* a legatee of the dissenting radical, liberal tradition, was forced to close in 1960 with a circulation six times that of the *Guardian,* and over double that of *The Times* and the *Guardian* combined. It paid a heavy price for appealing to an inferior quality of reader (even though its readers were almost as devoted as *Herald* readers).[48] It was sold, like a job lot in an auction, to the high Tory *Daily Mail.* The radical *Sunday Citizen* (formerly the *Reynolds' News*) also finally succumbed in 1967, after being progressively strangulated by lack of advertising support. Officially classified as a quality newspaper,[49] it received per 1000 copies (a basis of comparison that takes into account differences in circulation) one-tenth of the net advertising revenue of the *Sunday Times* and one-seventh of the net advertising revenue of the *Observer* in 1965.[50] By 1967, its average editorial load was only 37 per cent of that of the *Sunday Times* and 45 per cent of that of the *Observer*.[51] Deprived of the same level of subsidy, it inevitably offered an editorial service that was, in some respects, markedly inferior to that of its quality newspaper competitors.

The death of the *Daily Herald, News Chronicle* and *Sunday Citizen* decimated the social democratic press. It meant the loss of the only social democratic papers with a large readership which devoted serious attention to current affairs. The surviving pro-Labour papers are first and foremost entertainment sheets: devoting less than 10 per cent of their editorial space to political, social and economic news,[52] they scarcely constitute an alternative political voice.

The wider implications of this destruction are perhaps best highlighted by briefly considering the *Daily Herald*. Partly owned by the T.U.C., the *Daily Herald* reached the vanguard of the mass working-class movement – concentrated in the industrial heartlands of Britain, pro-trade union, overwhelmingly Labour (90 per cent in 1963), self-consciously working-class, and remarkably radical in their attitudes to a wide range of economic and political issues.[53] To judge from unpublished survey research undertaken by Odhams, the *Daily Herald* played an important role in fortifying the radical commitment of its readers and allaying a growing sense of their isolation within the working class.[54] For the *Daily Herald* provided an alternative framework of analysis and understanding that contested the dominant systems of representation in both broadcasting and the mainstream press. In its pages, trade unions, for instance, did not make 'demands' that were 'conceded' or 'rejected' in a world where the subordination of working people was accepted as natural and inevitable: trade unions represented the interests of working people who were morally entitled to a greater share of the wealth they created and a greater say in its allocation. Managements were not portrayed as largely invisible or secondary elements in industrial disputes – a frequent distortion in media coverage of industrial disputes in which groups of workers are characteristically portrayed as being in conflict not with their employers but with the general public.[55] And trade unions were not regularly protrayed in a negative context as 'bad news', causing social disruption, loss of production and damage to the economy, but as organisations fighting for the welfare of working people. The *Daily Herald* was a social democratic paper which negotiated rather than rejected the dominant ideology. But the commitments and perspectives that shaped its selection and treatment of news, and its relatively detailed political commentary and analysis, helped daily to sustain a social democratic sub-culture within the working class. The *Daily Herald* devoted more of its space to political, social and economic affairs than any other mass circulation daily, and at one time during the post-war period more than any other quality daily.[56] It was, in fact, the foremost quality newspaper of the working class.

Its death, and those of the *News Chronicle* and *Sunday Citizen,* was a symptom of the progressive erosion in post-war Britain of a popular radical tradition. But the loss of all three papers, which had helped to sustain this tradition with an aggregate average issue readership of 9.3 million people in their last full year of publication,[57] has also accelerated this erosion and contributed to the cumulative crisis within the Labour movement. The cultural base that has sustained active participation within the Labour movement has been slowly disintegrating. The Labour Party has ceased to exist as a mass movement in most parts of the country: individual membership of the Labour Party has declined by as much as two-thirds since 1952, while attendance at most branch meetings has fallen sharply.[58] Active participation in many unions has also declined, contrary to popular belief. Of course, the loss of these social democratic papers, including one that was essentially liberal, has been only one factor in the crisis of social democracy in Britain. But it is not something that democratic socialists – or those of whatever persuasion who want to maintain a healthy democratic system – can afford to ignore.

The deaths of these three papers, and the increased political imbalance within the press that they have caused, raise a puzzling question. What has happened to the advertising redistribution in favour of working-class publications proclaimed by those who argue that advertising does not significantly distort the market structure of the press, and hence what is published? The answer would seem to be that no such systematic redistribution has taken place in the national newspaper press. Indeed, if anything, rather the reverse has happened in the post-war period. A comprehensive analysis of the changing pattern of advertising distribution between individual newspapers is not possible because a small minority of publishing houses – including one whose papers regularly proclaim 'the public's right to know' and the need for greater public disclosure – declined to disclose past revenue figures. Caution must also be exercised in interpreting changes over time since the social class of readers, and its correlates, is only one factor influencing the distribution of advertising expenditure between newspapers. The available data, of which illustrative fiures are provided in Table 11.7, suggest none the less that the gap between up-market, middle-market and down-market Sunday newspapers, as measured by the comparable index of net advertising revenue per 1000 copies, increased between 1945 and 1975: in other words, the weighting of advertising subsidies in favour of the more affluent readerships has increased rather than declined, with much of the increase taking place in the 1950s. The pattern is rather different in the case of dailies because of the generous newsprint quotas obtained by quality papers during rationing. But between 1955 and 1975 the difference in advertising support for up-market quality papers compared with the rest has substantially increased (see Table 11.7).

The effect of more systematic media planning and increased working-class affluence has been offset by a number of factors. First and foremost, the lifting of government economic controls caused a less equitable distribution of advertising subsidies against a background of remarkably stable inequalities in the distribution of disposable wealth and income in post-war British society.[59] In addition, quality newspapers have benefited disproportionately from the massive increase in classified and financial advertising; suffered less from competition from commercial TV, partly because its readers tend to be light I.T.V. viewers; and suffered less from the decline of manufacturers' consumer advertising as a proportion of display advertising.[60] Thus, an exclusive focus on the growth of consumption and laudable changes in the process of media planning has served to obscure the continuing advertising discrimination against predominantly working-class publications in the national newspaper press.

Operating under License

According to the conventional wisdom, advertising dependency does not influence the market orientation of newspapers except

	1945 £	1955 £	1965 £	1975 £
Dailies				
The Times (up-market)				
Net advertising revenue	63,900	1,542,600	3,215,000	8,963,000
Net advertising per 1000 copies	10.20	24.4	40.51	90.64
Daily Express (middle-market)				
Net advertising revenue	382,764	5,373,430	13,193,786	14,520,994
Net advertising per 1000 copies	0.38	4.61	10.05	16.25
Daily Herald/Sun (down-market)				
Net advertising revenue	321,251	1,965,241	1,678,373	12,612,000
Net advertising per 1000 copies	0.52	3.86	4.28	11.81
Sundays				
Sunday Times (up-market)				
Net advertising revenue	100,017	664,100	7,615,000	16,713,000
Net advertising per 1000 copies	4.18	22.83	116.38	232.90
Sunday Express (middle-market)				
Net advertising revenue	99,837	1,179,635	5,290,532	10,347,188
Net advertising per 1000 copies	0.91	7.60	24.77	53.56
Sunday Pictorial/Sunday Mirror (down-market)				
Net advertising revenue	148,000	981,000	2,390,000	4,404,000
Net advertising per 1000 copies	1.14	3.69	9.28	19.92

* All figures for net advertising revenue are supplied by publishers save for the figure for the *Sun* in 1975, which has been estimated on the basis of detailed information. All advertising figures relate to publishers' financial years, unless otherwise stated, although they have been treated as if they corresponded to calendar years when calculating estimates of net advertisement revenue per 1000 copies. These have been calculated by dividing the annual net advertising revenue of each newspaper by the number of days on which it was published, and by dividing the product by its annual net circulation and multiplying by a 1000. All circulation estimates are the average of two six-monthly average circulations derived from the Audit Bureau of Circulation except in the case of the *Daily Herald* and *Sunday Pictorial* in 1945, when no audited figures are available and consequently publishers' figures have been used.

possibly by making newspapermen pay more attention to their readers. 'To attract advertisements newspapers have to attract readers', proclaims the Advertising Association, 'but this presumably is the purpose of their editorial activities in the first place'.[61] The underlying assumption, is, of course, that advertisers are neutral intermediaries between the press and the public: 'Advertising', writes John Whale, for instance 'doubles the price on each new reader's head ... but there is not much a newspaperman can do to differentiate a double from a single dose of zeal to attract new readers'.[62]

But the strength of the dose varies considerably, as we have seen, since some readers are more valuable to advertisers – and hence to publishers – than others. Indeed, in some circumstances, the attraction of new readers of the wrong sort can lose money. The classic illustration of this is the strange career of *The Times* in the late 1960s and early 1970s, documented in an admirable study by Fred Hirsch and David Gordon.[63] Between 1965 and 1969, *The Times* increased its circulation by a remarkable 69 per cent in an aggressive promotion campaign that recruited large numbers of lower-middle and even working-class readers to the paper. These additional sales increased losses because the inferior quality of the new readership failed to generate a corresponding increase in advertising. The success of *The Times* in attracting more readers of the wrong sort was its undoing. Saddled with a massive loss, it was forced to set about shedding part of its new readership as a conscious act of management policy initiated in the early 1970s in order to improve its financial position.

This highlights one important effect of advertising on the conduct of newspapers. The large advertising subsidies of quality newspapers are their reward for attracting a predominantly middle-class audience. A marked dilution in the social quality of their readers carries, on the other hand, a heavy penalty – a reduction in the level of subsidy per reader and, because quality papers cost much more than their net retail price to produce, heavy losses on copies sold to the public that are not fully recouped by advertising. The system of rewards and punishments institutionalised by advertising finance of the press thus helps to restrict the circulation of quality newspapers to the upper stratum of society.

Market specialisation is not undesirable in itself. There is, in fact, a lot to be said for a system of support that encourages quality provision for relatively small, homogeneous audiences. Much of the character of the *Daily Telegraph* or *Financial Times,* both important and distinguished papers, would be lost, for instance, if their economic survival depended upon maximising their appeal to the largest possible audience. An acute problem arises, however, because a different set of pressures operates on the popular press. Whereas advertising encourages audience specialisation at the top end of the market, it has the opposite effect at the bottom end of the market. This has resulted in the progressive cultural polarisation of journalism between quality newspapers for élites and increasingly tabloid-style journalism for the mass market. For the effect of advertising on the popular newspaper press is to encourage an orientation towards either a larger, less differentiated audience (and resulting stress on material that is of universal appeal to people with dissimilar interests and backgrounds) or, in some instances, a deliberate move up-market oriented towards more affluent readers. Both these marketing orientations are profoundly de-radicalising.

The impact of advertising on the market orientation of the popular press is well illustrated by the troubled post-war career of the *Daily Herald.* When economic controls on the press were enforced (1940–56) the management of the *Daily Herald* was able to pursue a policy of relative editorial integrity in which the business of collecting advertisements was kept largely separate from the editorial task of running a newspaper. Its management sought to maximise advertising revenue by selling the attributes of its existing readership rather than chasing after the sort of readership that would generate most advertising revenue. An imaginative advertising promotion campaign was initiated from the late 1940s onwards that sought to sell the working class as such by emphasising the growing affluence of working people; that focused attention upon heavy spending by *Daily Herald* readers on certain commodities (such as cereals, fats, desserts, beer, sugar preservatives and canned meat); that tried to sell the *Daily Herald's* influence as the paper read by councillors; and, increasingly desperately and disingenuously, as the paper primarily of the labour aristocracy (the skilled worker or worker in high-wage occupations).[64]

The diminishing success of these efforts was an important factor in causing the *Daily Herald's* management to reconsider the paper's editorial strategy. Two basic options were discussed in the mid-1950s – both of which were attempted during the next two decades. The first option was the Murdoch's *Sun* in embryo, the basic ingredients of which were less politics and current affairs coverage, and more human interest stories, more photographs and strips.[65] Its inspiration sprang from the recurrent market research finding that human interest stories to do with sex, love, romance, crime, celebrities, accidents and humorous incidents are of universal appeal: they are read almost equally by men and women, young and old alike, whereas home and international affairs appeal primarily to men and to the older age group.[66] Yet it was young people and women – particularly women – that would help sell more advertising. The new approach, according to a memorandum that landed on the editor's desk in May 1955, would 'bring in women – vital to the advertising department'.[67]

The second option, and the one that was adopted after a period of uncertainty, was to push the *Daily Herald* up-market in an attempt to attract middle-class readers that would generate more advertising. Cautiously pursued under John Beavan's editorship (1960–4) with the full approval of the paper's new commercial proprietors from 1961, Daily Mirror Newspapers, it involved adding new features (such as features about books, opera, ballet and classical music) aimed primarily at a middle-class audience, as well as loosening the paper's ties with the T.U.C. and Labour Party. While the change did not alienate traditional *Daily Herald* readers, it did not succeed in attracting the middle-class readers and additional advertising revenue that had been hoped for.

Heavy losses compelled a reassessment culminating in a relaunch of the *Daily Herald* as the *Sun* in 1964 – a new paper in which the T.U.C. no longer had a 49 per cent shareholding. The relaunch carried the John Beavan concept of the *Daily Herald* to its logical marketing conclusion. The new *Sun* was designed as a middle-market paper that would appeal to a new coalition of readers consisting of working class, politically radical, *Herald* readers, and young middle-class 'social radicals' – an alliance that would be socially balanced in terms of class, age and sex. 'The new paper', confided an internal memorandum in January 1964, 'is to have the more representative make-up essential to advertisers'.[68] The implications of this were spelt out in extensive pre-launch research into 'social radicalism' – defined by attitudes to sex before marriage, capital punishment, wider public access to (but not abolition of) public schools, and other liberal issues. Social radicals by this definition turned out to be only marginally more inclined to vote Labour than Liberal and Conservative, to constitute almost as high a proportion of *Daily Telegraph* as of *Daily Herald* readers, and to include amongst their favourite reading the society gossip columns of William Hickey in the *Daily Express* and Paul Tanfield in the *Daily Mail*.[69] A paper that would have a balanced profile pleasing to advertisers would clearly have a very different character from the cloth-cap militancy of the *Daily Herald*.

The new mutation pleased few people. The *Sun* alienated *Daily Herald* readers, yet failed to recruit in sufficient numbers young readers from the middle and lower middle class.[70] The only remaining option – to brush the dust off the 1955 proposal – was rejected because it meant competing with the *Daily Mirror,* another paper owned by the same group.[71] It was left to Murdoch, who took over the *Sun* in 1969, to interpret in his own inimitable style the ideas that had been put forward by the Odhams marketing department fourteen years before. These ideas were not particularly original, of course, since they represented a literal market research reading of how best to maximise sales in the mass market, with priority given to women and young people. The result was a newspaper given over almost entirely to human interest stories, sport and entertainment features, in which home and international affairs news coverage (a minority interest in mass marketing terms as much before as after the introduction of T.V.) was allocated a mere 7 per cent of editorial space in 1976 (see Table 11.8). The *Sun's* commercial formula proved successful, resulting in rising sales, increased penetration of the female and youth markets, and increasing advertising receipts per reader. But it was a very different paper from its predecessor, a point that was emphasised when it weighed in strongly behind the Conservative Party in the divisive miners' General Election of 1974.

The transition from the *Daily Herald* to the *Sun* illustrates the dynamics of the popular newspaper market. The characteristics of the old *Daily Herald* that commanded intense loyalty amongst its regular readers and made it such a distinctive voice in popular journalism rested on a market base similar to that of all quality newspapers – a socially homogeneous audience with shared values and understandings. Its reduction to a well-processed commodity with a universalised appeal to a heterogeneous mass audience was the inevitable price that had to be paid in a market where quantity is the only bankable alternative to social quality.

What happened to the *Daily Herald* was merely an exaggerated version of what happened to many other popular daily and Sunday newspapers during the post-war period. News coverage of home and international affairs was progressively downgraded to becoming a still more minor and trivial feature of popular journalism. Admittedly, part of this decline was a consequence of the distortion caused by newsprint rationing when the space shortage resulted in a larger proportion of space being given to coverage of current affairs. But it also reflected the growing commercial pressure on popular newspapers to maximise their sales and advertising revenue by gaining the largest possible audience with a balanced profile (including women and young people who, in terms of general market preferences, show limited interest in current affairs). As a result, public affairs news coverage has fallen to below 10 per cent in many popular papers and, in the case of all popular papers save one that were examined,

TABLE 11.8   *Home and international news coverage* in popular national newspapers, 1936 – 76, as a percentage of editorial space*

	1936 %	1946 %	1976 %
Daily Herald/Sun	22	33	7
Daily Mail	15	27	12
Daily Express	15	28	11
Daily Mirror	9	17	9
Sunday Express	8	20	5
Sunday Pictorial/Sunday Mirror	7	15	5
Sunday People	10	15	2

Sample: 198 issues

* Including (*a*) news about social, economic and political affairs; (*b*) industrial news; (*c*) financial/commercial news; (*d*) medical, scientific and technical news; (*e*) news about other public affairs.

to a level below that in 1936. 'News', in its traditional sense, is no longer what newspapers mainly report or, for that matter, what they comment upon – outside the quality press.[72]

The Crisis of the Subsidy System

Objections have been raised to various public subsidy schemes for the press on the grounds that they would lead to 'feather-bedding' and inflated costs, help the strong at the expense of the weak, and undermine the economic stability of the press. These objections apply with even greater force to the existing support system – commercial advertising in its unregulated form – than to many of the schemes that have been put forward. What follows, given the space available, is necessarily only a brief summary.

The growth of advertising expenditure on the press has exerted an upwards pressure on newspaper costs. It has helped to fund higher paging levels, the recruitment of more journalist staff, larger administration and promotion costs, and far from parsimonious pay and manning agreements amongst production staff. Between 1948 and 1975, advertising spending on national newspapers increased from £10 million to £162 million.[73] This has helped to finance a massive increase in the annual costs of the average London daily (excluding the *Daily Worker/Morning Star*) from £1,570,363 in 1946 to £28,140,111 in 1974.[74]

But the growth in advertising patronage has, generally speaking, helped the strong at the expense of the weak. A detailed analysis reveals that it has been usually the market leaders, buoyed up by rising advertising receipts, who have set the pace in terms of rising paging levels. Increased editorial outlay has not only helped to enhance their market appeal, it has also forced weaker papers to increase their paging and costs in order to stay competitive without being able to draw upon the same level of advertising support.[75]

Advertising funding has not only contributed to a deterioration in the economic position of vulnerable papers, over the long term it has also contributed to a deterioration in the economic position of the national press as a whole. Structural changes in advertising expenditure and competition from T.V. have contributed to a weakening of demand for display advertising space in the national press at a time of sharply rising costs.[76] Newspaper managements have sought to maintain their market share by keeping their advertising rates low in relation to costs. The result has been a steady decline in the real return on advertising in the national newspaper press.

Thus national popular dailies obtained an estimated average 40 per cent surplus on advertising published in 1960, 15 per cent surplus by 1973 and no surplus at all in 1975. National quality dailies suffered a less marked decline in their advertisement profit margins during the same period, falling from 60 per cent in 1960 to 35 per cent in 1975. Popular Sunday papers fared rather worse, and some popular Sunday papers probably published advertisements at a loss in 1975.[77] It is perhaps scarcely surprising that in 1975 only four dailies and one Sunday paper – out of a total of seventeen national papers – made a profit.[78] The whole economic structure of the national press industry has been based on high costs fuelled by rising advertising receipts. The reduction in the real value of these receipts has resulted, notwithstanding some cost saving and more aggressive cover pricing policies, in a cumulative economic crisis in Fleet Street, which the downturn in the economy and in advertising budgets has served merely to exacerbate.

It is against this wider background that the changes in the post-war press must be seen. The reason why the loss of advertising sustained by papers like the *Daily Herald* and *News Chronicle* was so disastrous was because their costs were rising partly in competitive response to richer rivals. And the underlying cause of the growing commercialisation of the popular press – and its increasingly frantic pursuit of the common denominator of the mass market – is the long-term deterioration of national newspapers' financial position, and the increasingly desperate survival strategies they have been forced to adopt.

It is tempting to hope that the subsidy crisis will resolve itself by newspapers breaking free of advertising dependence, and all the distortions that it produces. Unfortunately this is wish-fulfilment, since the overwhelming majority of press publications – quality daily and Sunday papers, regional daily and local weekly papers, and most categories of magazine – continue to make a large surplus from advertising, and continue to depend upon this surplus for their profitability. Indeed, the surplus on advertisement production has scarcely declined in many sectors of the press during the last two decades.[79] Only in the case of established, mass circulation national newspapers, enjoying large-scale economies, has the real value of advertising subsidies become temporarily marginal during the period 1974–5 as a result of a self-defeating competitive policy the full implications of which were concealed from some managements.[80] An adjustment is currently taking place in Fleet Street but it is an adjustment that is restoring the profit margins of popular newspaper advertising rather than creating a move towards emancipation from advertising dependence.

Reform

In a survey conducted by the McGregor Commission, more journalists named advertisers as an 'undesirable influence' on their work than anything else.[81] Their assessment is more sensible than the ill-considered and complacent judgement of the McGregor Commission.

The problems identified in this essay are none the less relatively intractable. Within the existing framework of a market-based, advertising-funded press, there can be no complete solution to them. There is, however, one important measure that can be adopted within the existing framework which would help to ameliorate perhaps the most serious problem that has been discussed – the unequal distribution of advertising subsidies between élite and working-class audiences. This commercial discrimination has been crucially important, as we have seen, in creating a national press that is politically unbalanced and culturally polarised.

Any reform of the role of advertising in the press must address itself to the question of how to compensate for the unequal distribution of advertising subsidies between middle-class and working-class minority audiences. The current crisis of the advertising funding system does not make this question redundant. Thus, to take but one example, if a new quality daily paper was to be established with a circulation comparable to that of *The Times* but with a predominantly working-class audience, it would be forced to close as soon as its launch subsidy ran out. *The Times* makes an annual *surplus* on its advertising of over £3 million and still makes a loss.[82] Without something like comparable support, a working-class quality newspaper of comparable stature is doomed.

Furthermore, the need to redress the political imbalance of the national newspaper press is not offset by the residual presence of a radical weekly press. Radical weeklies do not and cannot provide a substitute for a radical national daily with resources at least comparable to its rivals with a similar circulation. Indeed, radical weeklies are themselves the victims of the advertising system. Whereas advertising provides massive subsidies for magazines like *The Economist* and *Homes and Gardens* that deliver specialised markets advertisers want to reach, it provides practically no support for small-circulation political weeklies like *Tribune*. This has helped to contain the development of radical political opinion weeklies by denying them the support necessary to develop their editorial service and to reduce their very high prices, while fostering the development of magazines of greater utility to advertisers.

Perhaps the best solution lies in establishing an Advertising Deficit Fund that would partially compensate publications which, because of their character and audience, are unable to attract substantial advertising. The fund would operate in only three priority sections of the press in order to concentrate limited funds where they would be most needed. In order to be eligible for assistance, publications would have to satisfy requirements in relation to the frequency of publication, the proportion of space devoted to current affairs news and comment (irrespective of its political orientation) and a minimum level of audited circulation. The purpose of these eligibility qualifications is to ensure that support would be given only to publications that fit into the quality newspaper (daily or Sunday) and political opinion weekly categories and are able to demonstrate a measurable level of public demand.

Publications exceeding an established circulation ceiling would also be ineligible for support in order to exclude mass circulation papers, enjoying big-scale economies, from the scheme. The level of support from the Advertising Deficit Fund would be fixed in relation to a specified ratio of advertising and sales subject to periodical review by the administering authority. A scheme operating on similar principles was introduced on a modest scale in France in 1973, and variations of the same scheme have been under active consideration in the Netherlands.

The administering authority would be appointed by the

government and accountable to Parliament. This makes it theoretically possible for the government to pack the authority with its own supporters and consequently for the ratio between sales and advertising determining the allocation of funds to be manipulated for political or ideological purposes. Similar problems of political manipulation arise in the appointments to the Independent Broadcasting Authority, the Board of Governors of the B.B.C. and the the judiciary, to mention only a few public bodies: we have managed to cope with these problems as have, incidentally, other governments in Europe operating selective press subsidy schemes. It need hardly be pointed out that untempered market allocation does not constitute a neutral alternative.

The overall funding of the authority would be determined by government, and its sources of finance would come from the Exchequer. The cost of the fund could be supported, in part at least, from within the newspaper industry.

A tax on press excess profits could be introduced on a broadly similar principle to the T.V. levy. The regional newspaper monopolies are mostly highly profitable and enjoy an impregnable market position in many ways comparable to that of T.V. companies.[83] The excess profits of monopoly should be harnessed to promote diversity.

The proposal for an Advertising Deficit Fund should not be considered in isolation. It is complementary to proposals outlined elsewhere in this book to facilitate the launch and establishment of new publications. Taken together they represent the first step towards creating a more representative and diverse press.

Part 5

The Future of the Press

Chapter 12

New Print Technology and Newspaper Culture

Bruce Page

The bloodline of the Royal Commission on the Press is visible in every page of its report – by Expediency out of Academic Sociology, a familiar couple of gallopers. From the female parent comes its principal characteristic: the laborious identification of the obvious. A voice which usually informs us that a large majority of marriages are between heterosexual pairs, or that more economists than foremen decorators have been to Oxford, tells us a number of things about British newspapers. There are quite a lot of them. Fewer these days, of course. One can't say how many there will be soon. The popular ones publish less foreign news than the posh ones. 'In the *Sun* and the *Daily Mirror* pictures of naked girls are prominent' (p.78). Some say the newspapers are rather good. Others say they are rather bad. On questions like this we have tended – well, to take up a position between these two extremes.

There is only one funny moment: a dissenting sermon by Mr Malcolm Horsman saying that his colleagues aren't fierce enough about conflcts of interest. People may remember Mr Horsman as the jovial soul who, when boss of Bowater–Ralli, organised certain share options which – to the extent of some £750,000 – were in the potential interest of himself and other directors, but, arguably at least, against the interests of the shareholders, who were given no information about this intriguing apparatus when it was set up. (When this matter was discussed in the *Sunday Times,* Mr Horsman announced that his part – £500,000 – was to be given to a charity, which he did not name.) Otherwise, the report is dedicated to the highly respectable proposition that the truth is an average.

One of the obviousnesses upon which the Commission stumbled is that something called New Technology is about to happen to Fleet Street. This, it thought, might do something to gee up the profitability of national newspapers. How much, it would be hard to say. The literary material being processed by these new devices would of course be the mixture as at present. One cannot expect much more from folk whose idea of discussing the content of the national press didn't go much beyond hiring Professor Denis McQuail to apply tape measures to it. ('Quality papers devote roughly half as much editorial space as populars to pictures.') And as the intellectual condition of our national life is not too luminous just now, the grey outlook of the Royal Commission may well be justified by events. ('Pause. Look solemn. Return to Même Chose.') But if change is to occur, we must at least preserve it as an idea, and I would like to suggest that new technology presents some possibilities more interesting that a minor black shift in the financial spectrum of Fleet Street.

Despite the Royal Commission, the quality of newspaper language – which is a serious part of our national literary experience – does matter. It has been cogently argued by writers as diverse as Lawrence and Isherwood that the way words are treated in newspapers is a central defect in modern society. In *Ulysses* Joyce actually shows language disintegrating amid the operations of a newspaper office. Possibly, this has something to do with the mechanical conditions of production under the obsolescent linotype technology. Borrowing one of Joyce's celebrated cross-heads, we need to think carefully about How A Great Daily Organ Is Turned Out.

The striking difference between newspaper articles and other forms of writing is that they rarely have a beginning, a middle and an end. Stories told by traditional practitioners, from Homer onwards, may or may not start with a bang. But generally there is some ebb and flow of tension along the way, and something akin to a bang near the ending. In spite of certain interesting experiments, most of the human race still follow this sequence, whether writing a financial analysis or an erotic lyric. Newspaper stories, however, *always* start with a bang and conclude, after several diminuendo bangs, with a whimper. The primary skill drilled into a young journalist is 'putting on a punchy intro'. The technical ideal is to compose the first paragraph in such a way as to make all subsequent ones redundant. The trainee is told that this is necessary to seize the reader's attention, and there is something in this. It is no bad thing to start with something interesting. But the dynamics of the typical newspaper story exclude one of the writer's most reliable devices – the unresolved tension, which you must read on to resolve. Newspaper stories always say whodunnit at the start, which means that only frantic energy can prevent them from declining into tedium.

The form is called the 'inverted pyramid'. Much skill is needed to force the real world – which principally flows the other way – into this arsey-versey configuration, and the fit is rarely snug. It is a kind of mannerism – in the sense that the Mannerist artists largely employed their cunning to violate the known rules of picture-making. Of course, some pretty good writers have been attracted – or forced – into this mannerism, and some may have transcended it, in somewhat the way Michelangelo transcended visual mannerism. But it remains, on the whole, 'a style best suited to neurotic artists'.

* * *

To repeat, the practice is justified by literary theory; you have got to grab the reader. But the decisive cause, I think, is mechanical.

No literary theory prevents you from making a newspaper without inverted pyramids, and whether it would anaesthetise the readers would be interesting to know. (Television soap operas, which appear to grip with a hideous strength, do not bother to invert any pyramids.) But you could not produce such a paper with Fleet Street's present 'hot metal' technology. The inverted pyramid is there to make sure that every story can be 'cut from the bottom'. English is best written character by character, and at least word by word. Much newspaper prose, though, seems to have been assembled from large, pre-fabricated slabs – and so, in a sense, it has been.

It was hard to make big business out of newspapers while working with Caxton's system of moveable type. For each character in a piece of manuscript, someone had to hand-pick a piece of type from store, and hand-fit it to its place in a line. The cumbrousness of such a process can be verified by an experiment with a John Bull printing set. Mergenthaler began a profound change when he designed a machine to select – at keyboard command – not a piece of type, but a re-usable mould for a piece of type. This, followed by others, the machine would clamp together in a line of given length, thus making a continuous mould ready to form, say, forty characters. Injection and swift cooling of molten metal then produced the linotype slug. In speed, this was a great advance on Caxton. But in some respects it was a step back.

A column of type composed character by character from individual pieces is a precise and flexible analogue of a manuscript. If you delete one character from the manuscript you can delete its precise correspondent in the type-column without having to change much else. Indeed, if you don't mind leaving the right-hand margin ragged (as in typescript) you will probably not have any consequent alterations for the deletion of several characters. But to delete one character from a piece of linotype setting, you must discard a whole slug, and this may entail re-setting many of the subsequent ones. The machine sets news ones fairly fast, but all the same there are great problems about rapidly assembling a batch of linotype-set articles into a newspaper. A 1000-word article might contain some 5000 characters. If it is any good, it is a unique combination of several hundred component words: some interchangeable (prepositions, etc.) and some which in context are unique (adjectives, typically). Looked at another way, the article is a 5000-item pattern based on the 90-odd basic signs of the 'alphanumeric' keyboard. From any viewpoint, it is an intricate artefact. The linotype analogue exists as about 100 slugs of metal. Most, if not all, will be unique as signs. But from the viewpoint of print engineering – the cohesion to resist high pressure – they are all required to be identical. As an analogue for a piece of literary creation, a set of lino slugs is not ideal. In book production, where there is usually time available to make things fit – or to expand the dimensions of the book – this doesn't matter. But a newspaper must be assembled from many distinct items, without time to spare, and compressed into a most inflexible format. The pages are represented by shallow metal boxes ('formes'), which must be tight-packed with slugs, to a capacity which tolerates little variation.

In the writing and editing process, you can estimate roughly how many bits of metal a given number of words will 'make', but you cannot get it just right except by chance. Even if you counted every character and half-character, you would be defeated by the fact that linotype machines must have variable spacing, controlled by their operators. And no two operators set to the same density. So there is always an excess or surplus of metal parts when you come to 'put a page away'. Usually, lots of separate stories have been considered at the manuscript stage, and the (unknown) length of each one affects the (unknown) length of all the others. Because you cannot afford infinite linotype capacity, you have to set copy 'as it comes': therefore the slugs for the beginning of a story are apt to be packed into the forme before the final sections have even reached the lino keyboards.

Of course, when you work on manuscript, everything remains flexible. To reduce length, you can write in new and economical forms wherever you like, and compression may give more vigour to the writing. But this is not so with linotype slugs. You must look for 'clean cuts': that is, excisions which can be made with little or no re-setting of lines – in other words, cuts which are made for engineering reasons, decided by mechanical, not literary, criteria.

An example will illustrate the process. Imagine a piece of news agency copy which has originated in England and been linoset for inclusion in a Canadian paper:

1. Mr James Wallas, Prime Minister
2. of Canada, collapsed and died
3. last night while addressing in
4. full armor a meeting of the
5. Knights Whose Armor Never Did
6. Squeak. He was speaking at St
7. Paul's Cathedral.

This has made seven lines of metal (14 per cent over) and we have room only for six. The obvious cut, from a writing viewpoint, is the label 'Prime Minister of Canada'. That was inserted for British consumption, but is otiose in Canada. It should be dropped to preserve the remarkable image of a man armed cap-à-pie, addressing a meeting amid the baroque splendour of St. Paul's, and suddenly clanging down like Astur in the Lays of Ancient Rome. But observe the consequences of such a cut:

1. Mr James Wallas collapsed and
2. died last night while address
3. -ing in full armor a meeting
4. of the Knights Whose Armor
5. Never Did Squeak. He was speak
6. -ing at St Paul's Cathedral.

The length is all right, but every line has had to be re-set. This is expensive – but the greater problem is that re-setting for fit on such a scale will wreck the deadline of the newspaper. The only solution is to cut 'from the bottom':

1. Mr James Wallas, Prime Minister
2. of Canada, collapsed and died
3. last night while addressing in
4. full armor a meeting of the
5. Knights Whose Armor Never Did
6. Squeak.

We are in without re-setting, for the compositor at the forme can shear off the characters after 'Squeak' and pack out with blank metal. But the content of the paragraph has declined in quality.

'Clean' cuts on this scale are what is required to get a hot-metal newspaper safely through its production process, and it requires a kind of violence to the written word which does no good to those who practise it without intermission. (Done in moderation, it may even be good mental exercise, like composing verses in highly contrived forms.)

*   *   *

The chief raw material of the hot-metal paper, then, is a highly specialised kind of writing. Old hands used to take pride in producing copy which could not merely be cut from the bottom – but which could be cut anywhere without apparent damage. Certain words exhibit a similar quality. But their basic vitality is rarely impressive.

The role of the large forces of sub-editors who dominate the national newspaper industry is first to ensure that all material which is sent to the linotype keyboards possesses the necessary nondescript, plasma-like quality, and then in the composing room itself to assist the printers to slice and slot it into the machinery. To adapt a famous joke: newspaper writing is to writing as military music is to music. Given the conditions of production, the wonder is that it is not worse.

On the whole we have probably benefited from the expansion of the newspaper business which hot-metal technology procured, although it would be hard to draw up an accurate balance sheet. It would be a pity, however, if the ill-effects of its deficiencies should persist any longer than necessary. Unhappily, there is a pronounced tendency to make any new technology closely resemble old ones in its mode of operation – losing, therefore, many of the potential advantages. Very possibly, the intense conservatism of the newspaper culture will ensure that computerised newspapers will be just as fuzzily written, just as mannerist, as hot-metal newspapers – just as neurotic in their alternations between the tedious and the frantic.

Yet computerised text handling offers quite fresh possibilities. The computer's model of any story it is handling is a very accurate analogue indeed of the manuscript (I do not of course mean to imply that the machines used are analogue computers) – indeed in a properly employed system it *is* the manuscript, and has all and more of the flexibility possessed by paper manuscript.

Typically, a computerised system operates with a keyboard based on the ordinary alphanumeric system, but with a good many more controls. It is like a larger, more complex typewriter, with an electronic screen in place of a sheet of paper. Characters composed on the keyboard appear on the screen, moving off the top as the pile of writing builds up. (One set of controls exist to 'scroll' material backwards and forwards so that earlier sections may be examined.) The story exists not as marks on paper, nor as a tray of metal slugs, but as magnetic traces in the computer memory. The computer has no trouble changing one word, or one character, at the beginning of 2000 words of solid setting – or indeed at any point whatever. So far as human reaction times are concerned, all the consequent alterations are made instantaneously. If an article – like the example paragraph – is 14 per cent too long, or 40 per cent too short, it does not matter where and in how many places the adjustments are made. No engineering considerations obtrude upon the literary process. There is no re-setting problem, for nothing requires to be set until all the problems of fit that bedevil newspaper-making have been solved, or anyway brought as close as possible to solution. Once a text has been produced which is capable of fitting the available spaces – and the computer knows precisely how much type each and every article will make – then the text can be turned into phototype in a time-span which is operationally negligible.

Potentially, the newspaper culture, in its present form, is made obsolete. But discussion has centred on only one aspect of this – the proposed reduction in number of printers. It is perhaps to be expected in a society as thoroughly poisoned as is ours by class and privilege that economies arising from new processes are rarely seen otherwise than as occasions for redundancies among *manual* workers. The skills of the printer, to be sure, are undermined. But so, in logic, is much of the work of journalists, and very much less has been said about this.

The non-journalist generally assumes that the typical newspaper man or woman is a reporter: someone whose business is to go about in the world trying to discover what happens, and who then tries to describe in writing such discoveries as can be made. Sophisticated members of the public have no doubt noticed that many newspaper writers have slipped away from this difficult ideal – in which the tension between hypothesis and experience must be endlessly maintained – and have drifted into punditry – the dreary territories of Chalfont, Levin, Johnson and the country of the paranoid left, where hypotheses, scarcely touched by experience, proliferate like maggots in the sun. But not only is it the case that not all writers are reporters: a majority of national newspaper journalists do not claim to be writers at all. Like many armies, Fleet Street is much more tail then teeth.

In Appendix 16 the Royal Commission tabulates the results of analysing the full-time staffs of all national newspapers. Only 37.7 per cent were classed as 'reporters and correspondents'. The categories of 'senior editorial' (19.7 per cent and 'sub-editors'

(23.0 per cent) add up together to 56.7 per cent. I think it would be hard for people with Fleet Street experience to deny that the distinction between these two categories is a matter of status rather than of function: the 'senior editorial' being for the most part sub-editors who have been promoted. 'Other editorial', a seemingly miscellaneous category, accounts for 14 per cent. No significant numbers of these people are likely to resemble writers: a majority probably have functions similar to sub-editors (certainly desk-bound functions for the most part). The Commission's account therefore suggests that about 60 per cent of national newspaper journalists are engaged in the editing and production processes, in which the methods and values of the hot-metal system continue, naturally, to dominate. (Fresher technologies exist to some extent in the provinces. But Fleet Street, even if it makes little money these days, makes most of the journalistic values employed at present.)

Of course, computerised systems could not eliminate editing, nor should they. They might, however, eliminate the gross over-editing which accounts for perhaps half of all editorial expenditure.

I suspect the effect of editing upon quality of writing might be described in a fairly simple chart. One sensitive editing process, after the basic act of creation, produces a steep increase in quality. Further processes, however necessary they may be for legal and bureaucratic reasons, produce little if any further improvement, and after two or three processes a swift decline begins. Much newspaper language has to penetrate seven or eight editing processes, whereupon mere avoidance of disaster becomes a triumph. Some processes are inserted to try to minimise errors which are introduced by other editing processes – as in ill-designed medical systems, many doctors are employed in repairing the injuries inflicted by other doctors through misguided attempts to heal. There are complexities in this which the Commission did not try to resolve. All journalists *start* as reporters, but many specialise as sub-editors after as little as four or five years' reporting – which is about as long as it takes most of us to discover how bad we are at it. Not only are senior editors drawn largely from those who gave up reporting fairly young: the entire culture of an office tends to be dominated by sub-editors, because in the nature of the work, they are around the place, and the reporters who are any good are not. In Appendix 16. the Royal Commission shows that a good many of the reporters and correspondents are not even based in the main offices, but are 'elsewhere . . . and overseas'. Photographers, incidentally, are only 5.8 per cent. One final thought: journalism has long flattered itself because it has always paid men and women the same rates. And obviously many of the best reporters are women. But only recently have a very few women been allowed to work in sub-editing and production – almost incredibly, because in so far as production work must be done, it is much more suitable than reporting for women who want to bring up children. In sexist Britain, the absence of women from the subs' table and the composing room is perhaps as good a guide as anything to where power is actually concentrated.

*   *   *

Moral, industrial and intellectual problems ramify from these propositions. At present, the new technology debate is being conducted almost entirely in squalid terms of deciding which manual workers should be chucked out of the over-laden lifeboat. Indeed, the only real 'debate' is about the price the fellows might extract for co-operating in their own removal. Yet the work performed by many of those who intend to remain aboard the supposedly more commodious vessel is no less unnecessary than that of the manual workers who are to be eliminated, and is vastly more anti-social in its effects.

Much argument is focused onto the 'battle of the keystroke', in which the manual unions are naturally determined to take control of the keyboards which will 'enter' words into the computer system. Their desire is that all the work of creation, assessment and editing shall be done – as it is now – on paper, and then 'entered' by operators who would take no part in the creative process. By such means, of course, most of the interesting possibilities of the computer are minimised, if not eliminated.

Yet there is little energy being deployed on the other side of the keystroke argument. Generally, the case is put chiefly in terms of managements hoping to save a bit more cash, so that the startlingly ill-managed Fleet Street system may stagger on unchanged for a few more years. New technology is seen entirely in terms of shoring up what exists – however ramshackle – and not at all of building anything new.

Few of the people operating on the journalistic side of this divide are reporters or writers either by temperament, experience or ability. The dominance of the sub-editor in Fleet Street is large numerically; it is overwhelming in terms of hierachy and philosophy. The problem is compounded by the fact that many writers, sentimentally, affect to see the computer as a 'dehumanising influence', and have chosen to limit their knowledge to fat-headed gossip about erroneous bank statements and the like. (One wonders if such people think that the computers which help to bring a plane load of children safely down to a pitch-black, rain-swept runway are a 'dehumanising influence'.)

When Kipling wrote that '. . . the Jew shall forget Jerusalem, Ere we forget the Press' he was as usual saying something very precise: he meant that in so far as our nation has reserves of energy and virtue, they were largely formed in times when the freedom to write, to publish and to communicate seemed to exist in practical and expanding fact, as well as an abstract principle. In the era of the centrally-organised, mechanised and bureaucratic newspaper system, the freedom which Kipling thought necessary – if our right hand, as it were, is to preserve its cunning – has not totally vanished, but has become perilously abstract. Computer-based technology offers possibilities that might help to restore creativity. But the incurious gaze of the Royal Commission has done nothing to bring them to attention.

Chapter 13

Politics and the Technology Push

Luke Alexander

It is a cliché among progressive thinkers in the newspaper industry on both sides of the Atlantic that newspapers are, or ought to be, in the information business rather than the newspaper business. The death of paper as a medium for communicating news and views is often forecast. The newspaper industry meanwhile exhibits the classic signs of an industry in technological upheaval. The dramatic impact of the computer is nowhere better illustrated. Not only is the computer revolutionising the internal technical processes of the newspaper, and along with them the social and managerial processes as well (which means jobs and demarcation). But it is also revolutionising the external communications media available to – and on current theory vital to the future of – the newspaper companies. The internal use of computers and associated peripheral equipment like Video Display Terminals* and photo-composition equipment may be regarded as a parochial concern of the newspaper industry, of interest only to the professionals. Even this aspect however intrudes on the public domain when large

---

* Known as V.D.T. for short, this is a combined screen and keyboard, where the screen replaces paper as the way of displaying what you have typed, and more importantly, displaying information, text, etc., which you have requested from the computer.

numbers of jobs may be lost; or when application is made for public funds to help the process of technological modernisation (as Fleet Street recently applied to the European Social Fund via the British Government); or when a public body such as the Royal Commission on the Press recommends various forms of public assistance or subsidy (as the Commission did in its 1976 interim report, again with reference to Fleet Street).

But the larger, and much less explored issue is the external aspect. As newspapers become fundamentally electronic institutions based on the computer, and as they are then able to turn their attention not only to electronic means of storage and manipulation of data, but also to electronic means of distribution and marketing, the relationship between newspapers (still essentially private enterprise organisations with a private enterprise ethic) and the television and Post Office networks (public institutions with a public service ethic) is bound to change. Not only will the role of newspapers *vis-à-vis* television and radio alter, even more rapidly than it has up to now: but more importantly public decisions will have to be taken on the monopoly–oligopoly consequences of this technological convergence of the media, and about the placing of editorial responsibility and the definition of editorial freedom under this new hybrid situation formed by the electronic newspaper and its mirror image, the text broadcast. For this technology push is not coming merely from one side: it is coming also from the television side, as Ceefax and Oracle, the B.B.C. and I.T.V. text transmission systems, cross words with the newly digitised Grub Street.

With the Post Office Viewdata system (more fully described below) also due for full market trial in 1978, yet another public body with ambitions to become the great mother earth of British electronic communications enters the calculation. Here we find one clue to the poverty of public thought on the effect of the technology push on the information needs and uses of society. For we have had three separate public enquiries, into newspapers, broadcasting, and the Post Office respectively, with only limited cross-reference between them. A lot of issues may fall, indeed have fallen, into the gutters between these enquiries.

Any or all of them could have been forgiven for not making too firm a recommendation, or reaching too firm a conclusion, on the convergence of technology. What is disappointing is that they have not fully addressed themselves to the problem. They have not added their voice, which could have been an important voice, to the formulation of a new wisdom and a new definition of public policy not just towards broadcasting or the press or telecommunications taken separately, but towards the media as a whole. If tomorrow's landscape is to be criss-crossed by electronic data highways, then he who licenses the drivers and the cars and charges the tolls must be in a powerful and responsible position: and 'he' in this context is the government.

The signs and symptoms of 'media convergence' are multiplying. People who last year were still talking in terms of quires and ens and pars are now learning, painfully but of necessity, about bits per second and the X 25 protocol and packet switching. Swopping one jargon for another – and both old and new technologies are rich in jargon – is not the problem: the imaginative leap is. What is the role of the newspaper of the future, in a world where electronics are blurring and breaking down the traditional demarcation lines of the media?

The Royal Commission on the Press rightly notes (page 9) the profoundly different ideas that lie behind the laws affecting press and broadcasting, respectively: the one being an essentially free market idea dedicated to diversity, freedom to buy and launch news publications, and freedom from any formal editorial requirements other than libel and official secrets; the other being an essentially public service idea, deriving from scarcity (or alleged scarcity) of airspace, entailing control and limited access. The Commission acknowledges the heavy overlap of function of the two media, which causes expectations and standards applied to the one to be transferred to the other (for example, more editorial freedom for broadcasters, a 'socially responsible' press). But it does not discuss this 'overlap' as a dynamic development in which technological pressures, by driving the two media ever closer towards each other, will further enlarge the area of transfer and conflict between the two ideologies, and further strain the credibility of either in their purer forms. The separate ideologies derive from separate technical bases: with the removal of technical separateness, there will be increasing pressure for a new unified ethic.

This failure comes out plainly in the too brief discussion of Teletext on page 36 of the Commission report. It dismisses the fears voiced by the provincial press that Ceefax and Oracle* will damage circulations, on the grounds that these systems will provide only part of the information at present supplied by the local newspapers. But the particular sections of the local press that will be hit by direct competition from teletext (the generic term that includes Viewdata) are very important sections indeed for the financial health and circulation of these papers – small ads, weather, entertainments guide, schedules of local events, travel and transport information, sports results and fixtures, news headlines, public service messages. The Commission under-rates the likely impact of this competition. This is not a reason for giving in to the plea by the provincial press that development of teletext systems should be slowed down: on the contrary, the near-monopoly status of most of the provincial press makes it the more imperative to develop a rival and competitive medium. But it is a bit sad that the Commission did not see it even in that positive light, let alone take a view about how press and teletext might co-exist in the future.

The specific challenge of Viewdata, which is unique in that it will have theoretically unlimited capacity and will be interactive (that is, the user can quiz the computer, instead of being a passive recipient), is better acknowledged, though again too briefly. Similarly, the Commission's rejection of the contention by the Newspaper Society and the Newspaper Publishers' Association that newspaper publishers should have a prescriptive right to take part in teletext developments, is certainly correct as far as it goes. But it merely reflects the traditional policy, followed in all recent official reports on broadcasting and on the press, of keeping press and broadcasting organisationally separate. (Local commercial radio has been an exception to this policy, but even there Annan has recommended greater separation.)

What this line does not recognise is that organisational separation derives ultimately, as we have said, from technical separation. Once technical separation disappears, the basis for anti-monopoly policy towards the media will need rethinking –

* Ceefax and Oracle use some redundant lines at the top of the T.V. screen to send text – news, guides, recipes, timetables, sub-titles, etc. – which you need a special adaptor at present to read, but which will become a standard feature. The crux is that the B.B.C. and I.T.V. are no longer organisations which just send you pictures – like newspapers they send you words to read.

and it may no longer be as simple as trying to keep the press out of teletext development. The same argument is being held in Germany. There is, correctly, the desire to prevent concentration of power in the media – but there is also a need to give newspaper organisations the freedom of manoeuvre without which they may wilt and perish at an even faster rate than applies already.

The Press Commission does, it is true, devote some lines (pp. 148-9) to the policy issues arising from Viewdata in relation to the press and the other so-called 'information providers'. The summary of these issues by the Commission is excellent as far as it goes. But the Commission refuses actually to commit itself on any of the issues, when there was certainly scope for a body like the Commission to take a view, for example, on the editorial rights of the Post Office (as provider of the medium) as against the rights of the press and other parties (as providers of the information).

The Annan report is hardly more encouraging. It notes the blurring of the line between 'off-air' and cable technologies, without acknowledging the similar blurring between print and electronic. It also examines – and rightly rejects – the newspapers' plea for a five-year moratorium on the commercial development of teletext, and like the Press Commission rejects the notion of a prescriptive right for newspapers to take part in such developments. The main Annan report also rejects a minority suggestion that there should be an editorial board to oversee teletext, on which journalists would sit along with broadcasters. The useful suggestion made by Annan is that after some years' operation the whole question of teletext should be reviewed at a public enquiry, and this at least shows that the Annan committee took teletext somewhat more seriously than their press colleagues. Even so, the discussion is brief and bitty, and it is notable that Annan did not really analyse Viewdata (though the report did describe it well) presumably because as a Post Office development it fell outside the committee's terms of reference. It fell right into the gutter, since the Carter report on the Post Office also virtually ignored this side of the P.O.'s business.

Basically, Viewdata will be a set of computers distributed round the country on which the 'information providers' will put information and from which the users will get information via the ordinary telephone, linked to a T.V. set for display of the information and a special keypad with which to call up the information. What is entrancing about this system is, first of all, the enormous theoretical capacity of the system in terms of the sheer amount and variety of information that can be entered, stored and retrieved from it: and secondly, the prospect of a cheap, already installed electronic reception terminal being provided in the home and office by the simple means of linking telephone to T.V. screen. Such a cheap terminal could in principle receive data from a huge variety of sources, not just the Post Office's own Viewdata system, provided the Post Office would allow the information to be pumped out over its lines, and could at a stroke create the 'wired society' that the electronic futurists have been dreaming of. (It goes without saying that it might be a fairly primitive terminal in terms of its operating characteristics, compared to a more specialised but more expensive instrument: but once the use of a domestic/office terminal has been established as a social habit, the breakthrough will have been made.)

But whose property is the information on the Viewdata system? The Post Office has shifted its ground on that issue, in an interesting way. It began by seeking to make the information its own property, but that clearly did not please the organisations which have contracted to supply the information – and would in any case be a momentous departure for the Post Office, to be not simply the means of conveyance but also the owner of what was conveyed. By extension from this, who takes legal and editorial responsibility for the material on Viewdata? To an American, both these questions would seem nonsensical, because U.S. telecommunication networks are 'common carriers,' who simply act as a neutral transport system for data, and that status is fully recognised. But under British law, and with the present state of the act governing the Post Office, the Post Office is not a common carrier, and can be sued, just like any other publisher. Again, the Post Office has been shifting its ground on this issue, recognising the need to give information providers (IPs, as they are known in the jargon) as near as possible to total rights and responsibilities over the information they provide. But there will clearly have to be some method of adjudication on difficult cases.

A related set of questions concerns the users of Viewdata at both ends – that is, who has the right to put information on, and who has the right to take information off? It is easy to say that Viewdata is a social service, open to all to use on both the input and the output side. But once you start fixing charges for using it, problems arise. Can only those who 'rent' enough space on the Post Office's computers have access to the system? Can only those who make enough use of it, that is, make enough telephone calls to access the computer data bank, be allowed to benefit from the service? Both these apparently commercial decisions carry important consequences about limiting what ought surely to be a genuine public service utility (as the telephone itself ought to be). It could end up with a number of rich clients, who are mainly big organisations talking to each other or indeed carrying on internal communications, dominating a public resource.

Not dissimilar questions arise from developments at U.S. newspapers like the *New York Times,* which on the one hand represent a bold response to the challenges and opportunities offered to the newspaper industry by new computer-based technology, and on the other hand show the disquieting trend towards turning information from a cheap and freely available commodity (may one say, a democratic commodity?) into an expensive and therefore elitist commodity. For on the one hand there is the *New York Times* itself, a splendid world-view newspaper selling for a few cents on the streets of New York and elsewhere – a price at which, to all intents and purposes, information on a substantial scale is available without hindrance to every citizen and visitor: on the other hand, in the name of being 'in the information business', and to shore up the poor profitability of the newspaper itself, its publishers have set up an electronic information bank (called indeed 'The Information Bank') into which a large team of abstracters insert abstracts of articles from a wide range of publications every day, which can be accessed by display terminals at customer locations, via an index – and this service runs out at nearly $100 an hour to use, although a typical enquiry may only take a minute or two. But it is, deliberately, expensive information, and is making information into an 'upmarket' specialist commodity to be sold to the highest bidder.

Not so long ago, in a letter in the *Guardian* newspaper, Mr Colin Campbell of the University of York argued as follows:

> If the society of the future is to be one in which knowledge is the key ingredient in power then the unequal distribution of information is as grave a threat to democracy as the potential

misuse of information by government of big business. Thus if it is to be the case that an individual may, at the touch of a button or the turn of a knob, know the latest stockmarket prices, the weather prospects, or the *Guardian's* circulation figures, or obtain a print-out of last month's *Hansard* or the current edition of *Nature,* then surely it is vital that this should be recognised as every citizen's right and not a privilege of the rich and those employed by wealthy organisations.

At present this right is recognised in the provision of public libraries and to some extent through publicly supported information services and Citizens' Advice Bureaux. But how is it to be guaranteed in the forthcoming telecommunications revolution?

If books, magazines, and newspapers are to become redundant in 20–25 years from now, how shall we ensure that all citizens have equal access to all publicly available information?

A paper given by R. K. Stamper of the London School of Economics supports the point.

We now live in a post-industrial society. One of its outstanding characteristics is the role which information plays in our new kind of economy. It is therefore lamentable that, ostrich like, the government and the profession of economists disregard the need for a policy in this field. There is a tendency to assume that information systems are a minor auxiliary to the major activity of our economy which is physical production. This is misleading. Indeed, the reverse is likely to be the case in the near future: physical production will be the auxiliary activity in most developed economies. Already, approximately half the working population are wholly engaged in producing information.

For a century and a half now newspapers have played a particular and generally well-defined role in society, part information, part entertainment, part political 'fourth estate'. A shift towards newspapers, or newspaper companies, regarding themselves as 'data bases', or as organisations whose prime job is to collect and evaluate information for onward dissemination not necessarily on paper, would therefore raise several important questions:

1. It would further emphasise the neutrality of information as opposed to the political role of comment: in other words, it would consolidate an already existing trend, regarded by many as undesirable, towards the non-political, non-partisan approach to publishing. The British national press is still party-oriented, though far less firmly or consistently than previously. The provincial press has however almost entirely lost the strongly partisan political flavour which once it had (and which indeed caused the foundation of many papers). Some see this trend towards a sort of conservative neutrality as desirable: some see it as part of the enfeeblement of political life. But if even the big national newspapers begin to see news as a commodity to be sold on to whoever wants to pay the price, there will be even more reluctance to prejudice such sales by taking political sides. In other words, as newspapers move into the electronic era, and new forms of 'publishing' open up to them, and as the distinction between them and the rest of the electronic media breaks down, both technically and operationally, there may be a significant effect upon the role of the press as fourth estate.

2. The economics of all this are not at all clear. Development of new types of information services, more advanced in the U.S.A. than in Europe, tends to piggy-back on the existing printed media, in particular the newspapers and magazines (except in so far as such services draw on official statistics and other publicly available data). In other words, the news gathering and evaluation is still basically that of the traditional publishing concerns. These concerns will no doubt argue that they are merely capitalising on this effort, by finding extra ways of making money out of it. The problem is that if more and more users switch to using these newer services (e.g. in banks, brokers, companies, sports grounds, bars, in the home) it may so eat into the circulation and therefore the advertising appeal of the press that its already fragile economics will be further endangered. Publishers argue that this is just the point: they must be organised for the day when new types of information dissemination are the order of the day. Maybe, but the cost of present-day news gathering is largely defrayed by advertisement income: and this may be affected by the techno-logical shift as well.

3. The present advertising strength of the press depends on delivering to the advertiser agglomerations of readers – either in undifferentiated masses (undifferentiated, that is, except by market research) or at least in broad categories, like most top businessmen or most top people. The effect is gained by lumping together variegated groups of people who are attracted to the publication for different reasons – sports coverage, financial coverage, tits and bums, legal developments, arts reviews, etc. In this respect a newspaper is very like a television schedule. But the new types of information service have three interesting characteristics: (a) they are often aimed at very specific interest groups, for example sports fans or stockbrokers, and one service is quite separate from another, so the effect is to fragment the audience into small sectors; (b) advertisements will only be seen on demand, that is, when the reader/viewer chooses to ask to see them (if, that is, the particular system carries ads at all), and not as a by-product of scanning the editorial content of the newspaper or magazine page; (c) advertisements seem certain to be different in character on such systems, being almost purely informational in content – all to the good no doubt, but (as on the Reuters Monitor system) it may be hard to tell what is advertising and what is 'pure' news and information.

It may be noted that much the same fragmentation may take place in television with the advent of the videodisc and the videotape recorder or cassette, since they enable people to choose their own pattern of evening (or other) viewing, and the audience cannot therefore be 'delivered' in mass millions to the advertisers. However, for the press the corollary is that the actual news gathering and analysis must be charged at much nearer to its cost price, rather than its subsidised price. But will this make information a high-price commodity? And is that what publishers want, and if they do, would society at large really want it as well?

4. The tendency to regard information as just another (high price) commodity means that the marketing technique will be to sell information at the highest price that 'the market'(however it is defined) will bear. Traditionally, the attitude to information has been quite other. In the commercial area, it has been to provide information as near to free as possible, through the subsidy of advertising: in the public sphere, it has been to provide it absolutely for free, as with the public library system. Now the

trend is towards copyrighting information like any other product or invention, in order to exploit its own inherent marketing potential. No doubt under such a regime different types of information would find different levels of price and availability. But what exactly is society's interest in this process of 'fencing in' information? How far can the doctrine of property rights be applied to a 'commodity' like information? And can the process be taken as far as copyrighting not just the facts, but also the expression of the facts – in short, copyrighting the ideas and evaluation as well as the facts? Is the notion of intellectual property rights, so cogent in the case of, say, computer programmes and software, applicable or desirable when it comes to those types of information that normally enter the arena of public debate and political argument?

5. The language and values of a data base may be quite different from the language and values of a newspaper or of other forms of written publication. Data bases deal only in certainties, simple 'is it or isn't it' questions, neutral in terms of values and with standard definitions and standard routes and indices through the data. However practical, the data base is an unlovely animal in this respect.

6. Is not the moral of all this that we need not so much a media policy, but an information policy for society, revolving around the already established U.S. notion of 'the right to know'? Such a policy would have to try and perform the difficult balancing act between the right to know and the right to privacy: between the commercial and political values of information: and between the right to publish information (which belongs to many) and the right to distribute it (which may, with modern techniques, belong to the few).

In this new world, Reuters is an instructive phenomenon. It is hard to say what sort of an animal Reuters now is. Certainly it is no longer just a foreign news agency of the classic type, although it still fulfils that function. Rather, it is a technologically-based information business, for which newspapers now provide only a minority of the custom. Using computers and terminals, Reuters here and in the U.S. is now changing its stance to become (at a price) a supplier to anyone of information from anyone – news, financial or commodity figures, recipes, sports results, etc.

In the U.K., the Reuters Monitor service looks like developing into a unified business information service through a V.D.T.-type reception terminal with a screen and keypad. In the Reuters head office, plans are advanced for a fully computerised central newsroom using Video Display Terminals, giving faster turn-around of news and the final emergence of Reuters as an electronic information carrier. Already it is supplying business information direct to the user in offices and financial institutions – that is, it is a retailer of information rather than just a wholesaler, as it is when supplying newspapers. If Reuters can link its computer to the emerging Post Office data service, then the prospect of retailing news (and many other 'commodities') direct to a cheap domestic terminal in the home, also opens up.

In the U.S., Reuters has been experimenting with a cable T.V. channel in New York, to provide a so-called wideband information service, with the idea that eventually satellites should be used as inter-city links for distribution from central news and data points, using local cable systems as the final distributor to the user at his domestic or office terminal. Similarly, UPI news agency has been experimenting with the use of cheap antennae to receive the wire service direct into an office (or apartment) block off a satellite. What role are the so-called news agencies playing here? They are, actually or potentially, displacing newspapers and other publications as purveyors of news and other information direct to the man in the office and the women in the home: and on the other hand they are developing into a quite new animal, with a world-wide telecommunications network allied to a news gathering and editorial capability, perhaps to become the first true 'information companies' in the information business. Others, like I.B.M. or the Post Office, have the technology: newspapers have the information. News agencies, conceivably, have both.

To see how the satellite is impinging on the life of a newspaper as such, the best example is the *Wall Street Journal,* which shows an aggressive commercial policy towards the exploitation of new technology. Having already split the U.S. into several separate marketing areas, each getting a differently structured *Wall Street Journal,* with decentralised printing using in some cases direct satellite links to transfer pages from one location to another. Similar links using the latest technologies enable the *Wall Street Journal* to send material to Hong Kong for the new *Asian Wall Street Journal.* This is not as yet a commercial success, but it is a bold venture in multi-national publishing and portends a similar invasion of Europe in the future if it is successful (maybe, even if it is not). With its wire service and business information retrieval service, the *Wall Street Journal* is a clear example of harnessing the commercial and marketing opportunities offered by new forms of technology, at least in the U.S.A. where private telecommunications networks are legal and multiplying. In Europe, the attitude of public Post Office authorities will, willy nilly, impinge on commercial planning of this type of multi-national, multi-centre newspaper printing in pursuit of what the jargon has already labelled 'the global newspaper'. Even within Europe, the sending of the *Herald Tribune* from Paris by use of facsimile links to London and Switzerland to diversify its printing and distribution shows how new technology opens up the horizons for a newspaper. The decision of the French telecommunications authorities to start a newspaper page facsimile service between Paris and the south of France to facilitate distribution is another example of how public decisions on the means of communication impinge on what is communicated.

As office word-processing systems based on V.D.U.s and computers talk to each other across telecommunications links, instead of executives sending letters to each other, and as Ceefax, Oracle and Viewdata lead the ordinary person towards using a screen as a receiver of text, so one may see the shift into electronic forms of communications gathering pace – it is as much a question of social habits as technical advance. What is important is that increasingly large numbers of people are getting used to receiving data and sending it via these new devices, at the moment mainly in office, commercial and engineering contexts: but it is a habit of mind which, like pocket calculators or colour T.V., will suddenly take off, even if one cannot say quite when.

Newspapers, like other institutions, are being caught up in this change, some more than others, depending on their audience (the *Sun* may outlive them all – its kind of data is hardest to reproduce on a V.D.U.). That newspapers have to come to terms with the new world, is obvious. The nub is, what role do newspapers have in the future pattern of communications and information? Are they to become information gatherers and analysers, competing against organisations similarly described (news agencies, libraries, government departments, scientific agencies, specialist computer-based data bank companies, etc.) purely on their 'editorial and evaluative' skills? or is there to be a social policy aimed at preserving the newspaper as such, as a cheap means of maintaining informed citizenry and political debate? Will it be Milton Keynes, the wired city, writ large or just a jungle of competing and expensive data banks for those that can afford them? Somehow, society will have to grope its way towards an information policy – a process in which the Annan and McGregor reports have offered little help.

Chapter 14

Government Policy and the Mass Media

Jean Seaton

The printing of newspapers, the production of films and the provision of a broadcasting service are all intimately connected industries. They have created and shared audiences, competed for personnel, developed complementary social and political functions, adapted each other's content, and frequently have come to own each other or be owned in common. As Anthony Crosland wrote in 1962: 'We now have for the first time a centralized uniform communication industry, commanding a national audience.'[1] Yet in fifty years of decisive government intervention in the media there has been little recognition of the fundamental unity of these industries, or that action in one industry would have repercussions in another.

In addition, governments have been inconsistent in their attitudes towards the media. During some periods their policy has simply reflected general industrial strategy, at others it has marked a distinct break from it. There have also been ambiguities as to whether a 'good' or 'healthy' industry was distinct from a commercially successful one, or merely the same thing. Some reports have suggested that success in a media industry inevitably implies a degradation of quality, others that quality cannot be rewarded at the expense of commercial criteria.

Politicians have usually been concerned with immediate

problems in the performance of the media, arising from the belief that the press and broadcasting are capable of decisively affecting their careers. While civil servants, during those periodic crises when they have been required to review the industries, have tended to see them – accurately enough – at a particular moment subject to determined pressures and opportunities. Moreover, strong traditions have developed about the appropriate nature and limits of public policy in dealing with each industry, and these have rarely been questioned. Different traditions even seem to have developed about the kind of report or research that is commissioned for the various media, those on the press being structural reports depending on economics; those on broadcasting concerned with moral and philosophical questions about public taste; and those on the films depending on the insights of those engaged in the industry itself.

These traditions did not develop from a coherent plan for the management of a diverse communication industry, but from a series of accidents. This paper will briefly review public policy towards the press, broadcasting and films, and attempt to assess the inter-relation between intervention in the separate industries, as well as the effects of governments' *failure* to intervene in them.

The Film Industry

Governments have rarely recognised that films have any ideological role at all. British films only survived their first crisis in the 1920s because of the protection afforded by a Conservative government. By the 1960s it was possible to review four quite separate grants, subsidies and levies which had been introduced in attempts to make the industry viable. Government policy encouraged the American takeover of the industry, indeed subsidised it from public funds. Paradoxically it had been government patronage which had supported a new and influential genre of films in the British documentary movement. Governments do not seem to have been particularly anxious about the effects of economic power over artistic and political freedom in this media industry.

The film industry is remarkable for the persistence of its economic problems. In Britain the home market for films has never been large enough to recoup costs. The industry could only make profits if it was able to export. The Moyne Report noted this in 1936,[2] many books and articles pointed it out;[3] the Plant Report noted it in 1949;[4] in 1975 Harold Wilson's working party[5] commented on it. Unfortunately governments have never appeared to understand its consequences fully. In the 1930s and 1940s British films aped Hollywood productions in an attempt to break into the American market; in the 1950s a distinctly British style of film also failed to export. In these circumstances piecemeal financial support would never be adequate. The Chairman of the government enquiry into the industry argued: 'Should we be content if we depended upon a foreign literature or a foreign press in this country? How then can we accept the prospect of foreign films?'[6] As a result of this enquiry the 1927 Cinematograph Films Act[7] banned block and blind booking (the practices by which American companies persuaded exhibitors to buy a series of films before they had been made) and obliged exhibitors to screen quotas of British films. During a period when the only other protectionist legislation covered the great staple industries, steel, cotton and iron, this was strong action to take over an industry of such minor economic significance as films. It was taken partly because officials were shocked at the unscrupulous American trade practices, but also because it was accepted that the industry was of great national importance.

The next persistent problem was that of securing finance for film production. Baldwin's government suggested that the banks and insurance companies involve themselves in funding films. These gave spurious propriety to financial arrangements which would not have been tolerated in any other industry. Producers borrowed money, and then raised more money on the strength of the first loan. The only collateral was often the expected profits on as yet unmade films and between 1936 and 1937 production rose by 300 per cent,[8] and a tiny number of city financiers, none with any real knowledge of the industry, controlled all of its debts. The bubble burst in 1937, when a newspaper article revealed the full extent of the debt. The city panicked, mortgages were called in and then the companies went bankrupt. In the middle of the crisis a government report[9] was published, which seemed to be unaware of the scandal. One cause of this naïvety was an inability to understand the uniqueness of the industry; another was its domination by the members of the industry itself, yet the collapse ensured that industrial finance was never again available to fund films.

The full vertical integration of the industry and its monopolisation happened just before and during the Second World War. By 1940, J. Arthur Rank owned most of the London preview cinemas, two of the three exhibition circuits, distribution companies, and was the main source of production finance. Almost the entire industry had become dependent on the fortunes of one company. In 1947, when more people were going to the cinema than even before, the general economic crisis led the government to impose a 75 per cent duty on all imports including films. The Americans immediately banned all exports of films to Britain and the government encouraged Rank to increase his output of films in order to fill the gap. Unfortunately, the Americans threatened to withhold Marshall Aid unless the duty on films was raised, and Rank's hurriedly produced films reached the screens only in time to compete with two years' backlog of American production. They were a disaster; Rank's company and consequently the industry was again nearly bankrupted. Apart from the attention of a succession of prominant Labour leaders, Gaitskell, Cripps and Wilson,[10] no less than three government reports were commissioned on the industry during this period. The division of labour between these reports,[11] one to report on monpoly, another on production costs and the last to study distribution, appears rational: in fact it ensured that none of them examined the whole structure of the industry.

The only alternative these reports opposed to the monopolies, was the chimera of the independent producer. This model was technically and aesthetically unrealistic about how good films were made, and there were no independent producers in any case. By concentrating on a false remedy, the reports ignored the unique alternative model of the British documentary movement financed directly by the government. This had developed an influential style, news content, new venues and audiences, and while individuals produced distinct, indeed personal films, they did so within the development of a particular genre.

The subsequent stage of government policy was marked by the belief that the injection of cash into the industry would change its structure. With remarkable rapidity the National Film Finance Corporation and the Eady levy were introduced, and the entertainment tax on films lifted, in order to assist 'independent producers'. Not only did these arrangements fail to improve the structure of the industry, they made it worse, and they soon became a substantial government subsidy to American companies who made films in Britain.

In the 1950s and 1960s the growth of television led to a world-wide decline in cinema audiences, and American companies became more eager to take over the British industry; paradoxically quotas guaranteed the films they made here a secure place on British screens.[12] The government's only objective was to maintain employment in the industry. At a time when the amount of British material shown on television were being rigorously controlled, the protection of a native film industry was abandoned.

By 1960 precisely what constituted a 'British film' had become unclear, and attempts were made to define how much of a film had to be made here to qualify for the subsidies and quota concessions.[13] Eight years later Crosland's review of film legislation was pessimistic. 'Film production remains hazardous'[14] it commented, and a suggestion that special grants be awarded to films for merit was rejected as 'being likely to promote indifference to economic reality'.[15]

In the 1970s there was another crisis. The Americans simply stopped making films in the U.K., so the industry collapsed, and in 1976 Harold Wilson's working party started its report ominously, 'All is not well with the industry'.[16] It never had been. The only positive suggestion the report made was that film production should be subsidised by a levy from television. It suggested this without reference to the economic condition of television and with no research into the structure of either industry. It also proposed that the administration of film matters should be rationalised. Unfortunately by 1978 there is very little left of the industry for a rational ministry to administer.

The Press

Governments have seen the press as an industry of such exceptional political importance that during this century they have made a policy of having no policy for it at all. Before 1947, when the first Royal Commission[17] was set up, it was not thought proper even to investigate the conduct of the press. Since then it has been subject to repeated public reviews.[18]

Despite this continuous attention, and an equally continuous scandal about the closure of newspapers, governments have still refused to intervene in the industry. This is because it has been accepted that economic management of the press is tantamount to economic control, which in turn will inexorably lead to political control. Ironically, an argument identical in form about the effect of monopolistic and even foreign ownership of the press has not been accepted. The 1977 Commission argued: 'There is a consensus shared by almost all those who gave evidence to us that the press should neither be subject to state control, nor left entirely to the unregulated forces of the market.'[19] Nevertheless, it argues that it has discussed proposals for reform of the industry at length, only so that 'by arguing the pros and cons we have finally laid them to rest'.[20] The report finally recommends measures to strengthen the internal organisation of the industry to withstand market pressures, but rejects any attempt to ameliorate them.

No Royal Commission has ever attempted to distinguish between the varieties of economic intervention that are available, or the nature of their political effects on the content of papers. This is perhaps odd as the very first Commission reported at the end of seven years draconian government control of the economics of newspaper publishing during the Second World War. At the start of the war newsprint was rationed under a scheme administered by the press but directed by the government, and the size of papers was reduced dramatically.[21] In 1938 a Political and Economic Planning Report had remarked that 'the press could survive with no advertising if people would buy smaller papers'.[22] During the war people paid for less advertisements but only a little less news, and they bought more newspapers. Free from competition with each other, the number of papers printed was fixed at the start of the war: free from competition for advertising revenue, advertisers competed to get into the newspapers; free from competition for newsprint, the paper was allocated by the government. The newspapers were more successful than they had ever been before, as a consequence of government control.

This economic management was quite independent from the political control of censorship. Indeed it has been argued that papers like the *Daily Mirror* 'the daily paper of the other ranks',[23] established a particular intimacy with their audiences during this period. George Orwell wrote 'All the papers printed articles that would have been considered hopelessly above their readers' heads a couple of years ago'.[24] The homogeneity of readers' and papers' interests [25] may not be the only criterion of the quality of journalism, but there is general agreement that the press performed exceptionally well under government control. In addition the press was profitable.[26] Indeed the problems that arose from newsprint control highlighted the vulnerability of the press to commercial rather than political pressures.[27]

Neither the government nor the press recognised the potential significance of the experience which was seen as an abnormal consequence of wartime economic controls, not as a precedent for relations between governments and the press. Indeed the 1947 Royal Commission was prompted by anxieties which essentially pre-dated the war. During the 1930s most of the press had favoured the government's policy of appeasement (as had broadcasting and the film industry[28]), and in the 1940s this was felt to have been the direct result of the political interests of proprietors, or an indirect response to advertisers who were thought to prefer cheerful papers. Although the National Union of Journalists argued that 'It is not merely our point that proprietors have replaced the editor, our point is that the commercial interests of the paper have replaced the editor',[29] the Report concentrated on a narrower definition of editorial independence. Indeed the Report accepted evidence that editors *felt* free from proprietorial influence as proof that they were.[50] The Report concluded that the necessity of selling newspapers in itself constituted a check on proprietors' propagandist ambitions.

The war had exacerbated tendencies towards centralisation in Britain, and anxieties about this were expressed to both the Royal Commission, and the Beveridge Committee on Broadcasting. In the case of the press, despite evidence of the rapid development of local and regional monopolies, nothing was done, while the B.B.C. was directed to change its regional policy fundamentally. However by 1947, broadcasting also set standards of journalism which had come to be expected of newspapers. The Commission recommended that a Press Council be set up to investigate examples of 'inaccuracy, triviality and sensationalism'[30] and to encourage 'the growth of a sense of public service among all engaged in the profession of journalism'.[31] One member, commenting that 'misrepresentation is inherent in party government, and without it the whole thing would stop'[32] wondered whether political partisanship should necessarily be discouraged in the press. The majority of the Commission disagreed – the most important task of newspapers was to supply impartial information. The guardian of this independence was the conscience of the editor.

Even by 1947 newspapers were inefficiently run, with little professional management, ineffective cost control and antiquated labour practices. Indeed the structure of the industry, rather like that of films, remained very similar through a succession of reports, although the economic crises this caused got worse. Between 1947 and 1960 seventeen daily and Sunday papers closed and there had been a scandal about the amalgamation of the *News Chronicle,* a paper of the left, with the Conservative *Mail.* A new commission was asked to enquire, 'not into the rights and wrongs of these events but into the economic factors affecting the press generally'.[33]

The Shawcross Report is the first comprehensive analysis of the structure of any media industry. It investigated the effect of advertising on the choice of papers;[34] it reprimanded management and unions, for 'inefficiency is not turned into efficiency because the parties have agreed to it'.[35] Nevertheless, despite its brusque tone and its emphasis on objective analysis, it was also puzzled by the problems of assessing the quality of a newspaper. It argued, 'There is no way to success but through the quality of management and editorial direction. Legislation cannot produce these qualities.'[36] If a paper was declining, only editorial enterprise could save it. This notion of Herculean 'flair' was derived from the industries' own myths, but also illuminates the failure of this and most other reports to examine what in its relationship with an audience makes a paper successful.

The recommendations of the Report seem at odds with its analysis. While increasing monopolisation of the press was a cause for anxiety, press holdings in television companies were only inimical to the public interest if they were major. The press should establish a press council with lay membership as the 1947 Commission had urged it to do. These recommendations 'involved treating newspapers differently from industry in general',[37] but the effects of the market are not otherwise questioned.

Between 1962 and 1977, papers continued to close and neither production processes nor labour relations had been greatly modernised. In 1974, a Third Royal Commission[38] was set up, this time prompted by the Labour Party's concern about what it regarded as the overwhelmingly Conservative bias of the press.

The Report is concerned with the effect of market forces on the 'diversity of opinion'. Nevertheless it shares with the Shawcross Report a scepticism about the nature of the political effects of the press, and implies that it would be irrational to expect more than a very few papers in each class to survive.

The Report claims that its definition of the freedom of the press 'demonstrates our belief that the press cannot be treated like an ordinary industry'.[39] Indeed it regards it as such an exceptional industry that it bases some of its conclusions on the expectation that proprietors will continue to support unprofitable papers. While it is anxious about the effects of market pressures, and appalled by the industry's own failure to become more efficient, it rejects all proposals for reform as impractical. Indeed government policy towards the press could perhaps now be characterised as policical opposition to intervention disguised as despair of any ability to effect the market at all.

Broadcasting

Governments have always controlled the structure and financing of broadcasting. For its first thirty years the service was run as a state licensed monopoly; with the introduction of commercial broadcasting the monopoly was broken, but the right of governments to control the provision of the service and its funds remained unquestioned.

Originally the government was forced to intervene in the arrangements of broadcasting in order to regulate the national and international use of the air: as P. P. Eckersley wrote: 'The B.B.C. was formed as an expedient solution to a technical problem. It owes its existence solely to the scarcity of air waves'.[40] In the 1920s wireless was seen simply as an ingenious experimental toy. Governments did not foresee its political value, and it was thought too trivial to demand serious attention. 'A minister' it was argued 'might well shrink from the prospect of having to defend in parliament the various items in a government concert.'[41] The entertainment industry saw it as a competitor for existing audiences rather than a creator of a vast new body of consumers. Indeed it was only when Northcliffe, proprietor of the *Daily Mail* and an early industrialist of entertainment, organised a broadcasting stunt (Dame Nellie Melba singing), that the real possibilities of a general audience were recognised.

In 1923 the Sykes Report recommended that the monopoly should be financed by a licence fee, but the Treasury continued to take a share of the revenue. The ability of governments to control the funds available to broadcasting through their right to determine the level of the licence fee has always constituted a powerful, and covert, control of the service.

In 1925 the Crawford Committee[42] recommended that the company should become a public corporation, licensed under a charter by the Crown. The uniqueness of the institution lay in its original relationship to the state: not obliged to make profits, removed from the pressures of the market through its possession of a monopoly, it could John Reith its first director argued, manage the new service entirely for the public good, and yet unlike governments be free from the partisan politics of particular classes or interests.

The development of the B.B.C. as a 'public service utility' has usually been attributed to Reith's leadership. However, the public corporation as a form of administration pre-dated the First World War, and in the 1920s it was a form increasingly used to manage public resources. Even Asa Briggs points out that the acceptance of monopoly broadcasting occurred so swiftly because 'a large number of important people and a large section of the interested public felt that it was right that this should be so'.[43] Reith then was not isolated in his ideas, nor were they particularly original. There was a widespread dissatisfaction with the *ad hoc* nature of industrial competition, while the experience of the First World War had demonstrated the justice of centralised planning, and in rationing schemes the exceptional national importance of some resources. These views seemed particularly appropriate to broadcasting.

The political independence of the new service was soon tested during the General Strike, whose first effect for broadcasting was to create a new audience for radio, and a new attitude of dependence in that audience. People may have been sceptical of the politics of the 'British Falsehood Corporation' as it was sometimes known, but lacking all other sources of information they relied on it. During the strike the government prohibited any representative of labour from broadcasting and the B.B.C. also exercised its own censorship.[41] However, the radio did not lie or harangue; it was never commandeered by the government, and it did report news, even of the strikers' successes. Its achievement lay as much in its tone as in its content. Although the price of the B.B.C.'s independence was to do what the government wanted, the strike marks the end of propaganda based on lies. Anthony Smith has pointed out that there had been a reaction to the crude propaganda of the First World War,[45] but during the General Strike the technique of propaganda based on the selective use of objective fact, and a concern to protect the authority of sources was developed, and was only to be perfected during the Second World War.

The B.B.C. also developed a cultural strategy, and Reith argued that it was: 'The peculiar nature of broadcasting open to all to hear, yet individual and intimate which . . . inevitably transferred the choice from the listener himself to the broadcaster'.[46] A sound archive was established as a museum for the regional accents which it was assumed would disappear as speech and tastes were standardised by broadcasting. The corporation also exercised political discrimination and in the 1930's the expressive politics of the unemployed were considered illegitimate, as were the party dissidents who opposed appeasement (even though the corporation privately made extensive preparations for a possible war). However, as Scannell and Cardiff[47] have pointed out, the Fabian Left, in so far as its members were 'impartial' social researchers, broadcast frequently. It had been these groups who had supported the constitutional arrangements of broadcasting so enthusiastically when it was set up.[48]

Doubts about the corporation's monopoly centred on the treatment of its staff. It was felt that it exercised such comprehensive powers over their personal and professional conduct that this was an abuse of individual rights, and might impair the impartiality of producers' judgements. The Ullswater Committee was concerned to protect the 'independence, security and conscience of the producer'.[49]

In 1949, however, the Beveridge Report[50] emphasised a quite different aspect of the corporation's performance, its machinery of accountability; indeed it argued that 'the responsibility of broadcasters is responsibility to the community, not to their own consciences'.[51] Beveridge distrusted the B.B.C.'s paternalism. 'I am not attracted by the argument of compulsory uplift achieved by the brute force of monopoly', he wrote. 'If people are to be trusted with the franchise surely they should be able to decide for themselves whether they want to be educated or entertained.[52] However, the Report reluctantly recommended the extension of the monopoly. Indeed the B.B.C. by abandoning 'mixed' programming, and dividing the service between a 'home', 'light' and 'third' programme, was already relinquishing its original claim to cultural authority.

Commercial television was introduced in 1954, and the very basis of broadcasting was altered. It changed from providing for needs to satisfying wants. While it was argued that the introduction of competition in itself would make broadcasting more sensitive to public needs, the Pilkington Report later commented: 'the product of the companies is . . . desirable advertising time. As commercial organizations they exist to create and sell that product.'[53] Thus, the Report continued, the Independent Television Authority, obliged by government to control the standards of the service that was provided, was based on two apparently irreconcilable objectives: quality and profit. This is in contrast with other reports on the media which have usually assumed that these two objectives were mutually dependent.

The 1977 Annan Report[54] only deals briefly with the economic structure of the industry. Personal in style, with metaphors occasionally running for pages, its basic premise is that a new public attitude has recently developed: 'at once inflationary in the expectation of what political power could achieve, and deflationary towards those in power who failed to give effect to those expectations'.[55] This attitude has led to 'more critical, more hostile and more political'[56] questions about broadcasting, and a belief that changes in its arrangements will change society. The Report does not believe this to be the case, and suggests that 'there is a right to speak in a free democracy, but it does not follow from this that there is a right to be listened to',[57] and it concludes that broadcasters, in the end, must have the authority to decide what is broadcast.

The Report makes nice distinctions about the nature of impartiality – 'not synonymous with mathematical balance, nor should it be confused with neutrality or interpreted as indifference'[58] – but is less imaginative in its explanations of the institutional arrangements which might guarantee it.

Conclusion

Governments' policies towards the press, broadcasting and films have been contradictory. Governments have barely questioned traditions of policy which have grown from casual decisions regarded as minor when they were taken; and they have never comprehensively reviewed the effect of their policies on all of the media.

Governments have repeatedly intervened in the film industry, but have only attempted to improve its market position. As a consequence they have overseen and encouraged its absorption by American companies. In contrast the press has been seen as such a politically sensitive industry that governments have always refused to intervene in its economic structure at all. Ironically then, the development of the press has also been determined by market pressures, and legal safeguards used (rather as cash was used in the film industry) in an attempt to strengthen its ability to withstand them. Yet governments have always controlled broadcasting. Not only have they licensed the initial right to set up a service but they have controlled it financially through the licence fee and the limits imposed on commercial broadcasting profits, and they have even imposed obligations on the broadcasting authorities about the content of the service.

Governments have also confused 'successful' papers, films and programmes with 'good' ones. An unprofitable industry or product may imply a failure in the relationship between the media and its audience; a profitable service may well be the best evidence of a good relationship, but the connection is not inevitable in either case. The failure of governments to distinguish between kinds of success and varieties of failure, or even to examine the nature of the media's relationship with their consumers has confused the object of government intervention.

Governments have assumed that as the different media have different political significance, their policy has been determined by a recognition of this. Films, for example, have only ever been seen as having any political role during wars when public morale becomes a factor which politicians wish to calculate on. It is surprising then, to discover that policy towards the different media has been based on identical premises and similar remedies, although governments do not seem to have noticed or intended this.

Intervention in the film and broadcasting industries was originally accidental, and a matter of administrative convenience; but later it was based on a limited acceptance of their uniqueness. Governments were prepared to protect the development of the new media industries. However, policy towards films, broadcasting and the press demonstrated a remarkable consensus of concern for the freedom of the individual media producer during the late 1930s and the 1940s. The first investigation of the newspaper industry concluded that the political independence of the press depended on the acumen and freedom of editors. Although it was impossible to proscribe for their judgement, its protection was the only legitimate end of public policy. Doubts about the B.B.C.'s monopoly were expressed solely through a concern for the security and independence of its employees; while successive reports on the film industry interpreted its recurrent crises in terms of their effects on the independent producer. It is as if the academics and civil servants who wrote these reports felt that an enterprise would survive and do well if it were led by men like themselves: independent professionals. The integrity of the individual was the first and last defence against a whole variety of political, commercial and aesthetic pressures.

The over-emphasis on the power of the individual practitioner was succeeded (although it is still a common argument) by a reliance on a partially controlled market to produce successful media industries. The intention of the 1962 Royal Commission on the Press was to reveal the inefficiency of the newspaper industry, and it was believed that the adoption of normal industrial practice would improve both the economic and journalistic performance of the press. In the case of the film industry it was assumed that cash, in the form of grants, subsidies and levies, could transform an industrial structure, while commercial broadcasting was introduced both because it would be profitable, and on the grounds that competition would improve the service to the public.

The most recent generation of reports also share assumptions, but less positive ones. The problems of the media industries have proved to be intractable. Demonstrating that the press is run irrationally has not led to its reform. The history of I.T.V. has shown that competition no more guaranteed accountability, or a wider choice of content, than a state monopoly had done. These reports represent an uneasy retreat from the belief in the efficiency of competition, but reject attempts to interfere in it because they would be unwise politically, or now, more smugly, because they would be impractical.

Indeed fatalism has been the dominant tone of public reports on the media. Often concerned with the symptoms of crises rather than their causes, they reveal the forces which determine an industry at a particular moment. They rarely recognise that these pressures have developed historically and have not always been present. During the 1930s public policy overemphasised the role of the individual in the media, and failed to understand the structure of the industries. Recently the structure of the individual industries has been more thoroughly examined, yet a similar mistake is being made. By concentrating on the performance of the separate industries policy has failed to take account of their inter-relationship, and the problems and possibilities which they share.

If government policy towards the media had merely been contradictory and sanctified traditions whose origins were accidental, then this would be sufficient reason to demand a fundamental change in the way policy was formed. When the three major reports on the separate industries which have been published in the last two years fail to investigate the nature of their inter-relationship, although they have made recommendations based on assumptions about it, then this too intensifies the demand for a change in government policy. Finally when it is revealed that policy has been based unknowingly on similar premises, and that as a consequence the film industry has died, broadcasting remained unresponsive, and the press become increasingly frail, then the demand for a coherent policy that deals with all the media becomes even more urgent.

Notes on Contributors

LUKE ALEXANDER is a newspaper executive.

NEAL ASCHERSON writes on Scottish politics for *The Scotsman,* in Edinburgh. He entered journalism as a leader writer on the *Manchester Guardian,* but has spent most of this time since writing on foreign affairs. From 1963–8, he was Central European correspondent for the *Observer,* based on Bonn and Berlin. In 1969, he was named runner-up Foreign Reporter of the Year for his coverage of politics in the United States, a country he had never visited or written about, but raised no protest. Between 1969 and 1972, he was an active member of the Free Communications Group. He is author of *The King Incorporated* (1963), a study of Leopold II, King of Begium and the Congo.

JAMES CURRAN graduated at Cambridge University and was a Research Fellow at the Open University before becoming a Senior Lecturer at the School of Communication, Polytechnic of Central London. A member of the Labour Party's policy study group on the mass media, he was parliamentary Labour candidate for Huntingdon (1970) and Cambridge (February and October 1974). He is joint editor of *Mass Communication and Society* 1977) and *Newspaper History (1978). He was a consultant to the* Royal Commission on the Press.

PHILIP ELLIOTT is a media sociologist who has specialised in studies of production, organisation and occupations in broadcasting and the press. He is Research Fellow at the Centre for Mass Communication Research, University of Leicester. His published work includes monographs on *The Sociology of the Professions* (1972) and *The Making of a Television Series* (1972). He has recently completed a study of the reporting of Northern Ireland in London, Dublin and Belfast.

PETER GOLDING holds an external degree in sociology from London University, and a graduate degree in sociology from Essex University. He is a Research Associate at the Centre for Mass Communication Research, University of Leicester, where he is currently doing research on the media and the welfare state. He has published various articles on mass communications, and is the author of *The Mass Media* (1974) and co-author of a forthcoming study of broadcast journalism in three countries.

STUART HALL is Director of the Centre for Contemporary Cultural Studies at the University of Birmingham. He has written and researched in the area of the mass media and ideology, producing a book on black crime, the media and the state – *Policing the Crisis* (1978). A volume of media essays *(Reproducing Ideologies)* will form part of the Macmillan series 'Communications and Culture'.

STUART HOLLAND graduated in history and gained a doctorate in economics at Oxford University before going on to teach economics at Sussex University. He worked in the Cabinet Office and the Prime Minister's Political Office for half the lifetime of the 1964–70 Labour Governments, resigning in 1968. He was appointed special adviser to the Minister of Overseas Development, Judith Hart, resigning in 1975. A member of numerous policy committees of the Labour Party National Executive, he edited *The State as Capitalist Entrepreneur* (1972) and is the author of *The Socialist Challenge* (1975), *The Regional Problem* (1976) and *Capital versus the Regions* (1976).

HAROLD JACKSON is the Features Editor of the *Guardian*. After some years as a sub-editor he worked on the Home News Desk.

He then became the paper's roving foreign correspondent, travelling widely in Europe, the Middle East, the Far East, Africa, and North America. In 1969 he was named News Reporter of the Year. He is the author of *The Two Irelands* (1972), a study of the conflict in Ulster, on which he also reported extensively for the *Guardian*.

GRAHAM MURDOCK is a graduate of the London School of Economics and the University of Sussex and is currently a Research Associate at University of Leicester's Centre for Mass Communication Research, where his main interest is the political economy of the mass media. He has written widely on mass communications and is the co-author of two books: *Demonstrations, and Communication* (1970), and *Mass Media and the Secondary School* (1973).

DAVID MURPHY is a lecturer in sociology at the University of Manchester Institute of Science and Technology in the Management Sciences Department. Prior to going to university he worked as a reporter for Tillotsons Newspapers of Bolton. He spent two years at Salford University preparing a thesis on newspaper organisation for a Masters degree, and two years at Manchester carrying out a Social Science Research Council project on the press, local pressure groups and local politics. He is the author of *The Silent Watchdog* (1976), a study of the press in local politics.

BRUCE PAGE first learnt about journalism in Australia, and has worked for the *Melbourne Herald*, the *Evening Standard*, the *Daily Herald*, the *Sunday Times* and the *Daily Express*, besides contributing to the *New Statesman* and other journals and dabbling a little in television. He has written books about espionage, politics, international affairs, fraud and aeronautics – the qualities of which are probably due to various collaborators – and is now writing a work of military, political and literary history. He is Editor of the *New Statesman*.

GEOFFREY ROBERTSON practices as a barrister in London, and has been involved in a number of cases concerning the limits of press freedom. He is the author of *Reluctant Judas* (1976), a book about the life of a Special Branch informer, and a forthcoming work on

British censorship law. He is an executive member of the National Council of Civil Liberties, and a frequent contributor to the *New Statesman*.

JEAN SEATON teaches sociology at the Polytechnic of the South Bank. She was recently awarded a British Academy research grant to study the development of the Portuguese press and Broadcasting since the *coup*. She is working on a book with James Curran on the media in Britain.

ANTHONY SMITH, was a current affairs television producer before turning writer and campaigner for change in the organisation of broadcasting. Between 1971 and 1976 he held a Fellowship at St Antony's College, Oxford. Among his works are *The Shadow in the Cave – the broadcaster, the audience and the State* (1973), *British Broadcasting* (edited, 1974), *The British Press since the War* (edited, 1975) and *Subsidies and the Press in Europe* (1977).

RAYMOND WILLIAMS is a Fellow of Jesus College and Professor of Drama at Cambridge University. In 1973 he was Professor of Political Science in Stanford University, California. His published books include *Drama in Performance* (1954), *Culture and Society 1780 – 1950* (1958), *Border Country* (1960), *The Long Revolution* (1961), *Second Generation* (1964), *Communications* (1966), *Modern Tragedy* (1966), *The English Novel from Dickens to Lawrence* (1970), *The Country and the City* (1973) and *Marxism and Literature* (1977).

Notes and References

Introduction

1. 'A heavy wodge of platitudes and the blindingly obvious' was the *Daily Mirror's* verdict (8 July 1977) cf. *Daily Telegraph* (8 July 1977) *inter al.* This seems an ungrateful response to a report which largely accepted the representations it received from the press.

2. Royal Commission on the Press, *Final Report* (London: H.M.S.O., 1977) Cmnd. 6810, p. 112. (Royal Commission on the Press is henceforth abbreviated to R.C.P.)

3. The Commission was content merely to describe European press subsidy schemes, and elaborate upon them in terms of the McGregor principle, rather than conduct an empirical investigation into whether intervention had resulted in covert political censorship. See R.C.P., *Final Report*, 1977, pp. 113–15 and Appendix C, pp. 93–111.

4. Anthony Smith, 'Subsidies and the Press in Europe', *Political and Economic Planning*, vol. XLIII (1977) no. 569; cited R.C.P., *Final Report*, 1977, p. 245.

5. Brian Simon, *The Two Nations and the Educational Structure, 1780–1870* (London: Lawrence and Wishart, 1974). The main fear was that state funding would lead to a secularised education imposed centrally by the state.

6. Fears on these grounds were expressed by people on the left including Sir Charles Trevelyan, a member of the Sykes Committee, who eventually backed the B.B.C. (The Broadcasting Committee Report, Cmnd 1951, 1923) George Catlin (father of Shirley Williams) even argued against the B.B.C on the grounds that 'few of us would like to see a British Newspaper Corporation' in 'Broadcasting in the Democratic

State', *Listener,* June 1936. Their misgivings were justified in the short run.

7. William Altman, Denis Thomas and David Fawers, *T.V. from Monopoly to Competition – and Back?,* Hobart Research Paper 15 (Institute of Economic Affairs, 1962).

8. Indeed even the McGregor Commission itself does not seem to take itself seriously. It failed to recommend that local authorities be restrained from giving selective financial support to local publications – a form of unmediated patronage that is liable to abuse and which clearly transgresses the McGregor embargo on selective funding. It failed also to condemn the £60 million VAT concession (at 1975 current values) on press sales and advertising, which clearly makes a section of the press dependent on government for its financial viability, to say nothing of the concessionary postal rates granted by a public corporation to papers with not less than a third of its content devoted to 'political or other news or of articles relating thereto or other current topics'. Indeed the McGregor Commission's position seems to be that all schemes that contravene its guidelines are acceptable provided they are established practice and unacceptable, in principle, if they are being proposed.

9. R.C.P., *Final Report,* 1977, p. 117.

10. For instance, ibid., p. 55.

11. Ibid., pp. 112, 124, 126.

12. For instance, ibid., p. 48.

13. Ibid., p. 113.

14. Ibid., p. 48.

15. Ibid., p. 117.

16. Ibid., p. 104.

17. Ibid., p. 114.

18. Ibid., p. 48.

19. Ibid., p. 117.

20. Discussion was largely in terms of distribution between media and categories of publication. R.C.P., *Final Report,* 1977, p. 37 *et al.*

21. R.C.P., *Final Report,* 1977, pp. 114, 117. The suggestion of political bias is implicit rather than explicit.

22. The difference in allocation is mainly due to the difference in the advertising utility of middle-class compared with working-class readers, not partisan bias on the part of advertisers. But the motivation is irrelevant; it is the consequences for the political structure of the press that is important.

23. 'No public body should ever be put in a position of discriminating like a censor between one applicant and another' (R.C.P., *Final Report,* 1977, p. 126). One wonders how the Independent Broadcasting Authority, which does precisely this, copes.

24. Milner Gibson, *Hansard Parl. Deb.,* vol. 60 (16 April 1850) col. 378.

25. Sir George Lewis (Chancellor of Exchequer), *Hansard Parl. Deb.,* vol. 87. (19 March 1855) col. 786.

26. J. F. Stephen in *Cornhill Magazine,* vol. 6 (1862) pp.57-8.

27. For further details, see James Curran, 'The Press as an Agency of Social Control' in J. Curran, G. Boyce and P. Wingate (eds), *Newspaper History: Studies in the Historical Evolution of the British Press* (London: Constable, 1978).

28. This is a simplified version of an argument advanced in James Curran, 'Capitalism and Control of the Press 1800–1975' in J. Curran, M. Gurevitch and J. Woollacott (eds), *Mass Communication and Society* (London: Arnold/Open University Press, 1977). See also Alan Lee's admirable study, *The Origins of the Popular Press 1855–1914* (London: Croom Helm, 1976).

29. R.C.P., *Final Report*, 1977, p. 110.

30. Ibid., p. 9.

31. Ibid., pp. 52-3 rightly does not regard the transfer of the *Guardian* to London, and the launch and relaunch of the *Sun*, as examples of new market entry. The most recent examples are the *Daily Worker* (1930) and *Daily Herald* (1912).

32. R.C.P., *Final Report*, 1977, p. 110.

33. Ibid., p. 54, p. 118 *et al.*

34. It rightly concluded, however, that some sector of the magazine press and to a lesser extent, the local weekly press were relatively accessible markets.

35. R.C.P., *Final Report*, 1977, pp. 43–4, 111. See also R.C.P., *Interim Report* (London: H.M.S.O., 1976) Cmnd. 6433.

36. R.C.P., *Final Report*, 1977, p. 107.

37. For a critique of the ideological framework of the report, see James Curran, 'Press Freedom as Private Property', *Media, Culture and Society*, vol. 1 (forthcoming).

Chapter 2

1. K. Marx, *The Grundrisse* (Harmondsworth: Penguin, 1973) p. 649.

2. Marx, *The Grundrisse*, p. 649

3. Marx. *The German Ideology* (London: Lawrence and Wishart, 1970) p. 65.

4. L. Althusser, *For Marx* (London: Allen Lane, 1969) p. 233.

5. A, Granisci, *Prison Notebooks* (London: Lawrence and Wishart, 1968) p. 148.

Chapter 3

1. Much of the more detailed material relevant to the theme of this essay is to be found in: Anthony Smith, 'Subsidies and the Press in Europe', *Political and Economic Planning*, vol. XLIII, no. 569 (June 1977).

2. For example, in the Finnish debate as to whether to redistribute the national sums expended on reduced postal charges. Parts I and II of the *Report of the Government Committee on Communication Policy*, 91 I, (1973) and 148 II, (1973), abridged (Helsinki: 1974) pp. 22–5.

3. See Royal Commission on the Press (R.C.P.), *Final Report Appendices* (London: H.M.S.O., 1977) Cmnd. 6810-1, Appendix C; and *Final Report,* 1977, Cmnd. 6810, para. 11.17, p. 111.

4. *From Semaphore to Satellite, the History of the International Telecommunications Union, 1865–1965* (Geneva: I.T.U., 1966).

5. J. L. Kieve, A History of the Electric Telegraph: a Social and Economic History (Newton Abbot: David & Charles, 1973) pp. 119–53.

6. *From Semaphore to Satellite;* and see Edwin Emery and Henry Ladd Smith, *The Press and America* (new York: Prentice-Hall, 1954) pp. 386–94.

7. J. L. Kieve, *A History of the Electric Telegraph,* pp. 216–29.

8. *Samarbeid i Dagspressen* (Norges Offentilge Utredninger, 1974) 5.1.

9. See comparision of balance sheets for different Norwegian papers in *Dagspressens ekonomi* (Norges Offentlige Utredninger, 1973) tables 1–13, pp. 19–28.

10. *Rapport du Groupe de Travail sur les aides publiques aux entreprises de presse* – the Serisé Report (Paris: July 1972, p. 28.) (A French Government report.)

11. *La Presse Quotidienne* (Cahiers Français no. 178, Oct–Dec 1976) 'Un secteur en crise', table 3, p. 4. (A French Government report.)

12. P. Frederix, *Un siècle de chasse aux nouvelles – de L'Agence d'Information Havas à l'A. F. P.* (Paris: Flammarion, 1959).

13. I.P.T.C. Newsletter, no, 37 (May 1977) p. 11.

14. European Space Agency, *Remote Printing in Europe via Satellite,* vol. 1 'Summary' (London: Arthur D. Little Ltd. 1977).

15. *Telecommunications – National Policy and International Agreement,* a Briefing Paper in preparation for the World Administrative Radio Conference of 1979 (cyclostyled document, International Institute of Communications, London) Sept 1977.

16. P. J. Lèvèque, 'Remote Printing for Paris Newspapers', in *I.P.T.C. Newsletter,* no. 37 (May 1977) p. 6.

17. Anthony Smith, *Telecommunications and the Press* (British Post Office, Long-Range Research Report No. 15, 1977).

18. See A. J. P. Taylor, *Beaverbrook* (Harmondsworth: Penguins, 1974) p. 95, and Colin Seymour-Ure, 'Changing Partisanship in the British Press, 1890–1970' (paper prepared for the European Consortium for Political Research Workshop on the Political Role of Mass Media, Strasbourg, March 1974).

19. Sir Norman Angell, *The Press and the Organisation of Society* (London: Labour Publishing Co., 1922).

20. J. Edward Gerald, *The British Press under Government Economic Controls* (Minneapolis: University of Minnesota Press, 1960).

21. Ibid. table 8, p. 43.

22. R.C.P., *Report* (London: H.M.S.O., 1962) Cmnd. 1811, table 7, p. 173.

23. Monopolies Commission, *The Times Newspaper and the Sunday Times Newspaper* (London: H.M.S.O., 20 Dec. 1966).

24. Ibid, para 162.

25. Harford Thomas, *Newspaper Crisis – a Study of Development in the National Press of Britain, 1966–67* (Zurich: International Press Institute, 1967).

26. This was discussed in R.C.P., *Report*, 1962, which concluded: '. . . in view of the statutory monopoly enjoyed by television contract companies we consider it to be contrary to the public interest for such companies to be controlled by newspaper undertakings' (para. 244).

27. *Bericht der Bundesregierung über die Lage von Presse und Rundfunk in der Bundesrepublik Deutschland* (Bonn: Presse und Informationsamt der Bundesregierung, 1974) p. 45.

28. *Frankfurter Allgemeine Zeitung*, 6 Dec 1975.

29. *Deutsche Presse-Agentur*, March 1976.

30. Deutscher Presserat, Tätigkeitsbericht 1975–76.

31. See speech of Federal Minister for Internal Affairs, Gerhart Baum, 15 May 1975 (Pressedienst des Bundesministeriums des Innern).

32. *Fact Sheet/Denmark* (Copenhagen: Press and Cultural Relations Dept of Ministy of Foreign Affairs, 1977).

33. *Pressehandbuch 1975* (Austrian Press Handbook) (Vienna: Verband Oesterreichischer Zeitungsherausgeber und Zietungsverleger, 1976); and see article in *Suddeutsche Zeitung*, 3 June 1975.

34. Ulrich Saxer, *Medienpolitische Systeme: eine Analyse schweizerischer Medienpolitik*, Heft 1 (Publizistik, Drückerei und Verlagsanstalt Konstanz Universitätsverlag 1976).

35. Christian Padrutt, *Zur Lage der Schweizerischer Presse* (Zurich: Publizistisches Seminar der Universitat Zurich, 1975).

36. Report by the Nederlandse Vereniging van Journalisten (Amsterdam, 1975).

37. Centre du Recherche et d'Information Socio-politiques (C.R.I.S.P.), *Morphologie des groupes et entreprises de presse (III)*, 9 May 1975, *Courrier Hebdomadaire*, no. 682.

38. C.R.I.S.P., Annex sur 'DOC' no. 103. 1976.

39. *A Free and Responsible Press – a General Report on Mass Communication* (University of Chicago Press, 1947).

40. R.C.P., *Report* (London: H.M.S.O., 1949) Cmd. 7700, ch. XI.

41. The French newspapers received a once-only newsprint subsidy after the tremendous price rises of 1973. In Italy, the Ente Nazionale per la Celluloza e per la Carta (E.N.C.C.) distributes a subsidy to all newspapers according to newsprint consumed per page per thousand of circulation.

42. Statens Offentiliga Utredningar (Swedish Government Official Report), *Dagspressens ekonomiska villkor*, 1965:22.

43. Statens Offentliga Utredningar, *Dagspressens situation*, 1968:48.

44. Karl Erik Gustafsson and Stig Hadenius, *Swedish Press Policy* (Stockholm: Swedish Institute, 1976) p. 52.

45. Federazione Italiana Editorial Giornali (F.I.E.G.) *Ordinamento della professione di giornalista* (Rome: Industria tipografica Imperia, 1965).

46. See Stefano Merlini, 'Ordine dei giornalisti, Contrattazione collective, liberta a dignita professionale dei lavoratori nell' azienda giornalistica', and Pietro Zanelli, 'Aspetti particolari del trattamento economico-normativo dei giorhalisti', both in *La stampa quotidiana tra crisi e riforma*, ed. Paolo Barile and Enzo Cheli (Bologna: Societa editrice il Mulino, 1976).

47. Andrea Orsi Battaglini, 'L'integrazione del prezzo della carta: logica di mercato e politica dell'informazione', in Barile and Cheli, ibid.

48. Carlo Macchitella and Domenico Sorace, 'I problemi della distribuzione', in Barile and Cheli, ibid.

49. *Disegno di Legge concernente nuove norme per la Stampa* — cyclostyled Italian draft law, 1977.

50. These have been subjected to various proposals for further amendment at the time of writing. For discussion on the Arnaud draft law, see *Il Sole-24 Ore* (Milan), 8 Feb 1977.

51. The *Gazetta di Mantova*.

52. Svennik Hoyer, 'Temporal Patterns and Political Factors in the Diffusion of Newspaper Publishing – the Case of Norway', *Scandinavian Political Studies*, vol. 10 (1975) (Oslo: Universitetsforlaget and London: Sage Publications, 1976).

53. Allan Viranko, *Suomen sanomaelehdisto vakaanuttaa asemaansa, 1916–1966* (The Consolidation of the Finnish Press, 1916–1966) (Helsinki, 1970).

54. Report of the Government Committee on Communication Policy, p. 14.

55. S. Hoyer, 'Temporal Patterns.'.

56. Dick Leonard, 'Paying for Party Politics: the Case for Public Subsidies', *Political and Economic Planning*, vol. VLI, Broadsheet no. 555 September (1975).

57. For a description, see Anthony Smith, *The Shadow in the Cave* (London: Quartet, 1976).

58. *De Journalist* (Amsterdam), 15 Sept 1976.

59. Elisabeth Noelle-Neumann, Franz Ronneberger and Heinz Werner Stuiber, *Streitpunkt Lokales Pressemonopol – Untarsuchungen auz Alleinstellung von Tageszeiten* (Düsseldorf: Droste Verlag, 1976).

60. *Media Perspektiven* (Hamburg) 1977, no. 1.

61. Submission of the Dublin Newspaper Managers' Committee to the Minister of Finance, Dublin, June 1975 (prepared by P. A. Management Consultants (Ireland) Ltd).

62. To 5½ per cent on all papers sold by subscription.

63. *Bulletin de Documentation Pratique des Taxes*, no. 10. (Oct 1976) (article on 'La Presse et la T.V.A.') and Sénat, 106, *Rapport au nom de la Commission des Finances*, par M. Jean Francou, 3 Dec 1976.

64. See R.C.P., *Final Report*, 1977, para 11.13, p. 111.

65. *Dagspressens ekonomi* (Norges Offentlige Utredninger, 1973) pp. 48–55.

Chapter 4

1. Royal Commission on the Press (R.C.P.), *Final Report* (London: H.M.S.O., 1977) Cmnd. 6810.
2. R.C.P., *Report* (London: H.M.S.O., 1962) Cmnd. 1811.
3. R.C.P., *Final Report,* 1977, p. 14.
4. Ibid., p. 149.
5. For details of the major newspaper companies' other interests, see R.C.P., *Final Report Appendices,* 1977, Cmnd. 6810-1. Appendices A, B; G. Murdock and P. Golding, 'The ownership, structure and control of the press, 1914–1976', in J. Curran, G. Boyce and P. Wingate (eds), *Newspaper History: Studies in the Evolution of the British Press* (London: Constable, 1978).
6. R.C.P., *Final Report,* 1977, p. 154.
7. Ibid., p. 149.
8. Ibid., p. 105.
9. D. Hamilton, *Who is to Own the British Press?* (London: Birkbeck College, 1976) p. 18.
10. R.C.P., *Interim Report: The National Newspaper Industry* (London: H.M.S.O., 1976) Cmnd. 6433, p. 38.
11. R.C.P., *Final Report,* 1977, p. 109.
12. Ibid., pp. 98–9.
13. Ibid., p. 79.
14. Ibid., pp. 59 *et seq.*
15. Ibid., p. 9.
16. Ibid., p. 123.
17. Ibid., p. 126.
18. Ibid., p. 126.
19. N. Beloff, 'Has Fleet Street a Future?', *Encounter* (September 1977) pp. 82–8.
20. R.C.P., *Final Report,* 1977, p. 134.
21. G. Murdock and P. Golding, 'Beyond Monopoly: Mass Communications in an Age of Conglomerates', in *Trade Unions and the Media,* ed. P. Beharrell and G. Philo (London: Macmillan, 1977).
22. R.C.P., *Final Report,* 1977, p. 155.
23. Hamilton, *Who is to Own the British Press?,* p. 18.
24. R.C.P., *Final Report,* 1977, p. 39.
25. G. Cleverley, *The Fleet Street Disaster* (London: Constable, 1976) pp. 37–47.
26. R.C.P., *Final Report,* 1977, p. 32.
27. Ibid., pp. 241–50.
28. Well described by F. Hirsch and D. Gordon, *Newspaper Money* (London: Hutchinson, 1975), pp. 45–6.
29. See R.C.P., *Concentration of Ownership in the Provincial Press* (London: H.M.S.O., 1977) Cmnd. 6810-5, Appendix G.
30. Ibid., p. 120.
31. Ibid., p. 87.

Chapter 5

1. Jeremy Tunstall has pointed out that while the notion of editorial sovereignty is especially associated with *The Times* and its tradition, an examination of the history of *The Times* shows that even in the mid-nineteenth century the editor shared his responsibility with not only a proprietor but also a manager, while it was the manager who hired and posted foreign correspondents. While Dawson, in his second phase as Editor of *The Times* enshrined his sovereignty in a written contract, this has been the exception rather than the rule. Evidence to the Royal Commission on the Press, 1977 (mimeo).

2. Labour Party, Opposition Green Paper, *Capital and Equality* (London: 1973).

3. Bias or lack of bias cannot be determined simply on non-correlation between the share of papers favouring particular parties at general elections, and the share of the resulting vote. Quite simply, the vote may be expressed despite editorial bias, through openness of voters to other media, their innate feelings about bias itself, and so forth. None the less, there is no doubt that more papers have supported Conservatives rather than Labour at general elections since the war. Also, the Royal Commission shows itself concerned about the inadequacy of press reporting on trades unions. (Royal Commission on the Press (R.C.P.)), *Final Report* (London: H.M.S.O., 1977) pp. 96–100.)

4. See Chapter 4, by Peter Golding and Graham Murdock.

5. These forms of 'elimination' and 'no entry' pricing have been well established in the economic literature on oligopoly, or domination of markets by a few sellers, for many years. See *inter alia,* J. S. Bain, *Barriers to New Competition* (Harvard University Press, 1962) and Paolo Sylos Labini, *Oligopoly and Technical Progress,* 2nd edn. (Harvard University Press, 1969).

6. Fred Hirsch and David Gordon, *Newspaper Money* (London: Hutchinson, 1975) p. 12.

7. See G. Walshe, *Recent Trends in Monopoly in Great Britain* (National Institute of Economic and Social Research, Occasional Paper 27, 1974).

8. The Editorial Director of the Westminster Press Group, the Hon. Nicholas Herbert, has 'a major say in the appointment of all group editors' (R.C.P., *Final Report,* 1977, p. 130). Ironically he is also the joint editor (with Bob Taylor) of *Press Freedom: The Lifeblood of Democracy* (York: Westminster Press, 1974) in which editorial freedom is proclaimed as both real and crucial to the health of the body politic.

9. Lord Beaverbrook, Evidence to the Royal Commission on the Press, 1962.

10. Mervyn King, 'Fact and Fiction in Industry's Profits', *The Financial Times,* 21 October 1974.

11. Press concentration in developed countries circa 1969: how the total daily circulation is controlled is shown in the following table.

	Controlled by the 4 largest ownership units %	Controlled by the 8 largest ownership units %	Controlled by the 20 largest ownership units %	Average percentage
Ireland	81	100	–	91
Australia	74	90	96	87
United Kingdom	66	77	89	77
New Zealand	59	76	94	76
Austria	52	71	97	73
Japan	56	71	90	72
Belgium	49	69	94	71
Canada	53	70	89	71
Denmark	50	64	84	67
Netherlands	39	55	82	59
F. R. Germany	42	50	62	51
Italy	30	47	75	51
France	30	46	73	50
Spain	29	43	55	42
United States	18	28	43	30

Source: Raymond B. Nixon and Tae-youl Hahn, 'Concentration of Press Ownership: a comparison of 32 countries', *Journalism Quarterly,* 48 (Spring 1971) p. 13. Cited by Tunstall, Evidence to the Royal Commission on the Press, 1977.

12. S. J. Prais, *The Evolution of Giant Firms in Britain* (National Institute of Economic and Social Research and Cambridge University Press, 1976) chapter 1.
13. Tunstall, Evidence to the Royal Commission on the Press, 1977.
14. R.C.P., *Final Report,* 1977, p. 204.

Chapter 6

1. Ansgar Skriver, *Schreiben und schreiben lassen* (Karlsruhe: C. F. Mueller Verlag, 1970) p. 32.
2. Report of the Committee of Inquiry on Industrial Democracy *(Bullock Report)* (London: H.M.S.O., 1977) Cmnd. 6706, p. 130.
3. See for instance, the Labour Discussion Document *The People and the Media* (1974) p. 32, para. 3.

Chapter 7

1. Chapter and paragraph references in the text are to Royal Commission on the Press (R.C.P.), *Final Report* (London: H.M.S.O.,

1977) Cmnd. 6810. Appendices are published in a separate volume, Cmnd. 6810–1, 1977.

2. D. McQuail, *Review of Sociological Writing on the Press*, R.C.P. Working Paper No. 2 (London: H.M.S.O., 1976) p. 10.

3. Report of the Committee on the Future of Broadcasting (Annan Report) (London: H.M.S.O., 1977), Cmnd. 6753, 17. 11–13.

4. Much of the material for this critique is taken from my study of the reporting of Northern Ireland in the London, Dublin and Belfast media. A condensed version is to be found in Philip Elliott, 'Misreporting Ulster, News as a Field Dressing', *New Society*, 25 November 1976. The full report will be published by UNESCO under the title *Reporting Northern Ireland*.

5. Arthur Christiansen, *Headlines All My Life* (New York: Harper, 1961).

6. Simon Winchester, *In Holy Terror* (London: Faber and Faber, 1974).

7. As for example in Dave Clark, 'Here is the news from the Europa', *Time Out*, 17–23 June 1977.

8. On the tradition of English stereotypes of Ireland and the Irish see R. Taylor, 'Images of the Irish', *New Society*, 28 November 1974, pp. 556–7.

9. Economist Intelligence Unit, *The National Newspaper Industy: A Survey*, 1966.

10. 1975 figure from A.C.A.S., *Industrial Relations in the National Newspaper Industry* (London: H.M.S.O., 1976) Cmnd. 6680, Appendix 16. Table 2. Bruce Page in his chapter in this volume points out that the number of sub-editors, desk editors and editorial executives combined is even larger.

11. The work of the Centre for Contemporary Cultural Studies, University of Birmingham on mugging is summarised in Steve Chibnall, *Law and Order News* (London: Tavistock, 1977) which also provides an excellent survey of reporter–source relationships for this type of news.

12. Winchester, *In Holy Terror;* Simon Hoggart, 'The Army P.R. Men of Northern Ireland', *New Society*, 11 October 1973, pp. 79–80.

13. See Fisk's story in *The Times*, 8 February 1975.

14. Claud Cockburn, *I Claud* (Harmondsworth: Penguin, 1967).

15. Andrew Stephen, 'A Reporter's Life in Belfast', *Observer*, 29 February 1976.

16. Paul Johnson, 'The Resources of Civilisation', *New Statesman*, 31 October 1975.

17. For example Harold Evans, 'The Half Free Press', *Granada Guildhall Lecture*, 1974.

18. As for example the chapter by Peter Golding and Graham Murdock in this volume or Jeremy Tunstall, 'Will Fleet Street survive until 1984?' Evidence to the Royal Commission on the Press, 1977 (mimeo).

19. Jeremy Tunstall, *Journalists at Work* (London: Constable, 1971).

20. Ibid., pp. 267–8.

21. Winchester, *In Holy Terror,* pp. 210–11.

22. John Whale, 'The Press and Jeremy Thorpe', *Political Quarterly,* vol. 47, no. 4 (October–December 1976).

23. The relevant findings may be found in R.C.P., *Final Report,* 1977, chapter 18, and *Final Report Appendices,* Appendix H.

Chapter 9

1. *Studies on the Press,* R.C.P. Working Paper No. 3 (London: H.M.S.O., 1977).

2. *Analysis of Newspaper Content,* R.C.P. Research Series 4 (London: H.M.S.O., 1977).

3. *Studies on the Press.*

Chapter 10

1. Royal Commission on the Press, (R.C.P.), *Final Report* (London: H.M.S.O., 1977) Cmnd. 6810, chapter 19, para. 4.

2. Ibid., chapter 10, para. 63.

3. *Report of the Committee on the Official Secrets Act* (London: H.M.S.O., 1972) Cmnd. 5104.

4. *Report of the Committee on Defamation* (London: H.M.S.O., 1975) Cmnd. 5909.

5. *Report of the Committee on Contempt of Court* (London: H.M.S.O., 1974) Cmnd. 5794.

6. *Report of the Committee on Privacy* (London: H.M.S.O., 1972) Cmnd. 5012.

7. R.C.P., *Final Report,* 1977, chapter 10. para. 86.

8. See T. Bunyan, *The Political Police in Britain* (London: Julian Friedmann, 1976) p. 18.

9. *R.* v. *Cairns, Roberts and Aitken* (The *Sunday Telegraph* Case), described by defendant Jonathan Aitken in his book, *Officially Secret* (London: Weidenfeld & Nicolson, 1971).

10. See the oral evidence of Chapman Pincher, *Departmental Committee on Section 2 of the Official Secrets Act,* (London: H.M.S.O., 1972) volume 4, p. 234.

11. *Sunday Times* editorial on Crossman Diaries case.

12. H. C. Relyea, *The Administration of the Freedom of Information Act* (Washington, D.C.: U.S. Congressional Research Service, 1976).

13. C. M. Marwick (ed.), *Litigation under the Amended Federal Freedom of Information Act,* 2nd edn. (1976).

14. M. Halperin et al., *The Lawless State* (Harmondsworth: Penguin, 1976).

15. *Departmental Committee on Official Secrets Act,* vol. 3, p. 249.

16. *New York Times* v. *U.S.,* 403 U.S. 713, at p. 729.

17. Mr Justice Douglas, *E.P.A.* v. *Mink,* 410 U.S. 73 (1973).

18. C. Wright Mills, *The Power Elite* (New York: Oxford University Press, 1956) p. 355.

19. *Attorney General* v. *Jonathan Cape Ltd* (1975) 3 W.L.R. 606.

20. *New York Times* v. *U.S.*, 403 U.S. 713, at p. 729.

21. *Prince Albert* v. *Strange* (1849) 1 H & T 1.

22. *Duchess of Argyll* v. *Duke of Argyll* (1967) chapter 302.

23. *Attorney General* v. *Times Newspapers Ltd* (1974) AC 273, at p. 300 (per Lord Reid).

24. Ibid.

25. *The Times,* letter to the Editor, 22 June 1976.

26. *Report of the Committee on Defamation* (London: H.M.S.O., 1975) Cmnd 5909, p. 5.

27. R.C.P., *Final Report,* 1977, chapter 20. para. 39.

28. Speech to the Liverpool Press Club, March 1976.

29. R.C.P., *Final Report,* 1977, chapter 10, para. 135.

30. Ibid., chapter 20. para. 64.

31. *New Statesman,* 6 May 1977, p. 600.

32. Ibid.

33. See *Privacy & Publication – Proposals for Protection,* Discussion Paper No. 2, (Australian Law Reform Commission, 1977).

34. *Declaration on Privacy* (The Press Council, April 1976).

35. R.C.P., *Final Report,* 1977 chapter 10, para. 52.

36. Sir Denis Hamilton, *Who Is To Own The British Press* (London: Birkbeck College, 1976) p. 9.

37. R.C.P., *Final Report,* 1977, chapter 19, para. 40.

38. See Geoffrey Robertson, 'Badly Burned Books', *New Statesman,* 23 August 1974.

39. See *Goldsmith* v. *Sperrings Ltd* (1977) 1 W.L.R. 478.

40. R.C.P., *Final Report,* 1977, chapter 17, para. 4.

41. Ibid., chapter 17. para. 20.

42. Ibid., chapter 2. para. 3.

Chapter 11

1. Charles Wintour, *Pressures on the Press* (London: Andre Deutsche, 1972) pp. 35–6.

2. Royal Commission on the Press (R.C.P.), *Report* (London: H.M.S.O., 1949) Cmnd. 7700, p. 141–3, indicated only that some special advertising supplements and pages published in the 1930s were probably influenced by advertising and that some small provincial weeklies may also have accepted advertising 'puffs'.

3. Michael Foot, in R.C.P., *Report,* 1949, p. 139.

4. *Ibid.,* p. 143.

5. R.C.P., *Report* (London: H.M.S.O., 1962) Cmnd. 1811, p. 87.

6. R.C.P., *Final Report* (London: H.M.S.O., 1977) Cmnd. 6810, p. 104–5.

7. R.C.P., *Report,* 1949, para. 527; R.C.P., *Report,* 1962, para. 276.

8. *Ibid.,* and R.C.P., *Final Report,* 1977, para. 10.158.

9. R.C.P., *Minutes of Evidence,* 1949, eighth day, 13 November 1947, Q2174. Major Harrison's testimony covered both the 1930s and the 1940s.

10. *Outdoor Girl Beauty Products: Recommendations of Advertising,* August 1936, p. 13 (London Press Exchange Ltd., File 152); *Hospital Services for the Middle Classes.* July 1939, p. 7 (File 200) *inter alia.*

11. For instance, the relatively free and easy attitude to advertising pressure expressed in the classic advertising textbook of the 1930s – Harold Eley, *Advertising Media* (London: Butterworth, 1932) – is not reflected in any of the standard post-war text books on advertising.

12. R.C.P., *Final Report,* 1977, para. 10.154.

13. J. Edward Gerald, *The British Press Under Economic Controls* (Minneapolis: University of Minnesota Press, 1956).

14. R.C.P., *Final Report,* 1977, table 5.5. p. 39.

15. *Analysis of Newspaper Content,* R.C.P. Research Series 4, 1977, Cmnd. 6810-4, pp. 15–21. Some of these content changes are actually referred to earlier in R.C.P., *Final Report,* 1977, pp. 77–8.

16. *Analysis of Newspaper Content,* table A4, p. 19.

17. This is not to criticise Denis McQuail's analysis – or question the pragmatic and understandable reasons for basing his historical analysis on that of the first Royal Commission – but rather the way in which his analysis was interpreted by the McGregor Commission.

18. The McGregor Commission relied heavily upon an analysis of national daily party endorsements at General Elections. This classification system only provides a meaningful measure of political balance if it is assumed that there is a significant difference between the left of the Conservative Party and the right of the Labour Party. See R.C.P., *Final Report,* 1977, pp. 95–9.

19. A representative sample was selected on the same rotational principle as the Royal Commission's content analysis. The sample was necessarily small – 12 issues per year for each daily paper and six issues per year (the same as the Royal Commission's content analysis) for Sunday newspapers.

20. A code–recode comparison between the two coders revealed a 5.9 per cent deviation in coding classifications of items summarised in Table 11.1 and Table 11.2.

21. In most cases, however, there is a less clear distinction between those falling in and outside the target group: in these instances, some but a reduced weight is attached to reaching people outside the target group.

22. This was first confirmed in Britain as long ago as 1932 in a pioneering survey commissioned by the *Daily Herald,* which is now destroyed.

23. These observations are derived primarily from survey-based studies commissioned or conducted by three publishing corporations. Answers to 'topic satisfaction' questions need to be treated with caution, however, since they can be highly misleading.

24. Given the large number of variables that could affect the allocation of space over so long a time span, it is indeed surprising that a link should have emerged so strongly. Two examples must suffice. The *Daily Mail's* sponsored travel coverage declined by 74 per cent between 1936 and 1976 in response to a 94 per cent reduction in its related travel advertising. It

failed to regain its position as the market leader for travel advertising after the war, with the result that a growing volume of display travel advertising was distributed to its main rivals, whose volume of sponsored travel features was also much greater in 1976 than in 1936. Similarly, book coverage in quality Sunday newspapers fell sharply as a proportion of total editorial space between 1936 and 1976, in line with the relative decline in book advertising, whilst their sponsored financial coverage increased massively – in the case of the *Sunday Times* by 988 per cent – in response to a comparable increase in financial advertising between 1936 and 1976.

25. This was developed with some sophistication in 1934 in a pioneering survey report commissioned by the *News Chronicle,* called *A Survey of Reader Interest in the National Morning and London Evening Press* (1934). For both cost and methodological reasons this form of advertising research into 'attention value' went out of fashion in the early 1960s.

26. First and foremost, there is widespread journalistic resistance to advertising pressure when manifested in a crude form. The number of sponsors of features in the national newspaper press is also sufficiently large for it to be possible to risk alienating individual advertisers without dire financial consequences. The pressures exerted by some advertisers are also, to some extent, contradictory: the demand for an authoritative editorial context commanding high attention is not easily reconciled with transparently sycophantic journalism. Some advertisers are also dubious, probably quite rightly, about the 'dispositional' influence of editorial settings.

27. The fact that Distillers, to take only one example, was a heavy advertiser in the *Sunday Times* did not prevent the *Sunday Times* from launching a national campaign against Distillers over the thalidomide issue. (Incidentally, despite the bitter legal battle that ensued, Distillers continued to advertise heavily in the *Sunday Times.*) This is not to deny the influence of advertising, but only to suggest that this influence is of a rather more indirect and complex nature than is often supposed.

28. *Profile of the European Executive Market* (London: Newsweek International/Conrad Jameson Associates, 1973), *et al.*

29. A code–recode comparison between the two coders revealed a 4.6 per cent deviation in coding classifications of items summarised in Tables 11.3 and 11.4.

30. John Westergaard and Henrietta Resler, *Class in a Capitalist Society* (London: Heinemann, 1975) table 17, p. 116.

31. Average for six-year period derived from the quarterly estimates in *Financial Statistics* (London: H.M.S.O.). My thanks to Andy Thomson for drawing this to my attention.

32. Ernestine Carter, *Tongue in Chic* (London: Michael Joseph, 1973).

33. There are honourable exceptions to this characterisation. An unsystematic analysis also suggests that sex-role portrayals in women's features are less stereotyped than they used to be.

34. This is not to advance a monistic thesis: advertising is only one of a number of influences shaping the values, images and issue agendas of sponsored features.

35. For some recent examples of this research, see M. McCombs and D. L. Shaw, 'The Agenda Setting Function of the Mass Media', *Public Opinion Quarterly,* vol. 36, 1972; K. Siune and O. Borre, 'Setting the Agenda for a Danish Election', *Journal of Communication,* vol. 25, 1975; J. M. McLeod, L. B. Becker and J. E. Byrnes, 'Another Look at the Agenda-Setting Function of the Press', *Communication Research,* vol. 1, 1974; M. Benton and P. J. Frazier, 'The Agenda Setting Function of the Mass Media at Three Levels of "Information Holding" ', *Communications Research,* vol. 3, 1976. These suggest somewhat surprisingly greater press than T.V. influence.

36. R.C.P., *Interim Report,* 1976, table E5, p. 96; *Concentration of Ownership in the Provincial Press,* R.C.P. Research Series 5, 1977, Cmnd. 6810-5, tables 5.2 and 5.7, pp. 18 and 23; *Periodicals and the Alternative Press,* R.C.P. Research Series 6, 1977, Cmnd. 6810-6, table 24, p. 24; and *The Periodical Publishing Industry* (mimeo), Coopers and Lybrand, R.C.P., 1975. For the earlier period, see *Costs and Revenues of National Newspapers,* National Board for Prices and Incomes Report no. 141 (London: H.M.S.O., 1970) Cmnd. 4277, Appendix G, p. 34; *Costs and Revenue of National Daily Newspapers,* National Board of Prices and Incomes Report no. 43 (London: H.M.S.O., 1967) Cmnd. 3435, table 3, p. 24; R.C.P., *Report,* 1962, table 3, p. 187; *Survey of the National Newspaper Industry* (London: Economist Intelligence Unit, 1966) Part II b, tables 13 and 31; R.C.P., *Report,* 1949, tables 3 and 4, p. 82. Some popular papers in the 1940s made a profit on sales alone as a result of the reduction of costs caused by newsprint rationing.

37. This was the argument advanced, for instance, by the Advertising Association in its evidence to the Royal Commission on the Press, 1974–7.

38. For comments on the effect of the press on broadcasting news values, see Lord Windlesham, *Communication and Power* (London: Cape, 1966) and Jeremy Tunstall, *Journalists at Work* (London: Constable, 1971).

39. These changes are reviewed in James Curran, *Advertising Media Planning and the British Press, 1945—75* (mimeo).

40. R.C.P., *Final Report Appendices,* 1977, Appendix E, 'Advertising and the Press', p. 126–7.

41. All advertising figures are net advertising revenue figures supplied by publishers with the exception of that of the *Daily Mail,* the net advertising revenue of which was estimated by multiplying its annual volume of advertising by its standard column rate over the appropriate number of publishing days, less agency commission.

42. Annual advertising volume has been calculated by multiplying the *Daily Herald's* annual average net circulation by its annual issue advertising volume, details of which have been provided by Reed International.

43. Estimated net advertisement revenues for all national daily newspapers are derived from the *Statistical Review of Press Advertising,* less 15 per cent (modal commission). Since the *Statistical Review's* estimates did not include classified advertising at a time when classified advertising was growing rapidly in the quality dailies, the estimate probably understates the fall in the *Daily Herald's* market share. Advertising revenue figures for the *Daily Herald* and *Daily Mirror* have been supplied by Reed International.

44. Calculated from *National Readership Survey* (London: Institute of Practioners in Advertising, 1962) and advertising standard column inch rates, as tabulated in *Daily Mail* records.

45. Sir Denis Hamilton, *Who is to Own the British Press?* (London: Birkbeck College, 1976), p. 7.

46. *Report on Supplementary Questions: Readers' Attitudes to the Main Features of Daily Newspapers* (Research Department, Odhams, D.H. 31, 1955); *National Daily Newspaper Readership Studies (2): Attitudes to Newspapers and Newspaper Reading, Preliminary Report* (Research Department, International Publishing Corporation, D.H. 75, 1964). These surveys were carried out for internal editorial purposes only.

47. *Report on Supplementary Questions: Time Spent Reading Daily Newspapers* (Research Department, Odhams, D.H. 8, 1955); *et al.*

48. *Report on Supplementary Questions: Readers Attitudes to the Main Features of Daily Newspapers* (D.H. 31).

49. The National Board of Prices and Incomes flouted the Fleet Street tradition of classifying newspapers by the social quality of their readers rather than by the quality of their contents. *Costs and Revenue of National Newspapers* (Report no. 141) classified the *Sunday Citizen/ Reynolds News* as a quality paper, a label adopted in R.C.P., *Final Report,* 1977, p. 272.

50. Advertising revenue figures derived from the *Sunday Times* and *Observer,* and in the case of the *Sunday Citizen* on the same basis as in note 41, above.

51. Space figures derived from *Sunday Times* and the *Observer;* an estimate for the *Sunday Citizen* was obtained from Beaverbrook Newspapers.

52. See Table 11.8, p. 262.

53. *Daily Herald Image – Self Designation by Social Class* (Research Department, Odhams, D.H. 60, 1961); *A Survey of People's Knowledge of Labour Party Policy and the Voting Intentions of Readers of National Daily Newspapers* (Research Department, International Publishing Corporation, D.H. 72, 1963); *Readership of Daily Herald* (Research Department, Odhams, D.H. 42, 1958); *inter al.* Reference to voting intentions in the text excludes those who were undecided or refused to answer.

54. *Report on a Survey to Study Attitudes to Daily Newspapers* (Research Department, Odhams, N.R. 9 1958); *Report on Discussion Groups – Daily Newspapers* (Research Department, International Publishing Corporation, D.H. 75, 1964) *inter al.*

55. The relative 'invisibility' of management in industrial relations stories is demonstrated by Denis McQuail, *Analysis of Newspaper Content,* R.C.P. Research Series 4, table B8, p. 116; his analysis also demonstrates that press coverage of strikes is most frequently linked with three themes – loss of output, loss of work by non-disputants and inconvenience or danger to the public (table B14, p. 124), though references to explanatory themes were relatively low. For a revealing summary of his findings – revealing, that is, of the McGregor Commission's own bias not of what Denis McQuail found – see R.C.P., *Final Report,* 1977, p. 83.

56. R.C.P., *Report,* 1949, Appendix 7, table 9, p. 253; *Attitudes to Newspapers and Newspaper Reading* (D.H. 75); our own unpublished content analysis.

57. *National Readership Surveys,* January–December 1960, July 1963–June 1964, January–December 1966.

58. The official estimates of individual membership of the Labour Party record a decline from 1,015,000 in 1952 to 675,000 in 1975. However, each constituency party affiliated (that is, was counted) at a minimum of 1000 members in 1975, whereas in 1952 each constituency party affiliated at 240 members. Most constituency parties have long ceased to have 1000 members, or anything like their official number, whereas in 1954 the average individual membership per constituency was 1639 (more than six times the official minimum). See *Report of the Fifty Third Annual Conference of the Labour Party, 1954* (London: Labour Party, 1954) p. 10.

59. *Royal Commission on the Distribution of Income and Wealth,* Report no. 1 (London: H.M.S.O., 1975); *Royal Commission on the Distribution of Income and Wealth,* Report no. 4 (London: H.M.S.O., 1976).

60. Nicholas Kaldor and Rodney Silverman, *A Statistical Analysis of Advertising Expenditure and of the Revenue of the Press* (Cambridge University Press, 1948); Rodney Silverman, *Advertising Expenditure in 1948* (London: Advertising Association, 1950), *Advertising Expenditure in 1952* (London: Advertising Association, 1954), *Advertising Expenditure in 1960* (London: Advertising Association, 1962); R. A. Critchley, *UK Advertising Statistics* (London: Advertising Association, no date); *Advertising Expenditure 1966–1975* (London: Advertising Association, 1976) *et al.*

61. Evidence of Advertising Association to Royal Commission on the Press 1974–7, answer to question 2 (p. 8).

62. John Whale, *The Politics of the Media* (London: Fontana, 1977) p. 93.

63. Fred Hirsch and David Gordon, *Newspaper Money* (London: Hutchinson, 1975) pp. 22, 78–80.

64. This examination of the *Daily Herald's* promotion campaigns draws heavily upon an interview with Mr W. D. McLelland.

65. *Daily Herald Reader Interest Surveys Recommendations* (Research Department, Odhams, 9 May 1955) p. 1–2.

66. This has been a recurrent and a unchanging market research finding for over thirty years. For an unusually comprehensive analysis of popular national daily newspaper reading behaviour, see *National Daily Newspaper Readership Studies: Feature Readership in National Dailies* (Research Department, International Publishing Corporation, D.H. 77, 1964).

67. *Daily Herald Reader Interest Surveys Recommendations,* p. 8.

68. *Attitudes to Newspapers and Newspaper Reading* (D.H. 75) p. iii.

69. See notes 66, 68 above.

70. The failure of the *Sun* was monitored in survey research undertaken by I.P.C.'s marketing and research department. A useful summary of this research is provided in *Report of an investigation into the transition from the Daily Herald to the Sun* (Research Department, International Publishing Corporation, January 1968).

71. Hugh Cudlipp, *Walking on Water* (London: Bodley Head, 1976) p. 251. The strategy articulated by the 1955 proposal rather than the proposal itself was rejected.

72. The decline of current affairs news coverage in the press could be attributed to an adjustment to T.V. There is, however, no evidence to suggest that T.V. has displaced interest in current affairs coverage in the press – see James Curran, 'The Impact of TV on the Audience for National Newspapers 1945–68', in Jeremy Tunstall (ed.), *Media Sociology* (London: Constable, 1970) and reprinted in K. J. McGarry (ed.), *Mass Communications* (London: Bingley, 1972). Indeed, if anything, the opposite would seem to be true in that heavy consumers of T.V. current affairs tend also to be heavy consumers of current affairs material in the press, whilst light consumption of current affairs on T.V. is associated with light consumption of current affairs in the press. It could be argued, however, that the shift in the contents of the press resulted from a misreading by newspaper managements of the effect of T.V. competition. It should also be added that current affairs feature material (as distinct from news) has increased as a proportion of editorial space in some popular papers by comparison with the 1930s though not with the 1940s: but the amount of current affairs analysis and comment is still very small – for instance, 6 per cent of editorial content in the *Sun* in 1976.

73. R. A. Critchley, *UK Advertising Statistics,* table 5, p. 9; *Advertising Expenditure 1960–1975,* table 4, p. 41.

74. Estimated from R.C.P., *Report,* 1949, table 4, p. 82, and R.C.P., *Interim Report,* 1976, table E5, p. 96. For detailed evidence on the effect of the advertising bonanza in the crucial period 1957–64 on newspaper costs, see *Survey of National Newspaper Industry.*

75. Thus, to take but one example, the *News Chronicle* was forced to incur an uneconomic level of paging in response to paging increases by the *Daily Mail* and *Daily Express.* Yet even though its paging was uneconomic due to insufficient advertising support, its average issue paging was still 45 per cent less than that of the *Daily Express* in 1960.

76. See references in note 60 above, and a useful summary analysis,

'Advertising Trends and the Press', prepared by Nick Hartley of the Royal Commission on the Press Secretariat. (Memorandum R.C.P. (76) Ad 6, November 1976).

77. R.C.P., *Final Report,* 1977, p. 39.

78. R.C.P., *Interim Report,* 1976, p. 38.

79. *Ibid.,* table 5.5., p. 38.

80. Graham Cleverley, *The Fleet Street Disaster* (London: Constable, 1976) chapter 2.

81. *Attitudes to the Press,* R.C.P. Research Series 3, 1977, Cmnd. 6810-3, table 3.050, p. 341.

82. Estimated from revenue figures supplied by *The Times* and proportion of advertising revenue absorbed by costs by the average quality daily, reported in R.C.P., *Final Report,* 1977, p. 39. A new down-market quality daily could operate, however, on a more modest scale than *The Times* and perhaps take full advantage of new technology.

83. A report prepared by the McGregor Commission's secretariat (*Concentration of Ownership in the Provincial Press,* R.C.P. Research Series 5, 1977, Cmnd. 6810-5) found that provincial newspaper monopolies were generally highly profitable. They report, on the basis of a large sample of companies, that provincial newspaper publishers had an average 27.5 per cent return on capital at historic cost in 1974 (table 5.12); that three daily newspaper publishers in 1974 even had a return on capital at historic cost of over 50 per cent (table 5.13); and that profits in provincial newspaper publishing in terms of return on capital at either historic or replacement cost were higher than in manufacturing industry generally (p. 31). They also show that 'competition between daily provincial papers published in the same town has almost entirely disappeared' (p. 32), while R.C.P., *Final Report,* 1977, concluded that these market monopolies were mostly unassailable in terms of direct competition by the same class of publication in the same town (p. 118).

Chapter 14

1. C. A. R. Crosland, 'The Mass Media', *Encounter,* vol. XIX, no. 5 (November 1962), p. 3.

2. *The Moyne Report* (London: H.M.S.O., 1936), Cmnd. 2053.

3. e.g. S. Legg and F. Klingender, *Money Behind the Screen* (London: Lawrence & Wishart, 1937); N. Davenport and R. Winnington, *The Future of British Films* (A News Chronicle publication, 1951).

4. Plant Report (London: H.M.S.O., 1949) Cmnd. 7837.

5. The Prime Minister's Working Party on the Future of the Film Industry (London: H.M.S.O., 1976) Cmnd. 6372.

6. Board of Trade Enquiry into the Film Industry. Blue Books, 80, 63, p. 17.

7. Cinematograph Films Act, 1927. Cmnd. 2053.

8. Davenport, *Future of British Films,* p. 21.

9. The Moyne Report.

10. Paul Foot in the *Politics of Harold Wilson* (Harmondsworth:

Penguin, 1968), claims that Wilson devoted more time to speeches about the film industry when he was President of the Board of Trade than any other topic.

11. Palacke Report, *Tendencies to Monopoly in the Cinematograph Film Industry,* (London: H.M.S.O., 1944); Plant Report, *Board of Trade Enquiry into the Distribution and Exhibition of Cinematograph Films* (London: H.M.S.O., 1949) Cmnd. 7837; Gater Report, *Report of The Working Party on Film Production Costs* (London: H.M.S.O., 1949) Cmnd. 6510.

12. T. H. Guback, *The International Film Industry.*

13. Film Act 1960. House of Commons Paper 206.

14. *Board of Trade Review of Films Legislation* (London: H.M.S.O., 1968) Cmnd. 3584, para. 12.

15. Ibid., para. 97.

16. *The Prime Minister's Working Party of the Future of the Film Industry,* 1976.

17. Royal Commission on the Press (R.C.P.), *Report* (London: H.M.S.O., 1949) Cmnd. 7700.

18. R.C.P., *Report* (London: H.M.S.O., 1962) Cmnd. 1811; R.C.P., *Final Report* (London: H.M.S.O., 1977) Cmnd. 6810. The press has also been subject to major independent reviews, like that of the Economist Intelligence Unit, *Survey of the National Newspaper Industry* (1966).

19. R.C.P., *Final Report,* 1977, chapter 2, para. 12.

20. Ibid., chapter 13, para. 48.

21. By 1943 papers were 20 per cent of their pre-war size. R.C.P., *Report,* 1947, p. 192.

22. *P.E.P. Report on the British Press,* April 1938, p. 43.

23. A. J. P. Taylor, *English History 1914–1945* (O.U.P. 1965) p. 174.

24. George Orwell, *The Collected Essays, Journalism and Letters,* vol. II (London: Secker & Warburg, 1966) p. 215.

25. This is the general argument, and advanced in particular about the Second World War, of A. C. H. Smith, *Paper Voices* (London: Chatto & Windus, 1975).

26. Lord Beaverbrook, Oral Evidence to the Royal Commission on the Press, 15 June 1947, Cmnd. 7317.

27. J. Gerald, *The British Press under Government Economic Controls* (Minneapolis: University of Minnesota Press, 1956).

28. See M. Gilbert and R. Gott, *The Appeasers* (O.U.P., 1965 for the B.B.C.) and 'Without the Benefit of Hindsight', on the role of newsreel coverage in support of appeasement.

29. R.C.P., *Report,* 1947. Oral Evidence, 19 June, 1947.

30. Ibid., para. 492.

31. Ibid., para. 662.

32. Ibid., oral evidence, 17 June 1947.

33. R.C.P., *Report,* 1962, para. 5.

34. Ibid., para. 14.

35. Ibid., para. 39.

36. Ibid., para. 278.

37. R.C.P., *Report,* 1947.

38. R.C.P., *Final Report,* 1977.

39. Ibid., chapter 2, para. 17.

40. P. P. Eckersley, *Power Behind the Microphone* (London: Jonathan Cape, 1941) p. 4.

41. *Proceedings of the Sykes Committee* (London: H.M.S.O., 1923) Cmd. 1951, para. 14.

42. *Report of the Committee on Broadcasting* (London: H.M.S.O., 1925) Cmd. 2599.

43. Asa Briggs, *History of Broadcasting in the United Kingdom.* vol. I, *The Birth of Broadcasting* (O.U.P., 1961) p. 238.

44. By banning the Archbishop of Canterbury from broadcasting, and, even worse, allowing the Catholic Bishop Bourne to broadcast, telling his flock they should return to work. B.B.C. Sound Archives, 27.982 and B.P. D.3. vol. 18.75.

45. A. Smith, *The Shadow in the Cave* (London: George Allen & Unwin, 1973) p. 31.

46. J. C. W. Reith, 'Introduction', *B.B.C. Handbook* (1931).

47. P. Scannell and D. Cardiff, *The Social Foundations of British Broadcasting* (Milton Keynes: Open University Press, 1977) Mass Communication and Society DE 353 supplementary material.

48. The B.B.C. became a model for 'the public enterprise', which in turn was seen as 'the greatest sociological invention of this century'. W. A. Robson, *Public Enterprise* (Oxford University Press, 1947).

49. *The Ullswater Committee on Broadcasting,* (London: H.M.S.O., 1936) Cmd. 5091, para. 179.

50. *The Beveridge Report on Broadcasting,* (London: H.M.S.O., 1949) Cmd. 8116.

51. Ibid., para. 652.

52. Ibid., para. 582.

53. *Report of the Pilkington Committee on Broadcasting* (London: H.M.S.O., 1952) Cmnd. 1753, para. 358.

54. *The Annan Report on the Future of Broadcasting* (London: H.M.S.O., 1977) Cmnd. 6753.

55. Ibid., ch. 2, para. 26.

56. Ibid., ch. 1, para. 12.

57. Ibid., ch. 3, para. 14.

58. Ibid., ch. 17. para. 9.

Index